T0295026

LABOUR'S CIVIL WARS

LABOUR'S CIVIL WARS

How infighting has kept the left from power
(and what can be done about it)

PATRICK DIAMOND AND
GILES RADICE

First published in 2022 by
HAUS PUBLISHING LTD
4 Cinnamon Row
London SW11 3TW

Copyright © Patrick Diamond and Giles Radice, 2022

A CIP catalogue record for this book is available from the British Library

The moral right of the authors has been asserted

ISBN: 978-1-913368-59-3
eISBN 978-1-913368-60-9

Typeset in Garamond by MacGuru Ltd

Printed in the UK by Clays Ltd, Elcograf S.p.A.

www.hauspublishing.com
@HausPublishing

Contents

Foreword

The biblical adage that 'if a house be divided against itself, that house cannot stand' remains sound theological advice. It also provides essential counsel for any political party that aspires to win elections and govern in a liberal democracy. If a party is riven with division and ideological conflict, and if people therefore do not know what it stands for, it is unlikely to win voters' trust or demonstrate governing competence.

Though both major parties have been prone to internal conflict over the years, historically it is the Labour Party which has been more given to damaging splits. The divide exposed by the Corbyn insurgency after 2015 is the most recent example of a century of infighting. Indeed, Labour has often been more adept at battling itself than defeating the Conservatives. The party over decades has appeared chronically prone to ideological conflict. It was a former Labour prime minister, Harold Wilson, who remarked that 'the party is a bit like an old stagecoach. If you drive it along at a rapid rate everyone on board is either so exhilarated or so seasick that you do not have a lot of difficulty … but, if you stop, everyone gets out and argues about where to go next.'

This book examines the history of Labour's civil wars and the underlying causes of the party's schisms. It is a work of synthesis which draws on contemporary accounts, diaries, and political biography. We argue that there is a cyclical pattern in the party's history. Labour has had sustained periods in office (1945–51, 1964–70, 1974–9, and 1997–2010). Sadly, however, these governments ended too soon, engulfed by disillusion and disappointment. With the exception of 1997, Labour has been unable to win re-election to serve a full second term. Having lost the subsequent election, Labour invariably 'breaks into warring factions'.[1]

However, we also believe strongly that unity on its own is not enough. To be successful, a political party must be willing to confront internal differences and put forward a distinctive message, appeal, and programme that can win the trust of voters. Labour must have a political project for the future. In doing so it is the authors' fundamental hope that social democracy can break the historical pattern of defeat and division on the left, thereby displacing Conservatism as the natural governing ideology in Britain.

May 2022

Why Labour is Given to Civil Wars

The divisions that have bedevilled Labour over the last decade, particularly under the leadership of Jeremy Corbyn, have existed since the party's inception at the beginning of the twentieth century. Historical analysis demonstrates that as a political force Labour has long been prone to ideological conflict and organisational rupture. While it certainly has a tradition of loyalty which ensures Labour leaders are rarely, if ever, removed prematurely from office (George Lansbury is, thus far, the stand-out exception), since its birth at the beginning of the twentieth century the party has constantly teetered on the brink of civil war. This book seeks to explain why Labour has so often been divided.

The first explanation reflects the pluralist institutional structure of the party. Throughout Labour's existence, three separate powerbases have co-existed: the trade union movement, the Parliamentary Labour Party (PLP), and the grassroots among the constituency parties. The trade unions helped form the party in order to achieve improvements in the working conditions and pay of their members while protecting the legal right to organise. The PLP were predominantly concerned with attaining political power through the parliamentary system by electing a Labour government into office. The grassroots activists, meanwhile, served as both foot soldiers and the radical conscience of the party. The 1918 constitution had established the right of individual members to join local Labour parties. The membership supplied the election workers to get Labour candidates elected, while they sought to uphold the party's ethical beliefs and its commitment to socialism.

All three blocs performed an essential role in giving the party its distinctive voice and identity. Nor were they necessarily always at odds. For example, the trade unions acted pragmatically in the aftermath of the failed general strike of 1926, recognising that only political power could secure workers' interests. It was necessary to elect a Labour government to defend the legitimacy of collective organisation. Moreover, the balance of authority within the tripartite structure changed across time, especially after Labour's election victories in 1945, 1964, 1974, and 1997 when power shifted inevitably to the PLP.

Even so, the last century graphically illustrates that the interests of parliamentarians, trade unions, and activists within the party are not easily reconciled. Indeed, when Labour was in office and confronted by having to take painful economic decisions, explosive disagreements with the industrial wing and grassroots activists threatened the uneasy truce in the party, as occurred during the 1950s and the 1970s.

The second reason why Labour has been prone to conflict is that the ideological aims of the party, its core beliefs and ideals, have been contested throughout history. Although Labour has been characterised as a socialist party, its doctrine is a subtle blend of ideological traditions drawn from liberalism, ethical socialism, syndicalism, Marxism, and municipal 'gas and water' socialism. The party's founders, notably Keir Hardie and Ramsay MacDonald, emphasised the spiritual appeal of socialism as a collection of ethical ideals. Hardie and MacDonald were strongly committed to political liberalism, emphasising the primacy of parliamentary democracy. But they remained vague about the party's policy programme. In the aftermath of the First World War, Labour devised an economic prospectus that prioritised the nationalisation and state ownership of British industry and productive assets. Yet there was continuing disagreement about the significance assigned to public ownership and state planning. By the early 1950s, it was apparent that Labour's ideology would have to be revised in the wake of successive election defeats and disillusionment with state control.

In this climate, there were continuing battles to define the party's ideology between revisionists and fundamentalists, traditionalists and modernisers. The academic and former parliamentarian David Marquand wrote in *Encounter* magazine in the turbulent circumstances of the late 1970s:

To pretend, in this situation, that socialists and social democrats are all part of the same great Movement – that Shirley Williams and Bill Rodgers and Roy Hattersley really have more in common with Tony Benn and Eric Heffer and Stanley Orme than they do with Peter Walker or Ian Gilmour or Edward Heath – is to live a lie. But it is a lie which the Labour party has to live with if it is to live at all.[1]

Marquand's contention was that the liberal social democratic vision of the post-war revisionists could never be
reconciled with the statist instincts of traditional socialism on
the British left.

A third source of conflict has been disagreement over the
basic political strategy of the party. At its most elementary
level, is Labour's purpose to win parliamentary majorities and
govern by gaining control of the levers of the British state?
Or does the party exist to foment opposition to 'capitalist
exploitation' and 'imperialism' by challenging the existing
constitutional machinery? Is Labour's aim to make the liberal
democratic system work more effectively, or to create an alternative society which its proponents depict as 'socialism'? The
question of strategy relates to how the party should gain power
in a diverse and pluralist society. Is Labour a class-based socialist party committed to the radical transformation of Britain,
or a moderate, progressive, social democratic force that represents all classes and shades of opinion under the banner of
'conscience and reform'? Throughout Labour's history, conflict over these basic strategic questions has ensured discord is
never far away.

The final reason why Labour has appeared prone to civil
wars is the temperament and behaviour of leading politicians in the party. Whatever lip-service is paid to the official
rhetoric of unity and class solidarity, there has been a recurrent tendency to indulge in factional infighting as a means of
gaining political ascendency. At crucial points in its history,
the party has been overwhelmed by a 'them and us' mentality
where traitors and cowards are perceived to be waiting around
every corner, looking for the first opportunity to corrupt and

undermine the labour movement. The personality differences that split Labour Cabinets from MacDonald to Attlee, Wilson to Blair, have been legendary.

As Peter Clarke, the Cambridge historian of modern Britain, observed, Labour's recurring civil wars have been driven by four distinct sources of conflict:[2]

Table 1: Labour's Civil Wars

Type of political conflict	Nature of divide
Organisational e.g. party institutions	The co-existence of rival power blocs in the party including the trade unions, the PLP, and the constituency grassroots.
Ideological e.g. 'Left versus Right'	Differences over the fundamental direction of the party relating to its view of capitalism, the role of the state, and Britain's global role.
Strategic e.g. 'Fundamentalists versus Revisionists'	Disagreements about how the party should respond to, and deal with, the impact of social and economic change in post-war Britain.
Personality-oriented e.g. 'Bevanites versus Gaitskellites'	The breakdown of the relationship between key political figures mirrored in conflict at the party's grassroots.

These four causes of disagreement are closely interwoven. Differences of personality, for example, are exacerbated by, and in turn encourage, disagreements over ideology, organisation, and strategy. Personal relations are a distinctive source of conflict in themselves. How political actors work together and resolve differences is critical: the capacity for emotional intelligence can serve to mitigate division. At the heart of Labour politics for the last century have been long-running jealousies, hatreds, friendships, and loyalties.[3] The institutions and organisational culture of the party have the capacity to aggravate and intensify conflict. So too do quarrels over ideology. Throughout Labour's history, the division between left and right has shaped internal debate, allowing politicians to position themselves in the struggle for power that ensued. Finally, battles over strategy proved decisive. Should the party stick to its core beliefs, demonstrating steadfast commitment to its values? Or should Labour adapt in the face of an altered society and a changing economy? This basic strategic tension underlies the distinction between fundamentalists and revisionists in Labour's ranks.

Harold Wilson's biographer, Ben Pimlott, emphasised the complex motives that provoked Wilson's resignation and the Bevanite rift with Gaitskell in 1951 over NHS charges. Pimlott identifies the underlying causes of the dispute as, 'A divergence over policy, which included a shrewd assessment of the likely impact of defence spending on the economy, a personal rift, in which jealousy may have played a part, coupled with frustration at Gaitskell's style.'[4] In other words, Wilson's motives were not straightforward. The divide was not merely about policy and personal ambition but 'deep differences of culture and mood' which separated the Gaitskellites from the Bevanites.

Throughout the 1950s, Wilson fought to position himself as the conciliator in the party. Bevan and Wilson's dispute with Gaitskell concerned the determination of the Treasury to insist on cuts that would deliver only modest savings, and yet split the party by breaching the fundamental principle of an NHS provided free at the point of need. Moreover, Gaitskell and Bevan had conflicting personalities. Bevan thought Gaitskell was a soulless and technocratic 'desiccated calculating machine', while Gaitskell believed Bevan was gifted but ill-disciplined. In the course of the 1950s, this grew into more substantive doctrinal discord which destabilised the party, keeping it out of office throughout the next decade.

However, by the end of the 1950s, Bevan and Wilson were in agreement with Gaitskell over fundamental questions of policy, as Pimlott has demonstrated: all three politicians supported the North Atlantic Alliance; they were committed to a mixed economy with a substantial role for the private sector that retained a commitment to public ownership; and all three endorsed government intervention to create a more efficient economy that delivered a surplus for welfare spending.[5]

The contemporary case of the dispute between Tony Blair and Gordon Brown has similar complexities. What began essentially as a personal rivalry provoked by the leadership contest that followed John Smith's untimely death in 1994 became increasingly ideological. Questions of political and policy strategy grew to become a source of intense conflict as the two battled to control the party's governing agenda. Brown feared that Blair's ultra-modernising zeal was transforming the party's identity, diluting its core social democratic commitment to equality.

The explosive impact of the Corbyn insurgency has been the latest division in a century of conflict and schism. The long view of history indicates that Labour has always been more effective at fighting itself than defeating the Conservatives. Yet this book also demonstrates the inescapable dilemma that all modern political parties, including Labour, face in a liberal democracy. They have to remain united, otherwise they damage their 'image' and perceived credibility in the minds of voters. That said, party unity on its own is not enough to win. A party must have a distinctive message and appeal to win the trust of the British electorate. Shaping any political project means confronting differences, facing up to the implications of internal disagreement while hammering out a viable programme.

This book will examine the history of Labour's civil wars, the elements that link these internal hostilities including the decisive impact of electoral defeat and the constitutional structure of the labour movement, alongside the underlying causes of the party's divisions over the last century. It is comprised of seven distinctive chapters:

1: Why Labour is Given to Civil Wars
2: Government or Opposition: The 1931 Split and the Fall of Ramsay MacDonald
3: Revisionists versus Fundamentalists: Gaitskell and Bevan at War 1951–64
4: The Bennite Revolt and the Birth of the Social Democratic Party: Healey, Benn, and Jenkins 1964–87
5: New Labour at War: Blair and Brown's Dual Premiership 1997–2010
6: The Left Insurgency, Corbyn's Leadership, and the Succession of Keir Starmer
7: Conclusion: The Way Ahead

This introductory chapter briefly summarises the book's key themes and events. Each main period (1931–51; 1951–64; 1964–1987; 1987–2010 and after) fits within a recurrent cyclical pattern in the party's history.[6] Labour loses a general election decisively, often accompanied by further defeats. Eventually the penny drops and it begins a hesitant and protracted recovery. The party wins a parliamentary majority at a subsequent election and enters government. However, Labour's period of office is usually relatively brief and ends almost inevitably in disillusionment and disappointment. Having lost another election, 'Habits of restraint and deference [are] abandoned and ancient practices [are] resumed … the party breaks into warring factions.'[7] The schism created by defeat then leads to protracted internal conflict. However, this doctrinal dispute becomes the stimulus for political revival, compelling Labour to clarify its ideas, aiding the party's rebirth and renewal.[8] It is striking how this pattern of history repeated itself throughout the twentieth century.

The political crisis of 1931 led to the first of Labour's civil wars. Indeed, it almost broke the party apart. Ramsay MacDonald was a Scottish politician from an impoverished background, born out of wedlock. Yet he became a pivotal figure, transforming Labour from a marginal force into a serious contender for power after the First World War. Although subsequently condemned as a political traitor, MacDonald had impeccable working-class credentials and an instinctive connection to the labour movement. After watching him give a speech to the Labour Party conference, Egon Wertheimer remarked that MacDonald was 'the focus of the mute hopes of a whole class'.[9] He was a charismatic politician and a spellbinding orator who captivated working-class audiences. His political vision was of a 'greater Labour Party' that would replace the Liberals by appealing to all sections of progressive opinion in British society, acting as the custodian of liberal democracy. First and foremost, MacDonald believed that Labour had to project itself as a unified, disciplined, and competent force. He then brought the Labour Party into government, first in 1924, and again in 1929.

However, by the summer of 1931, MacDonald had split from Labour to form the National Government with Conservative support following the financial crisis and the Great Depression that had begun in 1929. The Labour administration's collapse was not altogether surprising. As the worldwide economic meltdown unfolded, it was apparent that the Labour government lacked a coherent financial policy. Even in 1929, Labour's plan to tackle mass unemployment was alarmingly threadbare. Much of the serious thinking on economic policy was undertaken by Lloyd George's Liberal Party with the input of John Maynard Keynes. MacDonald and his chancellor, Philip Snowden, were determined to do whatever was necessary to reassure the city and the financial markets. Government debt and the current account deficit rocketed as the economic situation deteriorated. However, the trade unions led by Ernest Bevin were not prepared to agree to drastic reductions in unemployment benefit which would inflict suffering on the Labour heartlands. Most of the Cabinet led by Arthur Henderson were sceptical of the call for 'tough remedies'. There was consideration of Keynesian reflationary thinking in Labour circles. Yet as chancellor,

Snowden did not believe the Labour government could defy the markets and reject the gold standard. Moreover, in 1931 Keynes' ideas were untested and although theoretically compelling, hardly constituted a coherent programme.

In August 1931, ministers were confronted by the need to take painful decisions to balance the budget. Most of the Cabinet, the PLP, and the unions thought it was better for Labour to go into opposition, avoiding the choice of cutting 'the dole', which would harm the party's core supporters. MacDonald rejected that argument without hesitation. He insisted if it were to be a serious party of government, Labour must have the courage to take difficult decisions. If Labour was unwilling to reduce the generosity of welfare payments, the Tories would do it anyway but much more harshly. Moreover, if Labour did not act as a responsible party of government, it would once again be eclipsed by the Liberals as the major opposition to the Conservatives in British politics.

The Labour movement was by now openly at war. Unable to agree on its core economic policy, MacDonald established a National Government with the support of the Conservatives, the Liberals, and a small minority of Labour MPs. He was expelled from Labour, condemned as a traitor to his party and class. Following the break up of the government, MacDonald called a general election in November 1931 which led to a devastating defeat for his former party and the return of only forty-seven Labour MPs. Henderson, an underestimated figure who became acting leader in traumatic circumstances, attempted to bring MacDonald back into the fold. Yet for MacDonald to return having set up the National Government with opposition MPs was unthinkable. The events established in Labour's folk memory the mythology of Mac-Donald's treachery which has lingered ever since.

Despite that, Labour's electoral and political position gradually recovered in the 1930s. A new generation of party intellectuals, notably Hugh Dalton, Evan Durbin, and Hugh Gaitskell, began to develop economic ideas focusing on the centrality of planning and nationalisation that had a decisive influence on the 1945 government. However, on the eve of the Second World War in 1939, Labour's return to power was hardly guaranteed. In 1931, the party had greatly damaged its credibility and reputation for governing competence, and the ensuing civil war left an indelible mark. It took the extraordinary circumstances created by the outbreak of World War Two and the formation of the wartime coalition, in which Labour played a leading role, to transform the party's prospects.

Labour achieved a landslide victory in 1945 and its governing achievements up to 1950 were remarkable. It embarked on an unprecedented phase of legislative activism, laying the foundations of the post-war welfare state and the National Health Service (NHS). Even so, by 1950 it was apparent Labour was running out of steam. As the historian Alan Bullock remarked, Labour 'could not recover its impetus without a period in opposition to settle its differences and give a new generation of leaders the chance to rise to the top'.[10] New divisions as to the party's purpose in government were emerging. The divide was encapsulated by the personal and political battle between two of the most formidable Labour politicians of the period, Hugh Gaitskell and Aneurin 'Nye' Bevan. Their dispute was to reverberate throughout the 1950s.

Although in the same party, Gaitskell and Bevan could

hardly have come from more contrasting backgrounds. Bevan was a romantic working-class socialist from the Welsh coal-fields who began work as a coal miner at the age of fourteen. Largely self-educated, he was a remarkable orator who saw himself as the keeper of the socialist flame. Indeed, Attlee initially regarded him as the party's natural future leader. But his increasingly erratic and volatile performance meant Bevan was expelled from the party on several occasions. He only enjoyed unqualified support from figures on the party's renegade left, a small rump in the PLP.

In background and personality, Hugh Gaitskell was the polar opposite of Bevan. An upper-middle-class socialist educated at Winchester and Oxford, he was not born into the labour movement. He chose the Labour Party because of his commitment to its ethical ideals and vision of a more egalitarian society. Gaitskell advanced quickly through Labour's ranks. He was a talented economist and administrator who rose rapidly as a minister through the 1945 administration, having served as a temporary civil servant during the war.

Yet while Gaitskell and Bevan had markedly contrasting early lives, both men were intense, passionate, uncompromising, and at times obstinate. By 1950, having implemented the measures contained in the 1945 manifesto, the stage was set for dramatic confrontation over Labour's direction, personified by the split between the two men.

The spark was eventually lit over the issue of charging for NHS dentistry and spectacles. As the minister who founded the NHS in 1948, Bevan refused to contemplate the introduction of charges which he believed undermined the fundamental principle that treatment must be available to all, irrespective of their ability to pay. Gaitskell, in contrast, thought the willingness to introduce charges was essential for Labour to maintain its reputation as a responsible governing party in the light of fiscal pressures. With the prospect of war in Korea and the requirement for Britain to play its part in post-war collective security, rearmament must be paid for. That meant adjusting Labour's programme of domestic reform, committing fewer resources, and tolerating a slower advance towards the New Jerusalem outlined in its 1945 manifesto. Attlee, who initially failed to provide a clear lead on health policy, felt he had little option but to support his chancellor. The dispute was finally settled in Gaitskell's favour. Yet the disagreement paved the way for a decade of schism and division.

Labour was then defeated in the 1951 election, having won only a narrow majority in 1950, leading to bitter arguments about the party's aims. There was little idealism in its 1951 manifesto: Labour predominantly looked backwards, basing its appeal on reminding voters of the hardship of the inter-war years and the 'hungry thirties'. The disagreement focused on the role of nationalisation in Labour's programme, and the debate about whether Clause IV socialism was viable in post-war Britain. It was apparent that the state ownership of productive assets was increasingly unpopular with the electorate, particularly working-class voters. The consumer's experience of public ownership was decidedly mixed, while there was growing disillusionment with statism. In any case, the arguments for nationalising industries such as steel and sugar production were by no means clear cut, even among socialist economists. The custodian of domestic policy Herbert Morrison sought to paper over the cracks of doctrinal discord in fashioning the strategy of 'consolidation': Labour should not try to extend government control over the commanding heights of the economy any further, he argued. Instead, it should allow the publicly owned industries to become more efficient and sensitive to consumer demands.

Gaitskell was increasingly doubtful that the long-standing commitment to nationalisation as the centrepiece of its programme provided Labour with a coherent future direction. The 1952 publication *The New Fabian Essays*, and Crosland's seminal 1956 book *The Future of Socialism*, outlined a 'revisionist' analysis where socialism was conceived as a set of ethical values rather than a commitment to the socialisation of industry.[11] This position inflamed the party's left, among whom Bevan was the chief protagonist. Consequently, Labour was again on the brink of civil war. When Attlee stood down as leader in 1955, the trade unions, who were alarmed by Bevan's unreliable behaviour, gradually swung their support behind Gaitskell. Revisionism became the dominant intellectual tendency in the party, since it provided both a powerful analysis and diagnosis of Labour's weakness, combined with solutions requiring the modernisation of the party's programme and appeal.

In the second half of the 1950s, Gaitskell and Bevan established an uneasy truce. Yet the dispute between the party's revisionists and fundamentalists rumbled on, reaching its crescendo after the electoral defeat of 1959. In the wake of defeat, Gaitskell proposed to rewrite Clause IV of the party's constitution, which committed the party to nationalisation. Gaitskell's allies believed that Labour had to embark on radical modernisation of policy in order to win elections in the newly affluent society. The proposal provoked a huge backlash that eventually forced the leadership to retreat. It was in attacking symbols (rather than changing party policy) that Gaitskell's leadership came under the greatest pressure. He believed in rational persuasion but underplayed the importance of emotion and myth within the Labour Party. To those 'reconcilers' in the centre of the party, Gaitskell was becoming 'an agent of disunity'.[12] The attempt to rewrite Clause IV, which destabilised Gaitskell's relationship with the moderate trade unions, was swiftly abandoned.

Yet by the time of Gaitskell's untimely death in 1963, the party's position had improved. After 1960, Gaitskell adopted a more conciliatory style of leadership. The leader's victory over defence policy weakened the party's commitment to unilateralism, while Gaitskell's opposition to the European Common Market strengthened his position among Labour's grassroots. The Conservative administration was showing all the signs of exhaustion. It appeared increasingly likely that Labour would win the forthcoming general election. The new leader, Harold Wilson, a grammar school boy and former student of William Beveridge at Oxford, born in Huddersfield in the North of England, temporarily succeeded in papering over the cracks of disharmony, leading to the historic election victory of 1964.

Indeed, Wilson (a former ally of Bevan's) succeeded in unifying the party behind a programme of economic modernisation. Yet despite significant successes in government, especially in social policy and education, the defeat of the administration in 1970 against the backdrop of economic failure exposed a new fault line in Labour's ideology. The 1974–9 Labour governments were then plagued by economic crises and the breakdown of their relationship with the trade unions. The roots of Labour's civil war in the early 1980s lay in this period, as two major issues bubbled to the surface: Labour's strategy for managing the economy, and party policy towards Europe.

On economic policy, Labour's programme adopted in 1973 represented a significant shift to the left, embracing policies known as the Alternative Economic Strategy that were reflected in the 1974 manifesto. After 1974, the left-wing minister Tony Benn (an upper-class public school socialist who had worked closely with Gaitskell in the 1950s) urged the government to stick to its manifesto commitments following the perceived failures and broken promises of the 1964–70 administrations.

Nonetheless, most of the Cabinet, including Wilson and Callaghan, strongly disagreed with Benn's approach. Only a few months after the February 1974 election, the PM told his staff that he intended to take over industrial policy from Benn to avoid a collapse of business confidence. Wilson's press secretary, Joe Haines, was then instructed to brief the *Financial Times* that Benn was being sidelined.[13] Senior ministers wanted the government to adopt more consensual and 'responsible' policies that maintained Labour's credibility. However, the refusal of the Wilson government to accede to Benn's strategy in implementing the 1973 programme led to accusations of heresy and betrayal among the grassroots that echoed throughout the next decade.

Britain's prospective membership of the European Community (EC) was another major fault line exposed in the early 1970s. The issue of Europe cut across the division between right and left. Under pressure to keep the party united, Wilson decided to hold a referendum as a means of managing growing divisions within his party. He skilfully suspended collective Cabinet responsibility to enable ministers to campaign on either side of the debate. Nevertheless, Europe continued to be a source of political disagreement throughout the 1970s.

Despite the crisis in 1975–6 which entailed major cuts in public expenditure, the Wilson and Callaghan administrations managed to remain broadly unified. There were no Cabinet resignations (in stark contrast to 1931 and 1951), even though the IMF bailout necessitated tough choices. By 1978, the economic indicators were moving in the right direction: 'green shoots' were visible in the British economy. Indeed, it is possible that Labour could have won a general election in the autumn of 1978. Yet on the advice of his polling strategist Sir Robert Worcester, who believed Labour was underperforming in key marginals, Callaghan chose to delay. The so-called 'winter of discontent' marked by trade union strikes then depleted the government's credibility. In retrospect, Labour's defeat at the 1979 general election appeared all but inevitable.

Meanwhile, over the course of the 1970s the atmosphere in the Constituency Labour Parties (CLPs) had deteriorated, and the mood became more rebellious. From the late 1960s, the culture of the party and its attitude towards the leadership became less deferential. A 'cultural revolution' was underway as middle-class, university-educated activists flooded into the party. The unions were also swinging to the left, notably after the failure of the government's *In Place of Strife* reforms in 1969. The row over *In Place of Strife* was the worst crisis Labour had faced since 1931. During that period, 'the delicate balance between trade unionists and politicians, realists and dreamers, radicals and moderates that is the secret of Labour's viability seemed threatened'.[14] This created a political opportunity for career-minded politicians, including Tony Benn, to exploit dissatisfaction with the performance of the governments of the 1960s and 1970s, a performance which had failed to satisfy the expectations of the party's radical wing.

In the aftermath of defeat in 1979, the conflict erupted into civil war. The cause was not merely disagreement over policy (where there had been a radical shift to the left with growing support for the Alternative Economic Strategy and unilateral nuclear disarmament), but over organisation and the party's constitution. The system in which MPs select the party leader was replaced by an electoral college of CLPs, trade unions, and the PLP at the 1980 Wembley Special Conference. In 1980, Michael Foot (a 'respectable' left romantic who idolised Bevan) was elected leader; Dennis Healey became his deputy, defeating Benn by a small but decisive margin.

Insisting that the situation inside the Labour Party was becoming intolerable, the so-called 'Gang of Four' (Roy Jenkins, Shirley Williams, Bill Rodgers, and David Owen) broke away to form the Social Democratic Party (SDP) in 1981. This move appeared to offer a resolution to the civil war raging inside the party. Yet the SDP was unable to unify the social democratic wing of the labour movement. Only a small minority of MPs and a handful of trade unionists defected. The new party had some remarkable by-election successes, while attracting support among heavyweight intellectuals. Even so, at the 1983 general election, Labour (despite its catastrophic defeat) was able to maintain its status as the major alternative to the Conservatives. Consolidating that progress in the general election of 1987, Labour slowly but surely, under Neil Kinnock's and then John Smith's leadership, began the protracted process of modernisation which eventually led to electoral recovery.

By the mid-1990s, a new generation of progressive leaders had taken over the helm of the party. On the face of it, Blair and Brown's 'dual premiership' was the most successful political marriage in the party's history. Blair and Brown were undeniably the joint architects of the New Labour project. Their partnership enabled the party to win two landslide victories, followed by a less decisive third win in 2005. After 1997, they governed for three full terms, by far the longest period in the party's history. Labour had the capacity to reshape the political landscape, broadening economic prosperity, tackling the roots of child and pensioner poverty, overhauling the British constitution, while transforming public services, particularly the NHS. Blair and Brown were a successful combination that not only created and sustained New Labour but gave the party the longest period of power in its history.

What was so striking about this partnership was their complementary political gifts. Blair was charming, stylish, and charismatic, the best political communicator of his age, who could dominate the House of Commons, set party conference alight with his oratory, and speak persuasively to voters on television. Yet he had little interest in the minutiae of social and economic policy. Brown, on the other hand, was a heavyweight thinker, the party's master strategist who provided Labour with a new approach to managing the economy after the manifest failures of the post-war decades. He was steeped in the traditions of the Scottish Labour Party, an incisive and stimulating companion, although not always a particularly effective communicator or wise interpreter of the public mood.

The political commentator Andrew Rawnsley describes the Blair/Brown partnership as 'the rock on which New Labour was built and the rock on which it so often threatened to break apart. When they were working together, their complementary skills created a synergy which made the Government pretty much unstoppable.'[15] What Blair and Brown understood was that for Labour to articulate its appeal to voters, the party had to be united and politically disciplined. Yet to be in power and govern in the national interest, Labour must also have clear policies and positions hammered out through internal discussion and debate.

While Blair and Brown's partnership was unquestionably successful in reshaping British politics, Brown's constant manoeuvring for the leadership eventually destabilised the party. From the outset, there were explosive rows that undermined and weakened the government. Although the arguments can be dismissed as trivial in their immediate impact, a product of personality differences which are inevitable at the very top of politics, the tone became increasingly ideological as Brown and Blair battled over the future of their political project. The longer that Labour remained in office, the more prone it became to bitter arguments that divided the party, pushing it to the brink of civil war. Meanwhile, the media reporting of the conflict wallowed in its 'soap opera' qualities, the melodrama of the 'TBs–GBs' – as civil servants liked to describe them. There were endless opportunities to speculate about the turf wars between Number 10 and Number 11 Downing Street.

Without question, an appetite for power played an important role. Blair and Brown were surrounded by personal entourages, rival courts who believed it was necessary to emphasise the political differences between them. Yet the divide between the men was not only about career and position. Ultimately, it was about how to *use* power for the public good, advancing social democracy in contemporary society. There were ideological differences that fuelled the growing chasm between the Blair and Brown camps. When Labour was defeated at the general election in 2010, it appeared an increasingly divided party. Not surprisingly, it spent the next decade in the political doldrums.

By the 2000s, it looked as if Labour would become the natural governing party, after achieving consecutive election victories for the first time in its history. Unlike the twentieth century, the twenty-first century would be a 'progressive' century. Yet in retrospect it is clear the Blair and Brown years were storing up major problems for the future. In particular, the Blair legacy led to the alienation of the party's grassroots, failing to reform Labour's structures after the initial wave of modernisation in the 1990s. Neither did Blair's party create new mechanisms of participation that would engage the membership and tolerate internal debate. Cumulatively, the so-called 'Blair–Brown wars' had a negative effect. Differences over policy were deliberately exaggerated to accentuate the depth of the divide. This created a febrile atmosphere of bitterness and division which sapped morale. In 2007, after Blair's resignation, Brown inherited an exhausted and divided party which struggled to cope with the financial crisis of 2008, alongside the troubled legacy of foreign wars in Iraq and Afghanistan.

In 2010, Ed Miliband was elected leader. Unwisely, Miliband was determined to disavow New Labour's record, playing down the achievements of past governments. This position gave the party carte blanche to ignore the accomplishments of the 1997–2010 administrations, particularly on the economy. Labour was encouraged to swallow the myth that ministers had made a 'Faustian pact' with financial markets and business. The party then swung sharply to the left, as Miliband embraced opposition to austerity. His electoral strategy centred on mobilising the party's supporters in 'heartland' seats, the so-called '35 per cent strategy'. In 2014, Miliband endorsed the creation of a new Electoral College which allowed any 'affiliated supporter' to participate in leadership elections, opening the floodgates to a more left-wing leadership. In the 2015 election, Labour went down to further defeat, despite an unpopular Conservative government and the meltdown of the Liberal Democrats, who were punished for propping up a Tory administration.

In 2015, with the new electoral college in place, Jeremy Corbyn astonished the political world by emerging as Labour leader. The factors driving the Corbyn insurgency were not dissimilar to those that stirred populist forces across the advanced democracies over the last decade: antipathy to austerity and market liberal economics; a disdain for the political establishment; a desire to hit back against the forces of capital and unaccountable financial elites. Whereas Miliband was judged to have offered an insipid, ambiguous prospectus,

Corbyn appeared to promise 'the real thing', a radical social-ist agenda. Corbyn was able to exploit activist dissatisfaction with New Labour's legacy, especially Blair's policies in Iraq, and the way the party membership was increasingly margin-alised by the central machine.

Corbyn's politics were very much the product of British culture and society in the 1960s and 1970s. He was a believer in internal party democratisation. He backed unilateral nuclear disarmament combined with a visceral anti-Americanism and the need for an 'alternative' economic strategy. In Corbyn's view, the EEC was merely a capitalist club. Yet his election to the leadership brought Labour to the brink of civil war. Many MPs were unwilling to support his leadership. In the summer of 2016, Corbyn was challenged for the leadership, as 172 (out of 233) MPs supported a motion of no confidence, following the party's weak performance in the European referendum campaign. The cause of the disagreement was multi-faceted: there were serious divides over policy, particularly over the case for intervention in Syria and the renewal of Trident. The PLP also felt it was being marginalised in the party's decision-making and feared being subject to mandatory reselection. Most Labour MPs felt Corbyn was incapable of winning an election, and after a creditable showing in 2017, two years later the party went down to a disastrous defeat.

Taken as a whole, this book reveals that parties such as Labour face an inescapable dilemma. To win votes and secure the confidence of the electorate, they have to project them-selves as unified and politically disciplined, able to govern competently and take firm decisions. On the other hand, social democratic parties must have clear goals, a vision, and a policy programme. Proclaiming party unity is not enough. Labour must hammer out and agree policies that face up to the nation's problems, a process that necessarily entails disagreement – sometimes even ideological confrontation – between rival wings of the party.

The mood of much of the membership is an understandable yearning for peace and tranquillity after years of conflict that became increasingly destructive, born of the fundamental division between the party leader and his parliamentary wing. Yet at the same time, if Corbyn's successor, Keir Starmer, is to win the next election, Labour will have to forge an alternative programme that will appeal to voters as a whole, and which projects its competence and capacity to deliver, particularly in managing the economy in the wake of a global pandemic and the Russian invasion of Ukraine.

Unity is, of course, important but if it means avoiding problems and facing up to painful realities, however difficult, the pursuit of party unity could ultimately be self-defeating. The leadership must be prepared to attack outdated shibboleths, forging an ideological position that accepts society as it is, not as the left would like it to be. One of Anthony Crosland's favourite quotations was from Joseph Conrad's *Typhoon*: 'Always facing it Captain McWhirr, that's the way to get through.' Labour has to understand and address the impact of rapid economic and social change in modern Britain. Above all, the authors conclude, the party must shape a compelling national story and governing prospectus, offering a persuasive analysis of the future of Britain.

2

Government or Opposition: The 1931 Split and the Fall of Ramsay MacDonald

The internal schisms that have beset Labour throughout its history have deep roots. Since its birth at the beginning of the twentieth century, the Labour Party has been prone to internal conflict and division. Throughout its early history, the party was divided between the 'ethical' tradition of Keir Hardie emphasising the spiritual qualities of socialism as fraternity and brotherhood, and the 'Fabian' tradition of the Webbs, focused on efficient planning through the centralised state. These disputes were aggravated at critical moments by the temperament and behaviour of Labour's leading politicians. The party prided itself on the image of unity and class solidarity in the face of industrial and political adversity. Yet key figures frequently resorted to factional infighting and sectarianism to gain political advantage within the movement.

These sources of conflict help to explain the 1931 crisis which threatened to tear the party apart. The consequences of the split in the face of the unprecedented economic meltdown have reverberated ever since. The then prime minister, Ramsay MacDonald, is judged harshly in official accounts of Labour history. Pilloried as a traitor to his party and class, he was unable to prevent underlying tensions from bringing Labour to the brink of civil war. The political crisis of the early 1930s exposed the discord between the party's industrial wing, shaped by the sectional interests of the unions, and the parliamentary party and ministers acting in the national economic interest. Moreover, there was confusion as to Labour's essential purpose. MacDonald's allies wanted to remain in office, even if that meant offending their natural supporters. Yet many in the unions and party grassroots preferred to go into opposition, protesting against the evils of unemployment and cuts. By 1931, Labour had not yet resolved whether it was a party of power or a party of principle, a pragmatic party or a visionary party, a party of government or a party of opposition.

Moreover, there was damaging division over Labour's identity. The crisis revealed the absence of any cogent ideology and underpinning programme. MacDonald wooed his party through an appeal to ethical socialism, yet in government he eschewed ideology in favour of realism and pragmatism. In addition, Labour had arrived in office in 1929 without a coherent economic programme. It was not until the mid-1930s that a more robust vision of 'Fabian' socialism emerged emphasising nationalisation, central planning, and macroeconomic stabilisation. Faced by the worldwide depression in 1929, Labour was unable to formulate a viable plan to conquer mass unemployment. At key moments, MacDonald's political style and temperament aggravated problems created by structural divisions that existed since the Labour Party's foundation. Nonetheless, it is debatable whether an alternative leader, such as the more emollient Arthur Henderson, could have achieved a fundamentally different outcome. Labour as a party was prone to damaging internal divisions and the sporadic eruption of civil wars, irrespective of the machinations of its leadership. The depth of the economic crisis in 1930–1 was unprecedented.

This chapter on the 1931 crisis begins by focusing on Ramsay MacDonald's background as Labour leader, briefly outlining his upbringing and early career. It is important to then address the strategy that MacDonald devised to fashion a 'greater Labour Party' as the main anti-Conservative force in British politics. The chapter analyses Labour's evolution as a party of power from the end of the First World War to the minority government of 1929. It had a brief taste of power in 1924 but suffered from the absence of rigorous thinking about policy, while the 1926 general strike undermined the labour movement's moderate credentials. Still, MacDonald's party came to power again in 1929 on a tide of optimism and political goodwill.

The chapter then turns to the economic crisis of 1929–31 which eventually destroyed the Labour government. It examines the roots of the crisis, and its denouement in the summer of 1931, and considers why MacDonald's administration failed to determine an alternative course of action that might have preserved the unity of the labour movement by adopting Keynesian remedies to alleviate unemployment. Finally, the chapter focuses on the period from 1931 to the outbreak of the Second World War. Despite the reverberations of the 1931 collapse, the party was able to reassert itself as a serious contender for power. It did so through co-operation between the unions and the leadership, a recommitment to being a party of government rather than opposition, and by devising an ideological vision of Fabian 'efficiency socialism'. Moreover, after 1935 Labour had a leader in Clement Attlee committed to maintaining party unity and offering a credible governing alternative.

Ramsay MacDonald: His Personal Story

The story of Labour's first prime minister, James Ramsay MacDonald, begins in Lossiemouth, Morayshire, on 12 October 1866.[1] Lossiemouth was a fishing port in north-east Scotland, surrounded by tight-knit rural farming communities. James never knew his father, John MacDonald, a casual labourer and ploughman who absconded after learning that James' mother, Anne, was pregnant. Being an 'illegitimate' child among the Scottish rural peasantry was a humiliating experience that scarred MacDonald for life, perhaps explaining his craving for respectability and acceptance in polite society (both Keir Hardie and Ernest Bevin were also born out of wedlock). MacDonald's biographer, David Marquand, speculates that illegitimacy made MacDonald particularly vulnerable to criticism.[2] As a young man he could be reserved and prickly, 'uncertain of his identity and unsure where he belonged'. Like the party he aspired to lead, MacDonald was never entirely confident of his place in the world.

That said, there can be little doubt that MacDonald received love and attention from his adoring mother and attentive grandmother. Their influence made MacDonald courageous and self-reliant, giving him the steely resolve to strive towards the very top of British politics. Anne was employed as a dressmaker and house servant. James was largely brought up by his grandmother, the formidable Bella Ramsay. As a young boy, he was raised in conditions of material hardship, although there was a deep appreciation of the importance of education. MacDonald attended the parish school at Drainie where the quality of teaching was regarded as outstanding. MacDonald later recalled that as a result of his training, 'every bolt in our intellect was tightened up'. A star pupil, MacDonald then spent four years as a 'pupil-teacher', giving him 'an education far superior to any Labour leader of his generation'.[3] As a young man, James then embarked on a life of political activity. He left Scotland and moved to Bristol in 1885, a city with a strong tradition of working-class radicalism. He soon joined the Social Democratic Federation (SDF). The following year, he arrived in London. MacDonald struggled to find employment during the trade depression but was eventually appointed as a clerk at the National Cyclists' Union. Even so, his early career was marked by regular bouts of unemployment.

In the late 1880s, MacDonald became a member of the Fabian Society, and was subsequently involved in the launch of the 'Lib–Lab' journal the *Progressive Review* alongside J. A. Hobson and the radical journalist William Clarke. London was at the centre of a vibrant network of political activity on the left. The aim of the *Progressive Review* was to forge links between the 'forces of progress' among liberals and social democrats. The critical event in his life, however, was his marriage to Margaret Gladstone in 1896. Margaret's family were far from wealthy, but the private income from her middle-class father gave MacDonald the financial independence to pursue a parliamentary career at a time when MPs were unpaid. The couple subsequently had five children. Margaret and her family provided MacDonald with the financial and emotional stability he had hitherto lacked as a young man. MacDonald then rose swiftly to become a key figure in the founding of the Labour Party. Following the launch of the Labour Representation Committee (LRC) in 1900, MacDonald became its first secretary.

MacDonald was undeniably a gifted strategist who contributed ideas to the development of socialist thought, focusing on how to strengthen Labour's appeal to the nation. One of his most important works, *Socialism and Society*, published in 1905, emphasised the virtues of evolutionary socialism, of reform over revolution. A prominent member of the Rainbow Circle, which in the 1890s had been dominated by the 'New Liberals', MacDonald believed socialism must arise out of liberalism, retaining its core commitment to parliamentary democracy. He understood that Labour could only succeed as a 'greater Labour party' that replaced the Liberals by appealing to all sections of progressive opinion in British society, notably the middle-class and rural interests. The party had to strike a delicate balance. It had to co-operate with the Liberal Party to build up its organisation and win seats in Parliament, while developing an approach distinct from the Liberals that would eventually displace them as the main anti-Conservative force in the British polity. In appealing to those who were sceptical of Labour's ability to rule and its narrow class consciousness, the party had to project itself as a unified, disciplined, and competent political force, a party of conscience as much as class. Labour's goal, MacDonald maintained, was to subordinate 'dogmatic Socialism to the practical possibilities of Socialistic change'.[4]

As such, MacDonald believed his party must eschew trade union militancy and industrial conflict, marginalising the British Communist Party while preventing infiltration by 'fellow travellers' on the left. It was clear that the pragmatism and moderation of the trade unions was coming under strain from the growth of syndicalism and direct action. He was criticised by more radical 'Red Clydeside' and ILP-affiliated MPs for lacking 'the instinct of agitation'. While the First World War improved Labour's prospects by widening the electoral franchise and emphasising the role of the state in the economy, incisive political leadership was necessary if the party was to advance through the ballot box. That the Liberal Party would eventually be replaced by the forward march of the working class and the Labour Party was hardly a foregone conclusion.

By 1918, Labour was an unwieldy assortment of trade unions, socialist societies, the Independent Labour Party (ILP), and middle-class intellectuals gathered around the Fabian Society. The trade unionists saw the party's purpose as defending labour interests rather than transforming society. Neither did the Labour Party have any coherent ideological identity. The most prominent tradition was 'Corporate Socialism' centred on the goal of public ownership of the national economy. These aims were formally enshrined in Clause IV of the party's constitution, drafted by the prominent Fabian Sidney Webb and adopted by Labour in 1918. Clause IV articulated a doctrine of social justice yet it was an inherently ambiguous statement. There was little indication from the debate at the 1918 conference that Labour intended to fundamentally redistribute economic power between the classes and alter existing democratic institutions. The document *Labour and the New Social Order* published in the same year was informed by similarly ambiguous assumptions.[5] It was premised on the belief that capitalism would be replaced by a 'new order', while socialism would lead to booming production and rising working-class living standards. The prosperity of workers would be secured by a universal national minimum, public control of industry, a capital levy, and the appropriation of unearned wealth.[6]

Undeniably, Corporate Socialism came closest to defining a practical agenda for the Labour Party in power. Alongside it was G. D. H. Cole's vision of Guild Socialism. This doctrine amounted to the rejection of centralisation and statism in economic life while emphasising workers' control and participatory democracy, policies dismissed by the Webbs as 'sheer chaotic anarchy'. Meanwhile, other ideological streams and traditions jostled for influence. There were residues of late-nineteenth-century social liberalism, emphasising individual rights alongside the 'positive freedom' afforded by state intervention and the welfare state. And there was 'gas and water socialism' pioneered by local government centred on the practical provision of municipal services. The problem for the party was that in this period, its socialism was 'fluid and unstable, the synthesis of a variety of distinct traditions'.[7] There were obvious tensions between these ideological tributaries which made it difficult to meld the different traditions together into a coherent ideology.

Moreover, despite the widening of the electoral franchise,

the party struggled to gain momentum in a two-party system that favoured the Conservative Party and the Liberals. Mac-Donald understood that to displace the Liberals, Labour had now to fulfil working-class aspirations for social reform and assert its claim to moderate reasonableness. He told the 1924 Labour Party conference: 'Communism, as we know it has nothing practical in common with us. It is a product of Czarism and war mentality, and as such we have nothing in common with it.' During a decade of escalating class conflict culminating in the 1926 general strike, MacDonald warned against 'the tempting but futile paths of revolution'. He believed that operating within established constitutional structures was vital in attracting the support of the skilled working class and the progressive middle class. The railway-man, trade unionist, and MacDonald ally J. H. Thomas, typified this mindset by paying tribute to the British constitutional system which 'enable[d] an engine-driver of yesterday to be a minister of today'.

In 1906, after several attempts at winning a seat in Parliament, MacDonald was elected as the MP for Leicester, the result of a pact with local Liberals that prevented the anti-Conservative vote from splitting. The *Leicester Mercury* described MacDonald as 'a tall, strong, vigorous young man', who had 'obviously got a lot of fight in him'. By 1911, MacDonald had become chairman of the PLP, succeeding Henderson (a former iron-moulder and Liberal Party agent representing Barnard Castle in County Durham), who retired from the role, as was customary, after two years in office. MacDonald brought to the chairmanship his belief in the virtues of strong leadership. Nevertheless, he was compelled to resign in 1914 because of his opposition to the outbreak of World War One. Labour was split between its pacifist wing, and those who were persuaded by a more nationalistic and jingoistic appeal. The Independent Labour Party (ILP) largely opposed the war whereas trade unionists were generally patriotic. While MacDonald's anti-war views were deeply unpopular, he was unwavering. He did not believe that war could be solely blamed on German aggression, and sought to use his contacts with other European socialists to broker an end to the hostilities. He was particularly close to the German revisionist intellectual Eduard Bernstein. Not surprisingly, MacDonald was heavily defeated in the subsequent 'khaki' election of 1918.

However, by November 1922 he was back in the House of Commons as MP for Aberavon and resumed his position as chair of the PLP. The role was previously held by J. R. Clynes, the competent but uncharismatic trade unionist who had begun work in a Lancashire cotton mill at the age of ten. In Parliament, MacDonald won the backing of the ILP left as the leading anti-war MP. He used the platform of PLP chairman to become the first 'modern' leader of the party, not only managing his MPs and parliamentary procedure, but enacting a strategy to win power through political organisation and policy. At this stage, MacDonald completely dominated the party, underlining the newly established importance of the leader.

MacDonald had quickly acquired the reputation of being a gifted parliamentarian. He was widely regarded as handsome, principled, eloquent, and persuasive. MacDonald was a remarkable public orator, 'the greatest artist of our time', according to the Fabian founder, Beatrice Webb. MacDonald's rhetoric emphasised the spiritual and ethical qualities of socialism in order to broaden the party's appeal. It was said that the main influences on Labour MPs prior to the First World War were Dickens, Carlyle, Ruskin – and the Bible.[8] If according to that renowned cliché Labour owed more to Methodism than to Marx, MacDonald (himself a non-believer) channelled the spiritual qualities of non-conformism into ethical socialism. Yet he blended a romantic and utopian style of politics with total adherence to existing constitutional norms.[9] Following the 1924 election, MacDonald was invited to become prime minister, thus marking the absorption of Labourism into the established governing system.

Labour's Evolution as a Party of Power 1918–29

The decade after the end of the First World War was crucial to the Labour Party's historic advance. The expansion of the franchise allowed Labour to replace the Liberals as the main opposition. At the general election of 1922, Labour won 191 seats to the Liberals' 158. Yet even by 1924, Labour made little progress in devising a plausible plan for government. The first minority Labour government came about following the defeat of Stanley Baldwin's legislative programme, and Asquith's agreement to allow Labour to form an alternative administration. Asquith told his followers: 'If a Labour Government is ever to be tried in this country, as it will be sooner or later, it could hardly be under safer conditions.'[10]

The king, George V, then invited MacDonald to form an administration. A few days earlier, at a dinner hosted by the

Webbs, the 'big six' of Labour's first generation of leaders, J. H. Thomas, MacDonald, Snowden, Henderson, J. R. Clynes, and Webb, agreed that if the opportunity arose Labour should take office, if necessary as a minority government. If Mac-Donald's party had refused to serve in those circumstances, it would have risked 'giving a new lease of life to the Liberal Party', concluded Attlee. Even so, ministers were able to advance few concrete reforms during their ten months in power. There was some progress in foreign affairs, and in housing through the passing of the Wheatley Act. They were undoubtedly hindered by the absence of a parliamentary majority, but Labour's manifesto was threadbare.

The party's sterility was reinforced by Labour's small-c conservative economic policies. As chancellor of the exchequer, Philip Snowden believed Britain must remain committed to the fundamental axioms of sound economic policy, not least free trade and return to the gold standard. Snowden's persona epitomised the non-conformist Yorkshire working class, and he detested the vices of alcohol and gambling. Born in a Pennine village near Keighley, Snowden had entered the lower ranks of the civil service as a young man. He was eventually elected as the MP for Blackburn. Snowden believed the purpose of socialism was to make capitalism function more efficiently, ensuring material and spiritual improvements in the lives of the working class. Significantly, little detailed work was done prior to 1924 concerning the parameters of Labour's plans for public ownership. The party's views on industrial policy were intellectually superficial. More seriously, the party had few concrete proposals to address rising unemployment. The government lasted barely ten months. Yet five years later when it returned to power, Labour's ideas had barely developed further.

The 1924 Labour government duly collapsed following a parliamentary debate in which the Conservatives and the Liberals accused MacDonald of exerting unconstitutional pressure on the attorney general to withdraw the prosecution of the editor of *Workers' Weekly* on a charge of incitement to mutiny. The prime minister declared that if the censure motion or amendment put down by the Conservatives and the Liberal Party was carried, the government would resign. MacDonald's administration lost the vote by 364 to 198, and the prime minister asked the king for a dissolution. The subsequent election was dominated by foreign policy and the rise of international communism, which the Tories used to put Labour on the back foot.

Following the 1924 defeat there was fierce criticism of the parliamentary leadership within the party. The rising star of the trade union movement Ernest Bevin wanted to replace MacDonald with Arthur Henderson (although Henderson refused to stand against MacDonald). To impose discipline on his party, MacDonald had ensured the details of Labour's programme remained vague and ambiguous. What British socialism actually meant still appeared woolly-minded and nebulous. The 1926 general strike did not help matters, as the unions were portrayed as undermining the democratic constitution of the country. The strike ended in failure after just nine days.

In 1928, the party published its first comprehensive policy statement, 'Labour and the Nation'.[11] The document emphasised public ownership of industry to promote 'co-operation' over competition while eliminating 'the sordid struggle for private gain' from the economy. It was nonetheless striking how few specifics it contained, saying little about which industries would be nationalised under Labour. The justification for public ownership still rested on ethical arguments rather than precise claims about the impact on industrial efficiency. R. H. Tawney's judgement was that Labour's 1928 programme was wildly unrealistic. It resembled 'a glittering forest of Christmas trees, with presents for all'.

At the same time, MacDonald's lofty style had the effect of concealing major ideological disagreements which then erupted in the wake of the Great Depression. The trade unions had been defeated in the disastrous strike of 1926. In the face of Conservative legislation that made strikes illegal, many trade unionists saw the Labour government's election as the only hope of protecting their right to organise. As leader, MacDonald appealed to the moral aspirations of his party, affirming that socialism was an ethical cause. There was purposeful avoidance of any detailed discussion of policy. This damaged Labour after 1929, when it became clear that painful choices were necessary for which the party and trade unions were ill-prepared. Ideological vacuity was an inadequate basis on which to deal with painful economic realities in government. The root of Labour's civil war in the early 1930s was the fact that, in Marquand's words, the party remained 'a strange mixture of Utopian rhetoric and conservative practice'.[12] Indeed, it is fair to say that when Labour came to power in 1929 it was 'totally unprepared for the actual responsibilities of government'. As a consequence, its failures 'multiplied popular scepticism about the objectives of socialism'.[13]

The Years of Crisis: 1929–31

Labour came to power in 1929 evincing optimism and confidence. While the Conservative campaign in that year's election was built around the image of 'safety first' personified by Stanley Baldwin, MacDonald's Labour Party made gains from the worsening economic situation. The party won 287 seats in the House of Commons to 260 for the Conservatives, a narrow but decisive victory. Having won by appealing to the 'practical men and women' of the nation, MacDonald's government initially displayed a spirit of self-assurance markedly absent in 1924. As Beatrice Webb observed in her diaries, 'The PLP has the air of being thoroughly established; all the Ministers are self-possessed and self-confident and just at present purring over the popularity of their Government.'[14] MacDonald's administration looked moderate, competent, trustworthy, and determined to act in dealing with the mounting problem of unemployment. Initially, the trade unions were anxious to be supportive, giving the government the benefit of the doubt.

Yet this propitious situation was not to last. The state of the economy quickly deteriorated. The financial crisis occurred as recession in the United States led to an unprecedented collapse of world trade. The Wall Street Crash cut off the American funding that had sustained European prosperity since the First World War; a depression set in. Unemployment was rising inexorably each month. In Britain, it was already above one million before the crisis struck. Cyclical unemployment arising from the slump in the world economy added to structural unemployment, leaving thousands out of work in the industrial areas. By the end of 1930, there were two and a half million British adults of working age who were unemployed. By the summer of 1931, the unemployment rate reached more than 15 per cent. The government initially responded to the downturn by providing relatively generous unemployment benefits. But there was little sign of concrete policy ideas to tackle the problem, while the policy of making the dole more generous became increasingly untenable as budgetary pressures mounted.

Having developed few novel ideas in economic strategy, ministers felt compelled to continue their predecessor's budgetary policies while upholding the commitment to free trade and the gold standard. In 1925, Winston Churchill had returned Britain to the gold standard at the pre-war parity of $4.86. As chancellor of the exchequer, Snowden remained an austere politician who cared little for utopian socialism. His budget in 1930 proposed tax increases to reduce the £42 million deficit, alongside a rise in death duties and taxes on beer. Snowden dismissed the case for counter-cyclical expansionary policy and loan-financed public works. In this period, free trade was 'an article of faith', even within the Labour leadership.

Although Clause IV committed the party to a sweeping programme of nationalisation, there were few concrete plans to bring key sectors into state ownership. Ministers defended the government by pointing out that they lacked a majority in the House of Commons and did not have a mandate to transform the existing economic order. The root cause of mass unemployment was the dysfunctional capitalist system. MacDonald told the Labour Party conference in 1930:

So, my friends, we are not on trial; it is the system under which we live. It has broken down, not only in this little island, it has broken down in Europe, in Asia, in America; it has broken down everywhere, as it was bound to break down. And the cure, the new path, the new idea is organization – organization which will protect life, not property; organization which may protect property, but protect property in proper relation to life; I appeal to you, my friends, today, with all that is going on outside – I appeal to you to go back on to your socialist faith. Do not mix that up with pettifogging patching, either of a Poor Law kind or of Relief Work kind. Construction, ideas, architecture, building line upon line, stone upon stone, storey upon storey; it will not be your happiness, and it will certainly not be mine, to see that every stone laid in sincerity has been well laid. But I think it will be your happiness, as it is mine, to go on convinced that the great foundations are being well laid ... and that by skilled craftsmen, confident in each other's goodwill and sincerity, the temple will rise and rise and rise until at last it is complete, and the genius of humanity will find within it an appropriate resting place.[15]

Yet for all the eloquence of MacDonald's rhetoric and his success in reshaping Labour into a party of power, the government was humiliatingly exposed during the political crisis that erupted in the summer of 1931. The problem was that as the situation deteriorated in July and August, it was increasingly apparent that the government lacked a credible programme, while ministers and the labour movement were divided about the unenviable political choices that lay ahead.

What triggered the collapse of MacDonald's administration was the budgetary problem rather than the Great Depression itself. The government was brought down by divisions in the Cabinet over proposals to cut public spending, especially unemployment benefit. It is certainly the case that the pressure on the public finances in 1930–1 was enormous. Early in 1931, Snowden established the May Committee to provide independent advice to ministers on how to secure efficiencies in expenditure. On 31 July, the committee chaired by George May, former secretary of the Prudential Assurance Company, published a report forecasting a budget deficit of £120 million, and recommending major cuts in spending. May was an unusual appointment for a Labour chancellor since he was a conventional upper-middle-class City financier. The proposed efficiencies included £67 million in welfare payments for the unemployed. The economist John Maynard Keynes dismissed the May Committee's recommendations as 'a most gross perversion of social justice'. Keynes believed that economy measures which cut household incomes would merely exacerbate the problem of insufficient aggregate demand. Indeed, the report became the trigger for a subsequent financial panic. There was no relief from the pressure on sterling. The City and international markets insisted that there had to be a major budgetary adjustment by the UK authorities.

Throughout the crisis, MacDonald and Snowden's instinct was to broker compromise with opposition parties. They sought to build a cross-party consensus for a modest package of efficiencies.[16] MacDonald and his chancellor were prepared to do whatever was necessary to reassure the City and the financial markets. They believed the Labour government's ability to continue in office depended on upholding economic confidence. Ministers acknowledged that Britain's economy was dependent on the City of London, and the in-flow of international money.

Even so, the financial markets and foreign investors had already taken fright. MacDonald and Snowden sought to reassure them by agreeing more drastic measures, including further cuts in welfare spending. Yet the failure to secure agreement with the opposition led to the collapse of confidence in the government's strategy. The consequence was further pressure from international banks, major financial turmoil, and subsequently the run on sterling. Despite the government's acceptance of a further £56 million of cuts in August 1931, it proved impossible to win the support of Conservative and Liberal MPs. In the meantime, unrest within the Labour Party was stirring.

In the months leading up to the crisis, there was no immediate or obvious threat to MacDonald's position as leader, even as the economic emergency grew worse. For all the difficulties Labour faced when the party came to power in 1929, the PLP's mindset was fundamentally loyalist, while the trade unions remained sympathetic. There was an attitude of intolerance towards dissenters in the party vilified as undermining the advance towards socialism. The union leadership detested public criticism of the government, even if Bevin and Walter Citrine became frustrated in private. It was accepted that NEC and PLP malcontents ought to be marginalised. Throughout the period, Labour conferences were tightly managed and orchestrated, enabling MacDonald to rally the party faithful in a display of public confidence. In 1930, Oswald Mosley's resignation and advocacy of an alternative programme centred on reflation and a public works programme spelt trouble for Labour ministers. Yet Mosley's reputation was soon tarnished despite the superficial attraction of his ideas on the British left; Henderson appealed to PLP loyalty and the imperative of collective responsibility in the face of the impending worldwide economic crisis.

Even so, as political pressure mounted the Cabinet became increasingly divided. The Bank of England continued to pressure Snowden to implement further budget cuts to restore confidence. Ministers led by the implacably moderate Henderson, alongside the trade unions corralled by Ernest Bevin, were unwilling to countenance drastic reductions in assistance for the unemployed that would have inflicted acute suffering in Labour's heartlands. Trade unionists felt that they had to protect the position of working-class electors, otherwise there was little point in pursuing parliamentary politics. Socialists were naturally resistant to any policy that betrayed their principles of protecting the vulnerable. Hugh Dalton, MP for Bishop Auckland, reflected the mood of despondency: 'I am going to Bishop Auckland in the first days of January and hate the prospect of meeting my constituents again. It is all tragically different, so far as economic questions go, from what one had hoped and dreamed a Labour government would be like.'[17] MacDonald himself admitted Labour now faced an impossible situation since cutting the dole negated everything the party stood for, yet he continued to believe that leaving the gold standard was simply too politically risky.

Given the lack of obvious alternatives, the worsening

economic situation led to inevitable confrontation. The international crisis was initially sparked by the collapse of the Austrian bank Credit Anstalt in May 1931. Panic spread like a virus through the financial system. Within weeks, the Bank of England was sustaining heavy losses in its efforts to defend sterling. By August 1931, as the crisis deepened, it was clear that MacDonald's ministers would have to take painful decisions if they were to fulfil their aim of balancing the budget. Keynes advised that Britain should leave the gold standard immediately. However, Snowden feared that departing the gold standard and devaluing sterling was an easy option that would quickly erode real wages and living standards. The political options were so unattractive that some Cabinet ministers, many of the PLP, and most of the trade unions believed Labour should go into opposition. No longer in power, they could avoid the invidious choice of cutting the dole, harming the party's natural supporters, and losing financial credibility in the face of an economic firestorm.

It was to MacDonald's credit that he refused to take the easy way out. He believed that if it were to be a serious party of government, Labour must have the courage to take tough decisions. If ministers did not make cuts, the Conservatives would do it themselves but more harshly and indiscriminately. Moreover, if Labour did not behave as a responsible party of government, it risked being eclipsed by the Liberals as the main opposition. The problem was that the labour movement was reluctant to face up to the grave economic circumstances confronting the nation. Moreover, MacDonald's skills in managing his party proved inadequate. The prime minister struggled to co-ordinate his Cabinet to drive his legislative agenda, while a unifying sense of purpose and energy at a time of national crisis was often absent.

The prime minister's instinct was to micromanage Whitehall departments, notably the Treasury. Yet his grasp of economic policy, and more particularly his understanding of the structural causes of unemployment, remained weak. Exhausted by the turn of events, ministers were inclined to accept the advice of civil servants, leading to too little creativity and imagination. When Walter Citrine and Ernest Bevin of the TUC protested against the cuts, MacDonald was dismissive and unsympathetic. Indeed, to many observers the prime minister displayed a remarkable lack of empathy towards the unemployed that was very surprising given his background (although it must be said not everyone in the party supported more generous unemployment relief, which they feared might be abused, thereby losing Labour support among the 'decent' working class). MacDonald had forgotten that Labour was not a liberal 'progressive' party, but a 'labourist' party that relied heavily on working-class identification.[18] Even if the government lacked confidence in the doctrines of Keynes, it urgently needed a compelling answer to address the problem of unemployment. The dominant theme of party policy was public ownership of major industries and utilities, largely an irrelevance in those circumstances. Bevin believed the government's deflationary policy was a historic error, arguing like Keynes for devaluation to avoid industrial collapse.

As events took their course, Labour edged ever closer to civil war. The divisions within the Cabinet had become unbridgeable. Opposition to cuts came principally from Christopher Addison, George Lansbury, and Arthur Greenwood.

MacDonald accused those ministers of being in the pocket of the TUC. He attacked the trade union position as being obsessed with superficial 'palliatives' rather than measures that would actually reduce unemployment. A cuts package was eventually agreed by eleven votes to nine in Cabinet. The rebellion against Snowden's programme of retrenchment was led by Henderson. Unable to agree measures that unified his colleagues and having the proposal of coalition rejected, Mac-Donald sought an audience with the king, advising him that the government could not continue.

MacDonald expected the king to accept his resignation, appointing Stanley Baldwin to replace him. Yet to MacDonald's great astonishment, George V requested that he continue as prime minister, insisting his leadership was necessary to get through the national crisis. Susceptible to the king's flattery, MacDonald agreed, although egotism and vanity were not his only motives. MacDonald genuinely believed that only his government could solve the crisis, while as a patriot he should do as the King asked, taking steps to avoid a financial calamity. The king's persuasive powers were more significant than MacDonald's alleged susceptibility to the 'aristocratic embrace'. The so-called emergency National Government was established with the support of the Conservatives, Liberals, and twelve Labour MPs who defected with him, including the Cabinet ministers Snowden, J. H. Thomas, and Lord Sankey. Baldwin and the acting Liberal leader, Herbert Samuel, were to serve under him. Macdonald had nonetheless badly misread the situation, wrongly expecting 100 Labour MPs to defect with him. Few Labour ministers or MPs were prepared to 'travel the same road' as MacDonald.

At the prompting of George V, the opposition were prepared to allow a 'socialist' prime minister to continue in office, which had the merit, for them, of making MacDonald responsible for the unpalatable decision to cut welfare support. As such, MacDonald became 'the prisoner of an overwhelmingly Conservative majority ... everyone knew Baldwin was the pivot around which the Government turned'.[19] Labour ministers were dumbfounded by MacDonald's actions. Attlee for one felt that Snowden and MacDonald had blocked concrete proposals to deal with the crisis, while the cuts package did not require enough sacrifice from the wealthy. Attlee, Dalton, and Bevin resolved to lead opposition to the National Government, rallying the Labour Party against the prime minister. They were soon joined by Herbert Morrison and Stafford Cripps, then solicitor-general, who refused to serve in the National Government, despite supporting MacDonald in Cabinet. Cripps deeply regretted the division. He wrote to MacDonald: 'My own personal hope is that the rift in the party may be quickly healed.'[20]

In contrast, it appears that Morrison hesitated over the question of whether he should join the National Government. After all, Morrison supported the budget cuts as a fiscal necessity, while he admired MacDonald's leadership and exceptional political courage during the crisis in the face of other ministers' 'timidity'. On 25 August 1931, *The Times* reported that Morrison remained 'a loyal supporter of Mr MacDonald'. Yet only a day later, *The Manchester Guardian* insisted, 'there has never been any question of his joining the National Government'.[21] Morrison's biographers came to the view that in his heart Morrison was with MacDonald and wanted to remain in the government, but he was eventually persuaded by the prime minister that to do so would be career suicide. He must bide his time. All in all, the main figures in the party stuck with Labour because they still believed in its long-term aims in the face of the 1931 crisis which affirmed the moral bankruptcy of the capitalist system: a fairer distribution of wealth, defeat of poverty, preservation of social welfare, economic planning, and nationalisation.

To secure support for the tough package of measures the National Government proposed, including a 10 per cent cut in unemployment benefit, MacDonald called a general election in October 1931 with Tory support. By now, MacDonald was despairing of Labour's situation: 'It looks as though all our work has gone into the creation of a petty and passionate class movement whose ideal of socialism is not much more than public subsidies', he wrote.[22] Campaigning on policies decried by Keynes as 'the most wrong and foolish things that Parliament has deliberately perpetrated in my lifetime', the National Government crushed the Labour Party in a coupon election. Labour's 1931 manifesto proclaimed the election was 'A decisive opportunity ... to reconstruct the foundations of the [nation's] life ... The capitalist system has broken down even in those countries where its authority was thought to be most secure.' Yet during the campaign itself, Labour representatives were attacked relentlessly for being economically incompetent and unpatriotic.

The consequence was a terrible defeat: only fifty-two Labour MPs were returned, a sharp decline from 287 seats in 1929 (even if the result partly reflected the inequities of the first-past-the-post system: Labour's share of the popular vote fell only 7 per cent). Labour now held no seats in Tyneside, the West Midlands, or the Lancashire cotton towns. It had pockets of electoral strength only in the East End of London and the big cities such as Glasgow. Henderson, who served in the coalition government during the First World War, became acting leader. The instinct of avuncular Uncle Arthur (as he was affectionately known) was to try to heal the wounds that divided the party. He acted bravely in traumatic circumstances, initially attempting to bring MacDonald back within the fold after the prime minister's expulsion.

Yet it was never realistic that MacDonald could return in the aftermath of the divisive 1931 election campaign in which the prime minister pilloried his former Labour colleagues. What followed was 'the swift, cold and practically unanimous repudiation of MacDonald, Snowdon and Thomas by the entire Labour world'.[23] In a symbolic act, Morrison turned MacDonald's photograph in the London Labour Party headquarters to face the wall. Consequently, the myth of MacDonald's treachery and betrayal was established permanently in Labour's folk-memory. The blame for the 1931 debacle was alleged to lay squarely with the former prime minister. MacDonald was said to have been entrapped in an 'aristocratic embrace' which made him ill-suited to managing an economic crisis, a charge made more plausible by revelations of his affair with Lady Londonderry. Nonetheless, as David Howell attests, MacDonald's betrayal merely provided the Labour leadership with an alibi, distracting attention from the substantive failures of the 1929–31 administration.

The Keynesian Alternative?

The most significant historical question arising from these events is why MacDonald's government was unable to devise an alternative programme to deal more effectively with the economic catastrophe? At first glance, Labour's inability to provide an effective response to soaring unemployment seems inexplicable. The fundamental error, it is claimed, was Mac-Donald's refusal to pursue the radical ideas of Keynes, notably to abandon the gold standard and impose a 10 per cent tariff on goods that might protect the domestic base of British industry. Snowden's Treasury was without doubt strongly opposed to such measures. Labour was hamstrung because of its attachment to economic orthodoxy. Following the Great Depression, the party missed its opportunity to respond by enacting a radical programme to expand the responsibilities of the state. Snowden did not believe the Labour administration could defy the markets and leave the gold standard. In his landmark work *Politicians and the Slump*, the historian Robert Skidelsky insists Labour suffered from an endemic poverty of intellectual imagination, chiefly because the party was resistant to the theories of Keynes.[24] Its flirtation with nebulous ideas about socialism, which assumed the existing economic system would one day be superseded or replaced, meant the party failed to recognise the political choice was between 'interventionist' and 'laissez-faire' capitalism. The government clung like a limpet to conventional wisdom. Its ignorance about the functioning of capitalism in fact became 'an alibi for inaction'. MacDonald's party was trapped between orthodoxy and militancy. On the one hand, it had little confidence in the alternative proposed by Keynes; on the other hand, it did not want to embrace policies that would undermine 'Labour's credentials as a fit party of government'.[25]

Keynes was not unsympathetic to the predicament of Labour ministers. He served diligently on the Macmillan Committee in 1930–1. Indeed, Keynes formed a constructive working relationship with MacDonald. It is unrealistic to believe the Labour government could have become wholesale converts to Keynesian thinking. For one, 'intellectual snobbery' prevented Keynes from committing to the Labour Party's success. There was mutual distrust as a result. As he put it, 'I do not believe that the intellectual elements in the Labour Party will ever exercise adequate control'. Ministers remained perplexed since while 'Mr Keynes' economic ideas ... imply socialism ... he fails to go on from the economic principles he has laid bare to the necessary institutions which embody them in society'.[26] The Labour Party remained uneasy about Keynes and his governing philosophy. After all, he was a Liberal rather than socialist. He was to the right of Labour in endorsing the market economy's profit motive, refusing to take a stand in the putative conflict between labour and capital. More controversially, Keynes dismissed nationalisation – the centrepiece of Labour's 1918 programme – as an irrelevance. Despite its dwindling fortunes in the 1920s, Keynes continued to work predominantly with the Liberal Party. He was unwilling to bend to the class-orientated outlook of the labour movement in exercising political influence. He believed ultimately that Labour's utopianism meant it would fail to address prevailing economic realities.

As importantly, Keynes' ideas were largely untested in the late 1920s. The government's opposition to tariffs was hardly surprising given that most Labour (and indeed Liberal) MPs had long been enthusiastic supporters of free trade to keep food prices as low as possible. The Labour politician Hugh Dalton, who was a trained academic economist, violently opposed the protectionist measures advocated by Keynes, believing that the stimulatory effect of public spending risked stoking inflation. Moreover, while the rationale for government intervention was persuasive, it hardly constituted a coherent programme in 1931. It was not until 1936 that Keynes published his famous treatise *The General Theory of Employment, Interest and Money*, supplying the theoretical justification for demand management and the post-war settlement in Western Europe. Even then, many of Keynes' supporters were arguing vociferously about the concepts underpinning his theories, not least the validity of the so-called 'multiplier effect'. Keynes had a habit of changing his views, which irritated policymakers in the Treasury. Only a year after publishing the general theory in 1936, Keynes appeared to change tack, insisting that the expansion of aggregate demand was merely one way to tackle unemployment; other remedies were required, notably regional assistance policies.[27]

Skidelsky's view that the 1929–31 government collapsed because it was unwilling to listen to Keynes is implausible. In fact, the Treasury under Snowden sought to take Keynes' proposals seriously. Even the Bank of England accepted the intellectual case for public works. More importantly, there was no readily available Keynesian alternative for Labour to pursue in 1930–1. In fact, the party performed relatively well in difficult circumstances while, 'by the standards of the time, the Labour Government was not particularly orthodox'. In the firestorm of the 1931 crisis, Labour had little choice but to adjust fiscal policy while cutting spending: further borrowing would have undermined confidence in sterling and the financial system.

Nor could MacDonald's administration have increased taxes to reduce the size of the deficit. As Keynes pointed out, tax rises would have reduced consumer demand further, undermining confidence. Oswald Mosley proposed interventionist measures including public works, raising the school leaving age, early retirement, loosening credit lines, and imposing tariffs. Yet Mosley's programme was scarcely plausible or realistic. Such ideas 'rode roughshod over the austere traditions upheld by the British Treasury'.[28] Even Hugh Dalton criticised the expansionary programme of Mosley and Lloyd George. He was sceptical about the long-term effect of protectionism and stimulatory policies. Similarly, the transport minister Herbert Morrison (who Beatrice Webb believed was one of the government's few really competent ministers) objected to Mosley's plans for a national roads agency, arguing that responsibility should remain with local authorities. He did not want a 'state dictator' trying to manage the transport network from Whitehall. In fact, spending on roads was at its highest ever level under Morrison, and he was preparing ambitious and detailed plans to nationalise London Transport and the electricity sector.

Morrison believed that Mosley and Lloyd George greatly exaggerated the economic gains that were likely to be yielded by spending on public works.[29] Above all, the fundamental issue was that Labour did not have a parliamentary majority in 1931. It was reliant on the tacit co-operation of other parties, notably the Liberals. Although Lloyd George campaigned for radical initiatives in economic policy, most Liberal MPs defended the conventional orthodoxies of the time.

Yet it seems clear that there was no straightforward Keynesian solution to which Labour could have turned. Douglas Jay, subsequently an economic adviser and then minister in the Wilson government, believed that Keynes' theories placed too much emphasis on stimulating investment during slumps, negating the role of increasing consumption through redistributive taxation.[30] Nor were other countries around the world freely pursuing Keynesian programmes. The exception was Sweden where four years before the publication of Keynes' *General Theory* the social democratic government introduced a strong counter-cyclical spending programme. Under the influence of the economist and theoretician Ernst Wigforss, the party devised a new strategy to boost consumption, investment, and employment through public works and deficit spending. This new economic policy greatly increased Swedish production and led to a dramatic reduction in unemployment.

While the US government adopted the New Deal in the mid-1930s to pump-prime the economy and offset the catastrophic weakness of aggregate demand, Roosevelt's policies were in reality 'a series of improvised responses'. Public works were never part of a coherent expansionary approach, while the measurable impact of the New Deal on American economic performance remained unclear. Indeed, like Snowden, President Roosevelt maintained the goal of a balanced budget throughout the thirties.[31] No other western government had a convincing reflationary alternative that could have been adopted in Britain, given the structural weaknesses of the

British economy and its unique role within the international system. The Labour government was constrained by domestic and international circumstances: at home, it needed to maintain business confidence without losing the support of the trade unions. Externally, as ministers recognised, financial markets would punish governments that deviated too far from the nostrums of economic orthodoxy.

Nor was there any real consensus that a fundamental rewriting of Britain's economic and political settlement was required in 1931, even if that had emerged by 1945. After all, the radical expansion of the powers of the state 'would have interfered not only with the normal course of British economic life, it could have upset the structure of British political power'.[32] The Bank of England, the Treasury, leading financial institutions, and 'conventional wisdom' were all against radical policy innovation, imposing significant constraints, whatever the political instincts of MacDonald's ministers. To contend that MacDonald could have kept his party united while conquering the problem of unemployment if only he embraced Keynesian theories is a naïve misjudgement. Labour was constitutionally prone to internal schism and division, particularly during an economic crisis. It appears unlikely that embracing Keynesianism would have fundamentally altered its prospects.

Postscript: Revival 1931–9

Although 1931 was unquestionably a disaster for Labour that threatened to destroy the party, ironically the sequence of events provided a stimulus to rethink Labour's economic and financial policy, forging a prospectus more likely to bring the party together, enabling it to govern in hard times. The collapse of the minority administration and the electoral disaster that followed in 1931 resulted in the emergence of a new generation of leaders. During the 1930s, the internal divisions that destabilised Labour since its birth gradually dissipated. There was a shift in the internal balance of power within the party towards the trade unions, spearheaded by Ernest Bevin. The unions and the party leadership began to cooperate more fruitfully, mainly as a result of Bevin's influence. All sections of the movement were now committed to Labour as a party of power operating within the norms of the British parliamentary system. The unions supported the efforts of Dalton and Morrison to modernise party policy, although tensions between the industrial and political wings did not disappear entirely.

Moreover, Labour began to develop a coherent ideological identity, advancing the vision of 'efficiency socialism' championed by the Fabian Society centred on forging a more productive economy, not simply redistributing the fruits of growth. Labour's ideas throughout its history have been shaped by the overall condition of the national economy. When capitalism appears to be in crisis and working-class prosperity is plummeting, Labour's mood about the potential for economic transformation is optimistic. Yet during periods of relative economic expansion and rising living standards, Labour's programme becomes much more cautious and circumspect.[33] After 1935, it was apparent that the capitalist system, which was convulsed by the great crash of 1929, had stabilised, requiring the party to rethink its approach.

Although Stafford Cripps and the LSE academic Harold Laski argued that Labour ought to reappraise its commitment to the existing parliamentary and constitutional system, trade union leaders such as Bevin dismissed such theoretical speculation, which they believed jeopardised the status of organised labour and the capacity to ameliorate economic hardship.

The remainder of this chapter focuses on how Labour over the course of the 1930s healed its ideological wounds and laid the foundations for the radical, reforming government of 1945. This transformation occurred because a new generation of Labour intellectuals and politicians emerged, in particular Hugh Dalton, Evan Durbin, and Hugh Gaitskell, who combined socialist principles with pragmatic understanding of the functioning of government. The New Fabian Research Bureau (NFRB) was established with constructive input from sympathetic academics, notably G. D. H. Cole and R. H. Tawney. The XYZ Club of Durbin, Dalton, Gaitskell, the academic economist Nicholas Kaldor, and the City financier Nicholas Davenport helped to put Labour in touch with sympathetic opinion in financial institutions. Together, these institutes and think tanks provided 'a much more effective fund of economic ideas' than existed previously.[34] They replaced 'the mish-mash of Utopian aspirations and conservative assumptions which had served the party so badly between 1929 and 1931'.[35] There was greater unanimity between left and right in the Labour Party on the question of economic strategy during this pre-World War Two period, particularly over the importance of nationalisation.[36] Consequently, 'Labour strove to fashion a credible, hard-headed social democratic programme, free from the time-worn Lib-Labism of the Philip Snowden type, and from the more doctrinaire or Marxist forms of socialism.'[37]

From the aftermath of the 1931 crisis until the Second World War, Labour enjoyed its most intellectually dynamic period in the twentieth century. Dalton, Durbin, Gaitskell, and Jay were crucial in translating Keynesian theories into workable policies, the basis of *Labour's Programme* (1937). As Freeden notes, 'Keynesian ideas had made a fair amount of headway in the Labour Party in the late 1930s.'[38] This advance entailed a huge intellectual effort. Initially, Keynesian approaches were dismissed by socialists as palliatives that propped up the failing capitalist order. Keynesianism had to be augmented by a doctrine of central planning through the state. Although there was flirtation with Marxist remedies in the immediate aftermath of the crisis, Labour thinkers by 1935 accepted the continuation of the capitalist economy. They believed the persistence of high unemployment was morally unacceptable, while the dominance of market forces led to industrial inefficiency. Nationalisation alongside macro-economic demand management was intended to achieve the goal of full employment. Meanwhile, social and economic planning emphasised 'the allocation of resources by means other than markets'.[39] Public ownership would abolish capitalist monopolies enabling the socialist organisation of industry while promoting technological advance given that 'socialism was rational, capitalism anarchic'. Planning would ensure the state achieved efficiency in the use of resources. In 1934, Labour published its revised programme affirming its commitment to government's role in the economy: not only was capitalism inefficient, but the success of the 'five-year plans' in Russia strengthened the attractions of centralised planning.[40] This strategy was supplemented by *Labour's Immediate Programme* (1937) including the commitment to wholesale nationalisation and improvements in working conditions. Combining Keynesian instincts on economic management with confidence in indicative planning, the 1937 programme was a major influence on Labour's 1945 manifesto, *Let Us Face the Future*.[41]

This ideological prospectus was spelt out most convincingly in Evan Durbin's work *The Politics of Democratic Socialism*.[42] More than any other thinker of the time, Durbin subtly married Keynesianism with the doctrine of Fabian planning. He wrote that planning was 'the indispensable preliminary means for the attainment of the new society', a countervailing power against the anarchism of market forces.[43] The book was 'one of the foundation texts of British democratic socialism, exceeding in eloquence, conviction and depth of thought anything from any other contemporary source'.[44]

Durbin believed Labour must accept that capitalism was able to generate stable growth and prosperity. But Durbin also demonstrated that socialist measures such as public ownership could co-exist with democratic institutions. He remarked:

We wish to use the power of the state to establish expansionist policies within the growing socialised sector of the economy; to restore and maintain a high level of active accumulation; to moderate insecurity still further; to curb the cyclical oscillations of economic activity by a control of the income and investment position of the community; and to secure much greater equality in the distribution of the product of industry. It is only possible to do this by the supersession of private property as the seat of industrial control, as distinct from property as a form of personal reserve.[45]

Durbin remained an implacable opponent of Soviet Russia, believing that 'to betray democracy is to betray socialism'.

As Durbin attested, for the Fabians planning remained 'the essential ingredient in the socialist economic alternative'. His writings offered 'a non-totalitarian socialist programme ... subtly tailored to the British political tradition ... [and] a much more effective fund of economic ideas'.[46] Durbin believed that the emerging disciplines of the social sciences, notably economics, could enable Labour to better understand society and govern effectively. The 1931 crisis had the long-term effect of removing the 'ethical socialism' of Keir Hardie and Ramsay MacDonald from the mainstream of Labour's thought, replaced by the growing emphasis on the 'economic theories' of Durbin, Dalton, and Jay.[47] Durbin sought to develop a 'socialist economic strategy' influenced not only by Keynes, but Hayek and Robbins, who taught Durbin at the London School of Economics (LSE). Although a socialist, Durbin was sensitive to criticisms of planning and the need to protect consumer sovereignty, claims advanced by Hayek in his intellectual duel with Keynes.[48] Durbin acknowledged that capitalism was likely to survive despite its tendency towards periodic crisis: 'Expansion is the great virtue of capitalism; inequality and insecurity are its great vices.'[49]

Yet Durbin's thinking went beyond economic policy in the wake of the 1931 debacle. He was concerned not only with fashioning a credible ideological appeal but devising a political strategy for the Labour Party in power. Like MacDonald, Durbin believed democratic socialism should be achieved through gradual change, winning the support of the middle class rather than repelling those wary of upheaval and social conflict. He maintained that capitalism was fundamentally democratic, whereas Marxism was 'un-British'. It undermined the tradition of 'peaceful transitions of government'. Durbin insisted a Labour government must establish its credentials for effective economic management before increasing social expenditure, despite the prevalence of material hardship. There were limits to how far taxes could rise, and if necessary, it was believed 'the economy must come before equality'.

Durbin acknowledged the class structure of British society was changing even in the late 1930s. The industrial proletariat was declining, and new middle-class professions were represented in 'the growing army of technicians', 'white collar workers', and 'suburban householders'. The party had to look beyond its ties to the trade unions and embrace the rising managerial classes: 'We are living in a society where class composition is shifting steadily against Marx's proletariat', he wrote.[50] Between 1881 and 1931, the middle class grew to nearly a third of the working-age population, while the working class was transformed by the emergence of the service sector and the growth of property ownership. Durbin was conscious of the impact of the changing class structure and the growth of affluence among Labour's support.[51] He believed:

A society in which the lower middle classes and the pre-capitalist classes – the clerk, the small shopkeeper, the waiter and the civil servant – are increasingly important as a group is not likely, short of defeat in war, to be a revolutionary society. Neither is a working class that is acquiring property at a more rapid rate than ever before likely to become a more revolutionary class than it has been previously ... The pace [of change] is bound to be moderate in the hands of an increasingly middle-class electorate and an increasingly respectable proletariat.

Aside from thinkers such as Durbin, the NFRB became the main vehicle for devising Labour's policies. Its work in the 1930s demonstrates that 'British democratic socialist thought has a rich tradition of designing realistic programmes'. The efforts of the New Fabian economists ensured that by 1945 Labour 'was intellectually prepared for the economic realities of power in a way inconceivable at any earlier time in its history'.[52] Moreover, the ideological and intellectual prescriptions of the Fabians could unite the party, enabling Labour to outline a distinctive vision of society and a viable programme for government. The commitment to planning co-ordinated by the state provided the ideological glue that Labour hitherto lacked. Durbin and Jay emphasised the need for practical policies of economic reconstruction in contrast to the vague utopianism of the Labour Party in 1929. This was an effort to reconcile British socialism with Keynesianism and counter-cyclical demand management, further influenced by the experience of the New Deal in the US.

As a consequence of the general improvement in the party's standing, Labour was able to make a modest recovery electorally: by 1935, it secured 154 seats and 38 per cent of the vote. In the 1931–5 Parliament, Labour gained ten seats through by-elections, although its support was still overwhelmingly concentrated in northern 'heartland' areas and the poorer parts of East London. In Attlee, the party had a vigorous and relatively youthful leader from a new political generation. Labour was assisted by the fact that the influence of figures such as Bevin maintained the Labour Party as a moderate force, preventing the drift towards radicalisation. This moderation was firmly the vision of leading politicians such as Dalton:

> Here [in Britain] it is possible to make a peaceful, orderly and smooth transition to a better social order; and with a working Labour majority in the House of Commons, five years of resolute Government could lay the foundations of that order. Thereafter, at the next election, the people would be free to choose whether or not the work of socialist construction should continue.[53]

Dalton believed socialism's purpose was 'the abolition of poverty and the establishment of social equality, to build a prosperous and classless society'. In truth, the left in the Labour Party and the ILP agitators lost ground because their key demand for a 'united front' with the Communists was overwhelmingly rejected.

Despite Labour's advance, had a general election taken place in 1940 the party would almost certainly have been defeated. Recent events and in particular the policy of appeasement pursued by Neville Chamberlain momentarily destroyed the reputation of the Conservative establishment's 'guilty men'.[54] Like the First World War, the dramatic change in circumstances transformed Labour's ability to compete with the Conservatives. Yet Labour was now a more united force, in contrast to 1914 when the party indulged in endless tergiversations over support for the war. In 1939, Labour believed war was necessary and unavoidable in the face of fascism and totalitarianism. Hitler had banned the Social Democratic Party (SPD) and installed an autocratic regime in Germany. 'For the first time in its history', claims Kenneth Morgan, 'the Labour Party took an informed interest in problems of defence and national security', deciding to abandon 'muddle-headed internationalist utopianism'.[55]

Labour's patriotism and commitment to the nation soon provided rich political opportunities. In the National Government that followed in 1940, the Labour leadership proved themselves able ministers at a time of national crisis. Ernest Bevin's appointment to the Ministry of Labour symbolised the party's adherence to established political values and institutions. Bevin believed the parliamentary system could deliver concrete improvements in the social welfare and living standards of the British working class. Political power was a tool to secure concessions, not to overthrow the established order. As Paul Addison notes in his seminal work *The Road to 1945*, the coalition years laid the foundations for the radical Labour government elected at the war's end. Labour used the development of wartime policies to sow the seeds of its 1945 victory.[56] The wartime experience reinforced the party's shift towards reasonableness and moderation buttressed by radical aspirations for social and economic reform. Indeed, the coalition period demonstrated that it was possible to reform the economy by imposing regulatory controls on industry and using the machinery of planning – rather than wholesale public ownership.[57] The deep ideological fissures in the party had at long last been overcome.

Conclusion

The Labour government's collapse in 1931 left an indelible mark. Labour had come to power ill-prepared to face up to harsh economic realities. Its policies were characterised by 'radiant ambiguity' while Tawney's verdict that Labour 'frets out of office and fumbles in it' remained apposite.[58] Utopian rhetoric masked lack of clarity about the government's approach to managing the economy. The warning signs were present in 1924 when the Labour government felt it had little choice but to remain on the gold standard and to maintain free trade. Worse was to come in 1929–31 when the worldwide financial collapse tested the political and intellectual capacity of ministers to breaking point. The language of ethical socialism became a cloak to conceal adherence to the dominant orthodoxies of the age. With little experience of government, Labour was constrained in deviating from policies favoured by the financial establishment, while its core voters grew disillusioned with resulting cuts in public expenditure. These circumstances made the party vulnerable to internal schism and explain MacDonald's rapid airbrushing from Labour history. Yet not even the economic crisis of 1931 can adequately justify the descent into civil war. This chapter has shown that Labour was institutionally predisposed to conflict and division because it consisted of three rival power-bases, namely the PLP, the unions, and the party grassroots.

There was profound disagreement among these interests as to Labour's fundamental purpose: was the party's role to win power in the parliamentary system or to oppose the dominant political order? Was Labour a socialist party or a working-class liberal party with aspirations to social reform? At the outset, the party had no consistent role or ideological direction.

After 1931, the rising generation of party intellectuals and powerbrokers sought to remedy these failings, fashioning a Labour programme that by 1940 ensured the party was relatively well-equipped for power. It was recognised that the preservation of party unity on its own was totally insufficient if a majority Labour government was to be a viable prospect ever again. Labour required a feasible governing prospectus, a programme of 'practical socialism', as Hugh Dalton described it. The Labour Party proposed the so-called Immediate Programme, which combined plans to expand social welfare and economic prosperity with the strategy of nationalisation, including public ownership of coal, electricity, gas, and the Bank of England. Labour's strategy blended policies that were intended to transform the economic order in the long term with measures to advance social welfare in the here and now.

This policy was to form the basis of Labour's 1945 manifesto, *Let Us Face the Future*. With its support for rearmament, Labour had emerged as an anti-appeasement patriotic party, able to ally with dissident Tories such as Winston Churchill and Anthony Eden in resisting the rise of Hitler. In 1931, the party gravely damaged its credibility and reputation for governing competence. The trauma of the early 1930s was severe. The coming intervention of the Second World War transformed Labour's prospects, creating the realistic possibility of

holding power. The Labour Party rose to the challenge, recognising unity was not enough, focusing instead on forging
credible governing ideas for the future.

3

Revisionists versus Fundamentalists:
Gaitskell and Bevan at War 1951–64

Hugh Dalton, elder statesman, former chancellor of the exchequer, and party grandee, wrote in his diary after Labour's 1951 defeat that 'the election results are wonderful. We are out just at the right moment and our casualties are wonderfully light.'[1] His assumption, shared by other leading Labour figures including Clement Attlee, the Labour prime minister, was that the party would soon be back in power. Indeed, the Attlee administration had at first glance a highly impressive record. The post-war Labour government has understandably been eulogised and exalted for the last seventy years. Dalton later reflected that there was 'A new society to be built; and we had the power to build it. There was exhilaration among us, joy and hope, determination and confidence. We felt exalted, dedicated, walking on air, walking with destiny.'[2] More than any other government in British political history, Attlee's ministry appeared to embody what it means to be Labour. Lord Morgan, summing up his history of Attlee's government, concluded that: 'It was without doubt the most effective of all Labour governments, perhaps the most effective of any British government since the passage of the 1832 Reform act.'[3] Attlee and his colleagues had great achievements to their credit, notably the creation of the welfare state, the establishment of the National Health Service, helping to establish NATO and the Marshall Plan (in both of which the foreign secretary, Ernest Bevin, played a key role), and giving independence to the Indian subcontinent. With only a touch of hyperbole, Sam Watson, secretary of the Durham miners, told the 1950 Labour Party conference: 'Poverty has been abolished. Hunger is unknown. The sick are tended. The old folks are cherished. Our children are growing up in a land of opportunity.'[4]

Nonetheless, if Labour leaders thought their record meant that they would soon be back in power, they were wrong. The Conservative Party, accepting much of what Labour had done, won three successive general elections, each one with increasingly large majorities – in 1951 under Winston Churchill, in 1955 under Anthony Eden, and in 1959 under Harold Macmillan. It proved to be a depressing thirteen years in opposition. The Labour Party spent too much time in the 1950s engulfed in internal conflict, and too little time adapting to the economic and social changes which the Labour government had done so much to bring about. The fall of Attlee's administration was followed by 'a decade of fragicide'.[5]

This chapter examines the growing divisions that engulfed Labour during the 1950s in the aftermath of the Attlee government's demise. It does so by considering the contrasting careers of Hugh Gaitskell and Aneurin Bevan, two of the party's leading politicians. The chapter addresses the main cause of the party's splits, and then examines why a rapprochement occurred between Gaitskell and Bevan at the end of the 1950s which ensured that by the time of Gaitskell's death in 1963, Labour was again on the brink of power. It explores why Gaitskell was so determined to end the damaging rift with the Bevanites without sacrificing the search for new ideas, a revised social democratic doctrine, and a modernised political image.

These two exceptionally able younger ministers were the figures on whom the party's hopes for the future should have rested. Unfortunately, a deterioration in the relationship between them over National Health Service charges led to a longer-term conflict that was to have disastrous consequences for the Labour Party. The resignation of Bevan himself, the Bevanite revolt, and continuing internecine warfare lasted until 1955, and reverberated until the end of the decade. Writing thirty years later, the historian of the Attlee governments Kenneth Morgan concluded: 'This destructive and bitter conflict between the two most gifted and eloquent of the younger socialists of the day has many of the overtones of a tragedy.'[6]

The key problem confronting Labour throughout the period was that, once the 1945 programme (based on Labour's manifesto *Let Us Face the Future*) had been successfully implemented, there was little agreement as to what to do next. The party leadership had little new or interesting to say. The two giants, Ernest Bevin and Stafford Cripps, were in very poor health, while Attlee, now in his late sixties, was slow to bring younger politicians into his government, and in any case had little enthusiasm for new ideas. Herbert Morrison spoke of the need for 'consolidation', but it was hardly a rallying cry for a centre-left party. At the beginning of the 1950s, Attlee's Labour Party could tell the world about its fine record in government but almost nothing about the future. It had self-evidently run out of steam.

The historian Peter Hennessy, who was a fervent admirer of Attlee's, wrote that 'he had all the presence of a gerbil'.[7] Yet key to Attlee's success had been choosing an able and accomplished team of ministers. He relied on Cabinet heavy-weights, especially Bevin, Morrison, Dalton, and Cripps, alongside Aneurin Bevan, to supply ideas and impetus. In 1945, Attlee's boldest gamble in selecting his Cabinet had been to make Bevan, an eloquent parliamentary rebel, the minister responsible for setting up the National Health Service. Until Bevan entered the Cabinet as its youngest member (aged forty-seven), he was the archetypal dissident, arguing for the most extreme positions and kicking against the constraints of political leadership and discipline.

Born in Tredegar, Monmouthshire, in 1897, son of a miner (who had died of pneumoconiosis), Aneurin 'Nye' Bevan went down the mines at the age of thirteen. He was chosen as the chair of his local trade union lodge at the age of nineteen, and in 1926 he was appointed as a full-time union official. Then in 1929 he was elected Labour MP for Ebbw Vale. Blessed with a natural wit and a silver tongue, he quickly made his mark in the House of Commons. On the big issues of the interwar period, he was always on the side of the radical left. During the 1930s, he was a close ally of Stafford Cripps, then a left-winger who Ernest Bevin once described as 'more than half-way to Moscow'.[8] In 1939 Bevan was expelled from the party, though, unlike his mentor, he quickly returned to the fold.

During the 1939–45 war, Bevan emerged as the most formidable critic of Churchill and the coalition government. Even its Labour ministers were not immune from his attacks. About Churchill he wrote: 'His ear is so sensitively attuned to the bugle note of history that it is often dead to the more raucous clamour of contemporary life.'[9] He accused Bevin of finding it 'easier to deceive the people than to offend the Tories', and described Attlee as bringing 'to the fierce struggle of politics the tepid enthusiasm of a lazy afternoon at a cricket match'.[10] In 1944 he was nearly expelled again from the party after another particularly ferocious attack on Bevin.

In his interview with Bevan in Number 10 Downing Street after Labour's 1945 victory, Attlee made it clear to the former rebel that he was starting with a clean sheet. 'You are the youngest member of the Cabinet. Now it's up to you. The more you can learn the better.'[11] Cynics suggested that Attlee chose Bevan for his Cabinet to shut up a dangerous critic. But the more likely reason was that the new prime minister recognised Bevan's outstanding ability and wanted to give him the opportunity to use his talents constructively by helping to build the National Health Service, a centrepiece of Labour's manifesto.

Bevan proved to be a superb minister, one of the best British democracy has ever produced. His main achievement was the setting up of a comprehensive, nationwide health service free at the point of delivery. He won the support of the Cabinet for his centralised model of healthcare provision, against the opposition of Morrison, who argued for the preservation of local and voluntary hospitals. He successfully negotiated with the British Medical Association (BMA), devising a compromise whereby general practitioners (GPs) retained their professional autonomy but worked within the structure of the NHS. He bought off private consultants by allowing them to keep their private practice, but offering them a salaried connection with NHS hospitals and the opportunity to use a proportion of beds for their own patients.

Bevan's National Health Service began on schedule on 5 July 1948. Around 90 per cent of doctors joined the NHS at the outset, while two months later more than 93 per cent of the population had signed up. It was a personal triumph for Bevan and an unforgettable moment for the Labour government and for the country, still celebrated over seventy years later.

Bevan was arguably less successful in carrying out his other main responsibility – that of housing (then attached to the Department of Health), at least in the first two years of the Labour government. In the 1945 election campaign, Labour had laid great emphasis on housing needs, especially for workers and their families, and so it was not surprising that Bevan was criticised for his ministry's failure to get a grip on the house building programme. However, from 1947 onwards, local authorities were building on average 200,000 homes a year, while more than one million new 'social' units were completed between 1945 and 1951. The houses were of high quality, spacious, well designed, often with gardens. Even so, the Conservatives made useful political capital out of their 1951 election promise of building 300,00 houses a year – a promise which, under their housing minister, Harold Macmillan, they were able to fulfil.

Nine years younger than Bevan, Hugh Gaitskell was not

born into the labour movement. He chose it himself. On his father's side, his immediate forebears were mostly in the military. His father was a civil servant in India, stationed in Burma. He died when Hugh was nine. His mother married again and stayed on in Burma, which meant that the Gaitskell children had no real home life. Indeed, Hugh's entire childhood from the age of two and a half was spent either with family relations or at boarding schools. He followed his elder brother Arthur, whom he adored, first to the Dragon School in Oxford and then to Winchester College, then as now an academic 'nursery' for the children of the professional middle classes. He much preferred Oxford, which, in contrast to Winchester, he found lively and stimulating.

It was the 1926 general strike, during which Gaitskell carried messages for the strikers between Oxford and London, which drove him towards socialist politics. It was a turning point in his life. He wrote to an astonished aunt: 'Henceforth my future is with the working classes.'[12] Leaving Oxford with a first-class degree, Gaitskell accepted an adult education post in the Nottinghamshire coalfield where he 'learnt' about the working lives of the miners. He wrote to his brother that the miners were 'the nicest sort of people – indeed I liked all the working people I have met ... more honest and natural than the middle class who are always trying to be something they aren't'.[13]

The next decade (from 1928 to 1939) saw Gaitskell's development as an aspiring front-line politician. He was appointed as an economics lecturer at University College London; played an active role in a number of political clubs and think tanks, including the New Fabian Research Bureau and the XYZ club; unsuccessfully stood as Labour candidate for Chatham in the 1935 election; and, two years later, was selected for the safe seat of Leeds South. He also spent a year in Vienna where he assisted more than a hundred Austrian socialists to escape from the fascists.

As an economist who spoke German, Gaitskell was put in a 'reserved' occupation so that when war was declared in 1939, he was asked to join the Ministry of Economic Welfare. Then, when the Churchill coalition was formed, he became private secretary to his friend and patron Hugh Dalton, whom he found 'exhausting, exhilarating and instructive'.[14] In 1942, Churchill promoted Dalton to the Board of Trade; Gaitskell went with him and, in the autumn of that year, was promoted to principal assistant secretary. Gaitskell was widely considered to be an outstanding administrator and awarded a CBE. In the spring of 1945, he suffered a slight heart attack and it seemed that he might not be able to stand as Labour candidate for Leeds South at the general election. However, with careful nursing by his wife, Dora, whom he had married in 1937, he managed to survive the campaign and was elected with a large majority, though, when the Labour government was formed, he was not yet considered fit enough to be appointed as a minister.

In May 1946, Attlee gave him his first government post as parliamentary secretary at the Ministry of Fuel and Power. In October 1947, he replaced the minister, Emanuel Shinwell, who was widely blamed for the fuel shortages earlier that year. In a characteristic Attlee interview, the prime minister said: 'I am reconstructing the government. I want you to be Fuel and Power.' Gaitskell replied: 'Oh! Well.' Attlee continued:

'It is not a bed of roses.' Gaitskell said: 'I know that already.'[15] And that was that! The young minister quickly built a reputation for competence at his job. Together with other economic ministers (including Harold Wilson and Douglas Jay) he worked with the chancellor, Stafford Cripps, to provide a new impetus and purpose to the government, somewhat battered by the economic crises of 1947.

When Cripps fell seriously ill in 1949, Attlee was in nominal charge but, in practice, the Treasury was overseen by three younger men, Gaitskell, Wilson, and Jay, dealing with the crucial issues – above all, the devaluation crisis. It was then that Gaitskell showed his decisiveness, making up his mind that devaluation was essential, and then seeing that it was carried through. So much so that when Cripps retired, Gaitskell had become the obvious choice for chancellor, though, in a harbinger of the coming clash between the two, Bevan wrote to Attlee: 'I think the appointment of Gaitskell to be a great mistake.'[16]

The background to Gaitskell's first and only budget was distinctly unpromising. Following the communist North Korean invasion of South Korea in June 1951, the Cabinet, at the request of the United States, agreed to a massive hike in defence spending, amounting to double the pre-Korea level. Acting almost as defence secretary rather than as chancellor of the exchequer, Gaitskell declared that the rearmament programme was now the 'first objective of economic policy'.

Inevitably, the new chancellor was then compelled to raise taxes. He was also determined to restrain the growth of public spending. Health spending was to be kept within a £400 million upper limit; to pay for rising hospital costs, Gaitskell proposed to charge directly for half the cost of false teeth and spectacles, raising £23 million in a full year. It was this relatively small sum which became the 'casus belli' between Gaitskell and Bevan, who, in 1950, Attlee had moved to the Ministry of Labour.

There had already been a long-running argument over health charges between the two men, probably exacerbated by Bevan's fury at the younger man's promotion as chancellor. Bevan told one of his Cabinet colleagues, John Strachey, that Gaitskell was 'nothing, nothing, nothing'.[17] According to his biographer, Michael Foot, Bevan's objection to Gaitskell was more sociological than personal. In Bevan's eyes, the former Wykehamist represented nothing 'unless it was the civil service-cum middle class which was already vastly overrepresented at Westminster'.[18] Yet as Lord Morgan has perceptively argued, Bevan's friends were almost invariably middle class. The difference was that Gaitskell's intimates were economists and administrators, while Bevan's were politicians, journalists, writers, and artists. For his part, Gaitskell admired Bevan for his brilliance and charisma. Gaitskell noted in his diary on 9 March 1951 that 'Bevan is so much the best debater; so much the most effective speaker on the front bench, indeed in the House, that he can always raise his prestige by a performance of this kind'.[19] Nevertheless, as the new chancellor, Gaitskell was determined to face down Bevan and bring health costs under control.

Several attempts were made to bring about a compromise between the two men. Gaitskell's friend and fellow Treasury minister Douglas Jay told him that, though he agreed on the merits of health charges, he did not think the money raised was worth the trouble it would cause. Dalton urged Bevan not to resign and told Gaitskell that he thought too little of the party and too much of the voters.

The prime minister, Clement Attlee, said later: 'It oughtn't to have gone so far, but both sides dug their feet in and took up positions and would not budge.' Yet the truth is that the main responsibility lay with the prime minister himself. Clearly, his ill health (he was in hospital with a suspected duodenal ulcer) did not help, reinforcing Attlee's passive style of leadership. But an earlier intervention before the issue came to Cabinet might have persuaded Gaitskell to adopt the formula already used for prescription charges, of accepting the principle but without setting a date for implementation. Clearly Attlee's illness was a factor, but an intervention by the prime minister before the dispute came to Cabinet would have had a positive effect. It is difficult not to conclude that, with the probability of an imminent election, Attlee could and should have done more to resolve the conflict between these two exceptionally able ministers, leading, as it did, to Bevan's resignation, which was to have such a damaging effect in the years ahead in opposition. As Morgan attests, the 'destructive and bitter conflict between the two most gifted and eloquent of the younger socialists was allowed to escalate provoking a damaging feud that split the party for much of the 1950s'.[20]

On the merits of the issue itself, Bevan's argument had weight, particularly over the exceptional increases in defence spending. Harold Wilson, who resigned along with Bevan and John Freeman, argued that the massive rise in defence expenditure would inflict grave damage on the British economy. Significantly, the incoming Tory government quickly scaled down the huge Labour rearmament plan. With respect to health charges, these were not essential to Gaitskell's budget. Bevan was right to see these issues as a 'symbol', in Gaitskell's case of his determination to bring health spending under control, and in Bevan's defending the principle of a free National Health Service.

Peter Hennessy argues that Bevan's earlier resignation, along with Freeman and Wilson, was the most dramatic of the post-war era. It was driven ultimately by the 'seething cocktail of [Bevan's] accumulated frustrations' – of being passed over for the chancellorship by a technocrat like Hugh Gaitskell; of a belief that Gaitskell had been promoted too quickly because of his superior education while the working class had to advance the hard way; and because Bevan, a natural rebel, felt frustrated by the strictures of Cabinet collective responsibility and the grind of running a government department.[21]

But, as too often was the case, Bevan's tactics were flawed. Bevan had already displayed his intemperate side during a speech at Belle Vue in 1948 where he disparaged the Tories as 'lower than vermin'. The remark not only infuriated the Conservatives but greatly annoyed Attlee, who wrote to his Cabinet colleague:

My Dear Aneurin, I have received a great deal of criticism of the passage in your speech in which you describe the Conservatives as vermin, including a good deal from your own party. It was, I think singularly ill-timed. It had been agreed that we wished to give the new scheme as good a send-off as possible and, to this end, a non-polemical broadcast. Your speech cut right across this. I had myself done as much as I could to point out the injustice of the attacks made upon you for your handling of the doctors, pointing out the difficulties experienced by your predecessors of various political colours in dealing with this profession ... These unfortunate remarks enable the doctors to stage a comeback and have given the general public the impression that there was more to their case than they had supposed ... It has drawn attention away from the excellent work you have done on the Health Bill. Please be a bit more careful, in your own interest. Yours ever, Clem.[22]

Bevan's public threat to resign in a speech at Bermondsey and his vicious personal attacks on Gaitskell in *Tribune* infuriated the rest of the Cabinet. Dalton wrote that 'he showed ... unbearable conceit, crass obstinacy and a totalitarian streak'. In his address to the parliamentary party, Bevan 'was sweating and shouting and seemed on the edge of a nervous breakdown'.[23] Gaitskell helped his own cause by coming across as at least reasonable and courteous.

In contrast, Bevan's political judgement was often questionable, especially in the case of his resignation with a general election looming. As in 1950, Labour won more votes than the Conservatives in 1951, the largest vote ever secured by a political party in Britain. But there was a small shift of opinion against the party and fewer Liberal candidates, which allowed the Conservatives to gain twenty-four seats from Labour. The Tories had an overall majority of seventeen. Although it was a 'close run thing', Labour was now out of power for a generation.

In opposition, Labour's internal politics were dominated

by the Bevanite revolt and the bitter quarrel between left and right which split the party from top to bottom. In fact, Labour in the 1950s was even more divided over foreign than domestic policy. In the depressing decade that followed, Labour was embroiled in bitter dispute, divisions that prevented the party from adapting to the economic and social changes that the Attlee governments themselves had helped to bring about – not least rising material affluence and the growth of working-class prosperity.

The key historical question is how far the Bevanite uprising was an attempt to take over the party and make Bevan leader, as Gaitskell claimed? It is certainly true that the loose alliance of semi-Marxists, left-wingers, pacifists, and assorted malcontents in the Keep Left group, which had been an annoyance to Ernest Bevin in the 1940s, was transformed by Bevan's resignation. The group became a serious challenge to the political position of the leadership, especially on foreign affairs. After the 1952 Morecombe conference, which Michael Foot described as 'rowdy, convulsive, vulgar, splenetic', the Bevanites formed their own parliamentary group, while the left-wing *Tribune* newspaper organised 'brains trust' meetings in constituency parties to promote their ideas.[24]

Gaitskell fought back. He gave an emotional speech at Stalybridge, alleging that communist influence had been evident at Morecombe, and concluded: 'Let no one say that in exercising the right to reply to Bevanites we are endangering the unity of the party. For there will be no unity on the terms dictated by *Tribune* ... It is time to end the attempt at mob rule by a group of frustrated journalists and restore the authority and leadership of the solid and sensible majority of the movement.'[25] The right believed that the Bevanite group in the PLP were disruptive and dangerous. The editors of the journal *Socialist Commentary* wrote that, '... there is one danger not to be lost sight of for a moment. It is the danger of an organised faction at work, which is bound in the end to poison party life.'[26]

Nonetheless, the predominant mood in the party remained in favour of unity. Efforts by Bevan and his allies to rewrite party policy were more often rejected. Most of the leading interests within the labour movement supported the strategy of using the parliamentary and administrative apparatus of the British state to bring about social reform.[27] The centre and right dominated the party's institutions while the PLP retained its 'moderate majority' which could be mobilised against the Bevanites. Mainstream trade union leaders such as Will Lawther, Arthur Deakin, and Tom Williamson were determined to crush the left. There was little attempt to question the basic purpose of the party to capture power within the parliamentary system. Nevertheless, conflict arose because the 1945–51 period confirmed that for a Labour government, pragmatism would always triumph over idealism. The promise of radical socialist transformation had essentially been jettisoned, a reality that some on the left found a bitter pill to swallow.

Dick Crossman, himself a Bevanite (along with roughly thirty other Labour MPs), wrote in his diaries that Bevan was in fact a reluctant rebel. Indeed, Attlee had viewed Bevan as Labour's natural leader had it not been for his fatal tendency to kick over the traces at the wrong moment. The prime minister believed that Bevan's wife, Jenny Lee, who was herself a left-wing Labour MP, was a bad influence on her husband, saying of their relationship: 'He needed a sedative. He got an irritant.'[28] Even so, while Bevan tended to use forceful social-ist rhetoric, he was not advocating any fundamental alteration in the basic strategy of the party. It was quite apparent that Bevan and his associates lacked a robust theoretical analysis of economic and social changes in post-war British society, while the intellectual case for public ownership was losing its resonance as full employment was achieved using Keynesian macro-economic management techniques.

The next few years of opposition were dominated by the continuing Bevanite revolt, the focus of which shifted to inter-national policy and foreign affairs. The Bevanites have been described as 'an army of individualists'. Attlee had decided to stay on as leader in 1951, but failed to heal the left/right split, or to provide any clear sense of direction to his defeated party, which drifted listlessly. Having implemented the 1945–50 manifesto, according to Richard Crossman the government had little idea what to do next given it had 'exhausted its capacity for creative thinking'. The Cabinet was weary. Herbert Morrison, once the most imaginative and dynamic force in the Labour Party, promised only 'consolidation' of the nationalisation programme. There was, Morrison wrote:

A school of thought in the Labour Party which takes the view that the electorate having apparently not been keen on a further socialisation programme at this stage, the remedy is to extend and feature those proposals in a bigger type than ever, and that if only we could bang at them hard enough, the electors will become enthusiasts for such a policy. I do follow this line of reasoning, and I believe it to be unrealistic. In effect, it will lead to reaction and defeat.[29]

Morrison insisted that the party had to free itself from traditional dogma in a society of growing consumerism and full employment. Labour's goal was to make society more efficient and humane rather than forcing the nation on the road to socialism. Yet the party's fundamental neglect of the importance of renewing its ideas in office was a major reason why Labour failed to establish lasting dominance in British politics. Under Attlee, Labour's mindset focused on defending its past record rather than forging a credible programme for the future.

In 1952, egged on by the Bevanites of 'Keep Left', Bevan again led a major revolt against the party leadership's position on the defence estimates. This kind of behaviour infuriated Attlee, who eventually forced through the PLP a resolution calling for the abandonment of all factional groupings. Bevan accepted the decision and the Bevanites no longer met officially (although its leaders held unofficial meetings in each other's houses). Bevan was then elected to the shadow cabinet, albeit in bottom place. It seemed that at long last, peace had 'broken out' following Attlee's efforts to impose an uneasy truce. At a meeting of the PLP, he implored the Bevanites: 'Turn your guns on the enemy, not on your friends.'

However, in April 1954 Bevan intervened intemperately and without warning from the front bench following Attlee's reply to the Tory government's statement announcing discussions by the British and American governments with

South-East Asian countries on the setting up of a collective defence system against the communists under Ho Chi Min. At a meeting of the shadow cabinet, Bevan, after a gentle rebuke from Attlee, flounced out of the room, announcing that he was resigning. Harold Wilson (who had resigned over health charges with Bevan in 1951) then took Bevan's place on the shadow cabinet, an augury for the future. As the Bevanite challenge began to fade, the ambitious Wilson moved hastily towards the party's centre-ground. Attlee was heard to remark about Bevan's resignation: 'Just when we were beginning to win the match, our inside left has scored against his own side.'[30] A year later, Bevan's conduct (he again intervened in the House against his own leader, this time on the question of the atomic bomb) nearly led to his expulsion from the party. Only Attlee's determined opposition saved him. It must be said that Labour's right expressed pathological, some would say even irrational, loathing of Bevan. In his diaries, Hugh Dalton complained of Bevan's 'increasingly evil face, both when silent and when speechifying'.[31] Gaitskell, it was said, saw 'extraordinary parallels between Nye and Adolf Hitler'.

Attlee's official biographer concluded: 'It had been a near thing, Attlee got his way ... he had brought Bevan back into the fold and he had reunited the party for the impending election.'[32] However, despite Attlee's ingenuity in papering over the cracks, the Conservatives, led by their new leader, Anthony Eden, and boosted by Rab Butler's reflationary economic policy, comfortably defeated the Labour Party at the May 1955 general election. Labour's hopes of a quick return to office in the 1951–5 period were dashed. Labour's faith in

British democracy reflected its belief in 'the swing of the pendulum'. It believed it would soon be Labour's turn to go back into government as the unpopularity of the Conservatives grew. The 1955 defeat shook that faith. The Tories had been relatively successful in government: economic growth was rising comparatively quickly, and deregulation of the economy rather than planning and controls appeared to be effective.

Gaitskell later explained why he got the leadership: 'The leadership came my way so early because Bevan threw it at me by his behaviour.'[33] Bevan may have been a wonderful orator, but he also had a remarkable propensity to offend his parliamentary colleagues and to turn off voters, so much so that a powerful group of trade union leaders decided to block Bevan from becoming leader when Attlee stepped down. To stop him, they first backed Gaitskell for the position of party treasurer, and subsequently for the leadership itself.

When, following a second election defeat in 1955, Attlee finally retired, Gaitskell, who had initially supported Morrison, was persuaded to throw his hat in the ring, led by his younger revisionist allies, Tony Crosland, Roy Jenkins, and Denis Healey. Two brilliant speeches helped create a groundswell in his favour. At the 1955 Margate conference, Gaitskell explained, in revisionist fashion, that he had become a socialist, not so much because of a belief in nationalisation but because of his faith in social justice and dislike of the class system. Then in the same month, he made a devastating attack in the House of Commons on the Tory chancellor, R. A. Butler, for his irresponsible and opportunistic management of the economy, proclaiming that Butler 'began in folly, he continued in deceit and he has ended in reaction'.[34] In December that year, Gaitskell easily won the leadership ballot with 157 votes to Bevan's 70 and Morrison's 40.

The new leader then got off to a flying start. He united the party by putting influential left wingers into prominent shadow cabinet positions. Gaitskell appointed Harold Wilson, who, despite resigning with Bevan in 1951, had voted for Gaitskell as leader, to the shadow chancellorship. He also brought Bevanites such as Crossman and Barbara Castle on to the front bench. Most significantly of all, he surprised Nye Bevan by offering him the important role of shadow colonial secretary – an offer which Bevan felt he could not refuse. It was the beginning of a new partnership between Gaitskell and Bevan at the top of the party.

The first big test of Gaitskell's leadership was the Suez crisis. Apart from the Iraq War, Suez divided British politics more deeply than any foreign policy issue since Munich. The verdict of Denis Healey (one of Gaitskell's leading foreign policy advisers) on the British government's action over Suez was that it was in conception 'a demonstration of moral and intellectual bankruptcy', and in execution 'a political, diplomatic and operational disgrace'.[35]

Following the takeover by the Egyptian leader, Gamal Abdel Nasser, of the Suez Canal on 26 July 1956, there was a Commons debate on 1 August. Gaitskell's opening speech was finely balanced. He condemned Nasser's action in seizing unilaterally the canal, which was an international waterway. However, though he agreed that military precautions were justified, he stressed that it was British policy not to use force in breach of international law or contrary to world public opinion: 'While force cannot be excluded, we must be sure that the circumstances justify it and that it is, if used, consistent with our belief in, and our pledges to, the Charter of the United Nations and not in conflict with them.'[36]

On 10 August, he followed this up with a firm letter to the British prime minister, Anthony Eden, in which he said:

If there still be doubt in your mind about my personal attitude, let me say that I could not regard an armed attack on Egypt by ourselves and the French as justified by anything that Nasser has done so far or as consistent with the Charter of the United Nations.[37]

Despite this letter and a warning from the Tory chief whip, Edward Heath, about Labour's attitude, Eden persisted in claiming that the government had the support of the opposition in using military force.

The truth was that, despite Gaitskell's warnings and above all the public opposition of the United States, Eden was determined to bring matters to a head. On 29 October, following secret collusion between the United Kingdom, France, and Israel, Israeli tanks, supported by French planes, invaded Sinai. On 30 October, an Anglo-French ultimatum, ostensibly issued to separate the participants, but in fact an outrageous ploy to justify seizing the canal, was rejected by Nasser, and British planes then proceeded to bomb Egyptian airfields. Then on 31 October, the British and French vetoed a resolution by their main ally, the United States, calling for a ceasefire; and at dawn on 5 November, British and French paratroopers landed in Port Said. However, at midnight on

5 November, the British were forced by American economic pressure to agree to a ceasefire, still 75 miles from Suez. Eden's Suez venture had ended in what the Tory chief whip called 'a humiliating failure'. On 9 January 1957, Eden, a broken man, resigned on grounds of ill health.

Gaitskell was outraged by the government's duplicity over Suez. In a series of passionate parliamentary speeches and in a powerful reply for the opposition on 4 November to a ministerial television broadcast by the prime minister, Gaitskell denounced the Conservative administration's 'criminal folly' in breaching the UN charter. He accused the government of undermining Anglo-American relations, dividing the Commonwealth, encouraging at least by example the Russian invasion of Hungary, while damaging the reputation of the United Kingdom abroad.

Gaitskell was fiercely attacked by many Tories on the grounds that he had undermined British troops in action. But for others, Gaitskell's powerful and principled oratory, combined with the eloquence of Bevan, helped restore a sense of national honour and pride which had been so badly shaken by the Eden government's duplicitous behaviour. Asquith's daughter, Lady Violet Bonham Carter, wrote to Gaitskell, thanking him for 'your magnificent speech. It was not only for your party you were speaking – you spoke for England, for England's real and best self.'[38] Michael Foot, in the biography of his hero Aneurin Bevan, judged that, 'the combination of Gaitskell's relentless, passionate marshalling of the whole legal and moral case against the Government's expedition to Suez and Bevan's sardonic and reflective commentary upon it – complemented one another and constitute together the most brilliant display of opposition in recent parliamentary history.'[39]

Suez brought Gaitskell and Bevan closer together. Indeed, Bevan's statesmanlike performance throughout the crisis so impressed Gaitskell that he appointed him shadow foreign secretary. Bevan carried out his new duties with distinction, including successful visits to India, Russia and the United States. At the beginning of the lengthy and bitter row over nuclear weapons, which in 1960–1 was to split the Labour Party so profoundly, it was Bevan who led the opposition to unilateralism. In a celebrated speech at the 1957 party conference at Brighton, Nye slapped down his former allies: 'If you carry this resolution and follow out all its implications … you will send a Foreign Secretary, whoever he may be, naked into the conference chamber.' It would not be statesmanship, he said, but merely 'an emotional spasm'. Bevan was not, as his critics claimed, betraying his principles. As a member of the Labour government, he had supported the production of a British atom bomb. However, it was certainly the case that Bevan's oratory had the effect of strengthening Gaitskell's leadership in the run up to the 1959 election.

Other than the 1992 result, the 1959 election was the most disappointing of Labour's post-war losses. The defeat underlined the need for a radical shift since it could not be blamed on a poorly executed campaign or an inept leader. The Labour Party was the unwitting victim of social change, the rise of affluence, and the numerical decline of the manual working class. As the authors of *Must Labour Lose?* stated: 'Labour is thought of as a predominantly class-based party and the class which it represents is – objectively and subjectively – on the wane. This stamps it with an aura of sectionalism and narrow-ness, at a time when people see opportunities for advancement opening before them as never before'.[40]

That said, since Bevan's appointment as shadow foreign secretary, the party had appeared united behind its leader and policies. Labour's programme, with its emphasis on economic growth and social spending, especially an increase in the state pension and a watered-down approach to nationalisation, appeared cautious and achievable. The party ran a vigorous and effective campaign, with Crossman, the campaign coor-dinator, and, above all, Gaitskell himself making outstanding contributions. Bevan's impact came through traditional cam-paign speeches in which he was scrupulous in sticking to the party line. The Labour leader was blamed for pledging in a speech in Newcastle not to put up income tax in normal peace-time circumstances (a commitment which was supported by the shadow chancellor, Harold Wilson). Macmillan pounced, declaring that it would be irresponsible for the Conservative Party to follow Gaitskell into an election auction. Yet even the left accepted that the real reason for Labour's defeat was the growing material affluence of the 1950s. When the wily Tory prime minister, Harold Macmillan, said 'most of our people have never had it so good', it struck a chord with many voters; for the prosperous majority, the Conservative jingle 'life's better under the Conservatives. Don't let Labour ruin it' was extremely persuasive. As Anthony Crosland later noted, Labour was viewed as 'pro-austerity and anti-prosperity', in a society where affluence 'is to be welcomed unreservedly since it widens the range of choice and opportunity open to the average family'.[41] When the votes were counted, they revealed a Tory landslide with notable gains in the South and the Midlands, and an overall majority of 100 seats.

Gaitskell, whose dignified acceptance of defeat initially enhanced his reputation, badly mishandled the aftermath of the election. Given the scale of the loss, there was a strong case for sending a signal to the electorate that Labour was now prepared to fully come to terms with changing social and economic conditions. But any reform needed to be cautiously prepared, on the lines of the 1959 German Social Democrats (SPD) Bad Godesberg programme, which, following their 1957 election defeat, moved the SPD decisively away from its Marxist inheritance. However, instead of planning a long-term campaign around a thought-out strategy, Gaitskell, perhaps due to post-election exhaustion, allowed his friends to sound off in public with their own views, which his critics then misrepresented as those held by the leader, thus helping to build up opposition to internal party reform.

An initial 'post-mortem' meeting of Gaitskell's allies, which included two of his closest younger friends, Tony Crosland, the author of the revisionist tour de force *The Future of Socialism*, and Roy Jenkins, the eloquent advocate of liberal reform, was held at his house in Frognal Gardens. The discussion, in Jenkins' judgement, 'was conducted much more casually than conspiratorially'.[42] The reasons given for Labour's defeat included the unpopularity of nationalisation, the disapproval of the trade unions, the negative image of local Labour councils, and more generally the party's 'cloth cap' mentality. Someone, probably Hugh Dalton, proposed that a new formula should replace the existing Clause IV of the Labour Party constitution, which called for the common ownership of the means of production, distribution, and exchange. By all accounts, Gaitskell said very little.

Unfortunately, news of the meeting quickly leaked and, for left-wing critics, it provided clear evidence of a 'right-wing' plot to change the nature of the party. Their suspicions were strengthened the following day by a BBC *Panorama* interview with Jenkins and an article by Douglas Jay, which proposed dropping steel nationalisation and adding 'Reform' or 'Radical' to the name of the party. Gaitskell himself favoured the idea of revising Clause IV, even if Crosland and Jenkins believed that changing the party's official aims might be more trouble than it was worth.

Indeed, by the time of the 1959 Blackpool party conference, the dice were already heavily loaded against the leadership. The left was uniformly hostile, while in the centre, Crossman was ambivalent, Wilson (who was worried about rumours of losing his shadow chancellorship) suspicious, while Nye Bevan (whose health was already failing) remained loyal to Gaitskell but was above the fray. Unwisely, Gaitskell did not take the trouble to speak to Wilson. Crucially, the unions, on whom Gaitskell had so often relied for support in the past, were strongly resistant to any constitutional change. Without directly challenging Gaitskell, Wilson established himself as an advocate of unity, arguing that the existing Clause IV ought to be kept, albeit with a fresh statement of the party's objects.

At the 1959 conference, Gaitskell's political position was unusually weak. He was speaking only for himself since there was no official NEC statement to rally behind. Gaitskell's criticism of Clause IV as it stood was unanswerable: 'It implies that we propose to nationalise everything, but we do not'; and his formulation of a new Clause IV was not so different from that which Tony Blair successfully carried through at the 1995 special conference. Yet the debates that followed were marred by extraordinary bitterness, a warning of battles to come. It was clear that in 1959 there was not yet enough support even among moderate trade unions for revising the clause. In the end, Gaitskell was forced to concede by the weakness of his position, a vulnerability that was accentuated by the divisive unilateralist debate. He was then compelled to accept an unsatisfactory compromise.

The current text of Clause IV was retained but supplemented by a new statement of aims. If there was to be a real chance of changing Clause IV, then the leader had to have both the major trade unions and potentially hostile rivals like Bevan, Wilson, and Crossman on side, as well as rallying moderates inside the party. Relying on his Frognal Gardens praetorian guard to turn opinion was never going to be sufficient. The debate about why Labour lost the 1959 election became so embittered as the defeat appeared to confirm the depth of the party's existential crisis.

Although the evidence pointed to deep-seated social and economic change, with rising affluence and the decline of traditional manual labour as key factors, sociologists disagreed among themselves about the implications of alterations in the class structure. John Goldthorpe and David Lockwood's study *The Affluent Worker* (1961) focused on the lives of Luton car workers. It found that although their material living standards were rising, those workers retained many traditional working-class attitudes and values, including their commitment to trade unionism. Other experts, including the social researcher

Mark Abrams, insisted that the British working class was becoming more 'instrumentalist', rejecting collectivism in favour of home ownership, consumerism, and foreign travel. If that was the case, the Labour Party was doomed to defeat unless it was prepared to alter radically its doctrine, ideology, and beliefs, a move which many in the party believed would be a betrayal of socialism.

Bevan's and Gaitskell's substantive positions were, in fact, not that far apart. In his renowned book *In Place of Fear*, published in 1952, Bevan had already outlined the beginnings of a revisionist analysis for the Labour Party. He wrote that:

> The philosophy of democratic socialism is essentially cool in temper … a child of modern society and so of relative philosophy. It seeks the truth in any given situation, knowing all the time that if this be pushed too far it falls into error … its chief enemy is vacillation, for it must achieve passion in action in pursuit of qualified judgements.[43]

In his last conference speech at Blackpool in 1959 in which he made a moving appeal for unity, Bevan made it clear that although he believed in the goal of public ownership, he did not believe in a monolithic state-controlled society. Although Bevan and Gaitskell had their differences, it is likely that they could have worked together in a future Labour government. It was not to be. On 6 July 1960, Nye Bevan died of cancer.

Following Gaitskell's defeat over Clause IV, a crisis over nuclear defence, which almost overwhelmed Gaitskell's leadership, erupted in Easter 1960. At the end of April, the Tory government, which three years before had abolished conscription and adopted a defence position that overwhelmingly relied on the nuclear deterrent, abandoned 'Blue Streak', the fixed land-based rocket system. The new policy amounted to the virtual end of a British delivery system, and therefore of a wholly independent British nuclear deterrent. That gave a major boost to unilateralism. The Campaign for Nuclear Disarmament (CND) held a highly successful third Aldermaston march that Easter which highlighted the issue, and had a major impact on the labour movement. Easter was also the start of the union conference season: three unions voted immediately for unilateral motions, while the largest, the Transport and General Workers' Union, was now led by a committed unilateralist, Frank Cousins. Consequently, it looked increasingly likely that Gaitskell would be defeated at conference, especially as Nye Bevan, who had opposed unilateralism so effectively in 1957, was dying.

Although Gaitskell lost, he refused to accept defeat. In a passionate speech at the Scarborough conference, he started the 'fight back'. He began by accepting that the cancellation of Blue Streak undermined the case for an independent British deterrent. He argued that the key issue was neutralism:

If you are a unilateralist in principle, you are driven to becoming a neutralist … either they (the unilateralists) mean that they will follow the cowardly hypocritical course of saying, we do not want nuclear bombs, but, for God's sake, Americans protect us, or they are saying we should get out of NATO. Supposing all of us, like well-behaved sheep, were to follow the policies of unilateralism and neutralism, what kind of impression would that make upon the British people?

Gaitskell believed that the conference could not impose unilateralism on Labour MPs, who would then be compelled to vote against their conscience in Parliament. Then came the famous call to arms: 'Do they think we can simply accept a decision of this kind … there are some of us, Mr Chairman, who will fight and fight and fight again to bring back sanity and honesty and dignity, so that our party with its great past may retain its glory and its greatness.' Such was the persuasive impact of his oratory that he won over many constituency delegates. *The Daily Herald*, a pro-leadership paper, called it 'Gaitskell's finest hour'.

When Labour MPs returned to Westminster, Wilson, despite being opposed to unilateralism, challenged Gaitskell for the leadership as a 'unity' candidate, in opposition to Gaitskell's 'confrontational' approach. Even so, Gaitskell's speech at Scarborough had given his supporters new heart. Gaitskell won the leadership ballot decisively by 166 MPs to 81 for Wilson. The fight back was now gathering momentum. Assisted by the efforts of trade union moderates and by the organisational work of the Campaign for Democratic Socialism (CDS), a pro-Gaitskell grouping launched soon after the Scarborough conference with Bill Rodgers and Dick Taverne amongst its supporters, the official multilateralist defence policy was carried by nearly three to one. The result was a triumph for Gaitskell, restoring his authority as leader and, for the first time, impressing his personality on the whole country.

The last great drama of Gaitskell's leadership related to the Common Market. On 22 July 1961, the Conservative Cabinet decided to apply for entry. Although Macmillan emphasised that he was entering negotiations only to see if the UK's terms could be met and safeguards secured, especially for the Commonwealth and British agriculture, it was his intention to take the United Kingdom in if he possibly could. Firstly, Macmillan hoped it would give his faltering government new momentum. Secondly, after the failure of the European Free Trade Association, Macmillan now believed that Britain's future lay decisively with the burgeoning European Economic Community.

Gaitskell was much more ambivalent. Intellectually, he could see the case for British entry, above all on political grounds, but he was at heart a supporter of the Common-wealth. Gaitskell was greatly influenced by the Commonwealth governments' sceptical reaction over the course of the nego-tiations. Despite his year in Vienna before the war, he never felt himself to be particularly European ('I probably feel that I have more in common with North Americans than with the Europeans,' he once said). Although he saw the merits of Franco–German understanding, he sometimes regretted the creation of the European Community, telling CDS support-ers who were European enthusiasts that the subject was 'a bore and nuisance and it has always been so'.[44] Significantly, Gaitskell was determined that, after the rows over Clause IV and unilateralism, he would seek to keep the Labour Party united as far as possible. He was keenly aware that, although there was a determined group of his closest supporters in favour, including Jenkins and Crosland, the majority was

REVISIONISTS VERSUS FUNDAMENTALISTS

probably instinctively against Britain's entry. Healey, a committed Eurosceptic, had advised Gaitskell that, in any case, De Gaulle would almost certainly veto British entry, while there might be an opportunity for Britain to join on better terms after De Gaulle had left the scene. All these factors pushed Gaitskell into opposing British entry on Macmillan's terms.

All the same, Jenkins, Crosland, and other pro-Europeans were deeply upset by Gaitskell's emotional speech on the Common Market at the 1962 Brighton conference. On the surface, it was a reasoned and careful analysis of the pros and cons of membership, leading to a rejection of British entry on the terms negotiated by the Conservative government. Yet in emotive passages that helped give the speech its dramatic force, he looked back to the contribution which the Dominions made in the First World War: 'We at least do not intend to forget Vimy Ridge and Gallipoli,' he said; and he accused the government of 'selling the Commonwealth down the river'. Using passionate although wildly exaggerated rhetoric, he said that joining the European Community could mean 'the end of Britain as an independent state ... the end of a thousand years of history'. When Gaitskell sat down, he received a lengthy standing ovation. However, as Dora Gaitskell said to Hugh's parliamentary colleague Charlie Parnell: 'All the wrong people are cheering.'[45] Jenkins stood without clapping, while Bill Rodgers remained in his seat.

Even so, after Brighton Gaitskell had the world at his feet. His party was united behind him. Gaitskell had apparently faced down the three fundamental challenges to the revisionist position within the Labour Party: opposition to nuclear weapons; the emergence of the intellectual critique provided by the New Left; and the entry of former communists who left the CPGB over the Soviet invasion of Hungry.[46] Many on the left were enthused by Gaitskell's anti-Common Market stance, while the pro-marketers were still bound to him by personal and political loyalty. Both Labour's leader and the party were riding high in the polls. It appeared that Gaitskell now had an excellent chance of becoming Britain's next prime minister. Jim Callaghan reflects that, 'By the time of his death, [Gaitskell] was leading a united Party that seemed poised for victory at the approaching general election ... his penetrating and informed mind would have shown itself in a clear vision of the direction in which he wanted to take a socialist Britain.'[47] Tragically, however, Gaitskell was struck down by a rare disease, lupus erythematosus (a condition that attacks the immune system). He died on the evening of 18 January 1963 in his fifty-seventh year. Harold Wilson, a rebel in 1951 but now projecting himself as a responsible politician and healer of entrenched ideological differences, seized the crown and became Labour leader.

Conclusion

A party determined on winning elections must be broadly united, a requirement of which Gaitskell was all too aware. The years between 1951 and 1955 were marked by 'personalised bitterness', which had the effect of diverting attention from the party's fundamental difficulties, notably the absence of a compelling vision for the future. That explains Gaitskell's uneasy rapprochement with Bevan in the late fifties, and his unexpected opposition to British entry into the Common

Market. But there was a stubbornness to Gaitskell's make-up that concerned even his most loyal supporters. Denis Healey wrote in his autobiography that he was worried by the 'streak of intolerance in Gaitskell's nature; he tended to believe that no one could disagree with him unless they were either knaves or fools'.[48] Crucially, while leaders such as Attlee and Wilson sought to rise above party factions, Gaitskell believed his central role was to revise party doctrine and overhaul Labour's political image. He hated ambiguity and believed, where necessary, in ideological confrontation.

As such, any definitive judgement on Gaitskell's leadership is not straightforward. Like John Smith, his career was cut tragically short. A man of government rather than of opposition, he died just at the point when it was likely that he would become the next prime minister. He was without question a highly controversial figure. To his critics on the left, he was a ruthless politician, 'a desiccated, calculating machine' who robbed Nye Bevan of the leadership, and would have been a technocratic and second-rate prime minister. By contrast, his supporters believed that his commitment, passion, and courage were qualities which would have made Gaitskell an outstanding prime minister. His friend Tony Crosland said that: 'He had that quality of leadership ... a man of total honesty, dogged bravery and iron will.'[49] Ultimately, Gaitskell did not believe that it was right to say one thing to party members and another to the voters. The leadership had to advocate feasible and credible policies that ensured Labour was perceived as a viable governing party, a real alternative to the Conservatives.

Arguably, Gaitskell was well-qualified by character,

experience, and intellect to lead a Labour government. He had shifted party policy, downgrading the centrality of nationalisation while recognising that Labour needed to manage the mixed economy efficiently to deliver growth and public sector expansion. Gaitskell's record in opposition indicates that, like Mrs Thatcher, he would have led from the front. His decisiveness, displayed over the 1949 devaluation crisis, would have made it likely that a Gaitskell administration would have devalued sooner rather than later in 1964, very much to the country's advantage. Some historians believe Gaitskell's Atlanticism would have pushed his government into a disastrous involvement in the Vietnam War. Yet one should not forget that in his 1957 Godkin lectures at Harvard, Gaitskell presciently warned against western military intervention in Asia. In relation to the EEC, the question is whether, like Harold Wilson, he would have changed his mind and later decided in favour of Britain remaining in the European Community. We should remember that he was against Macmillan's terms of entry, not against the principle of British membership.

These are the fascinating might-have-beens of history, to which, by definition, there can be no definite answers. There is little doubt, however, that Gaitskell left an important legacy not only to his able successor, Harold Wilson, but to today's Labour Party – namely that Labour must be a party of government or it will wither and die. This is not because Gaitskell believed in power for its own sake, but because he understood that, without power, it was impossible to put Labour's principles and policies into practice. He believed: 'Unity in the party can never be recreated by a series of uneasy compromises; the trouble goes too deep for that.'[50] Gaitskell ensured that revisionism became the dominant intellectual tendency in the party, reflected in the nine official policy documents published by the NEC between 1955 and 1958.[51]Above all, Gaitskell's insistence on the need for power contrasted with many of the Bevanites who (with the notable exception of Bevan himself) were far more comfortable in opposition.

It soon became apparent that Wilson's leadership style was different. He compared the Labour Party to a stagecoach: 'As long as you keep it rattling along at a quick pace, the occupants are either too exhilarated or too seasick to cause any trouble.' He also took immense pains to bring former Gaitskellites like Crosland, Jenkins, and Healey into his cabinet. He won the leadership in 1963 because he brought 'the stability and unifying influence that the Party needed'.[52] Wilson was certainly an adept tactician. The Labour MP Jimmy Maxton's view that 'a man who can't ride two horses at once has no right to a job in the bloody circus' is an apt commentary on Wilson's style of leadership.

However, as Gaitskell declared after Labour's 1959 election defeat, 'unity is not enough'. The most important lesson to be drawn from Gaitskell's leadership is that Labour must be an explicitly revisionist party, always ready to adapt to social and economic change. He may have failed to alter Clause IV in 1959, but he bequeathed to Harold Wilson a modernised party, capable of appealing to a majority of the British people. At the 1964 election, which Labour narrowly won, Wilson promoted the party as a force for modernisation and opportunity, intent on breaking down the barriers of class and privilege by aligning scientific and technological progress with socialism.

In reality, Labour had wasted much of the 1950s, first in fratricidal conflict and then in a failure to adapt fast enough to social change. The bitter civil war that engulfed the party in fact reflected deep divisions over its doctrine and political purpose. For the Bevanites, as David Marquand has written, the mixed economy was a staging post towards a fully socialised economy where the instruments of production were predominantly in the hands of the state. Furthermore, they believed strongly in a class-based electoral strategy. Yet Gaitskell's acolytes thought that public support for further advances towards 'socialism' was extremely limited. The Gaitskellites favoured a progressive electoral strategy based on the appeal to community rather than class, actively wooing the middle classes. This position is best captured by Herbert Morrison's exhortation that the party must 'Gain and keep the support, not only of the politically conscious organised workers but also of large numbers of professional, technical and administrative workers ... the soundest socialist appeal is that which is most universal in scope.'[53]

As Crosland subsequently highlighted in *The Future of Socialism* (1956), there were in any case practical problems with the commitment to wholesale nationalisation, notably the declining rate of public investment and growing consumer dissatisfaction. The revisionist case had been developed by the authors of *The New Fabian Essays* (1952), modelled on the original *Fabian Essays in Socialism* and published to address the Attlee government's record. Younger thinkers in the party, notably Crosland, Jenkins, and Healey, sought to identify a way ahead following the traumatic 1951 defeat. Crosland's essay, 'The Transition from Capitalism' was the most authoritative and original in the collection. He claimed that contrary to Marxist analysis, capitalism was not destined to collapse and was being transformed by the expansion of state intervention in the economy to secure full employment, alongside the rise of the managerial class, which tempered more aggressive forms of capitalism that were 'red in tooth and claw'. Crosland and his fellow authors sought to demonstrate that 'capitalism could do precisely what Marx said it could not do: it could provide the working class with continually rising standards of living'.[54] Crosland averred that the purpose of socialism was to eradicate inequalities of social status in order to create a genuinely classless society.

For Gaitskell's revisionist followers, the mixed economy in Britain was here to stay. Keynesian economic policies were the means to achieve full employment and rising living standards. Planning and controls had long been abandoned in favour of Keynesian demand management. In these circumstances, the gulf between 'revisionists' and 'fundamentalists' in the party was growing. Whereas in the period prior to World War Two there was a stronger degree of consensus about economic policy and the commitment to public ownership, by the late fifties new divisions were opening up over Labour's attitude to capitalism and the market.[55] Moreover, as David Marquand suggests, 'family quarrels are often bitter ... this one was no exception'. Labour in the 1950s was engulfed by 'a quarrel of factions', not only ideologies and ideas: Bevanites saw Gaitskellites as 'cliquish, self-righteous and intolerant' while Gaitskellites saw the Bevanite enemy as 'cliquish, disloyal and disruptive'.[56] The fault line between revisionists and fundamentalists was firmly rooted, continuing to haunt the party for the next three decades.

To be sure, by the mid-1960s Labour had apparently emerged as a successful reforming government, winning four out of the next five elections. Its new leader had learnt the painful lessons of the party's successive defeats in the 1950s. He appealed to 'the white heat of the technological revolution' and a sense of national purpose to paper over the deep fissures and cracks in Labour's ideological identity that had persisted since the Attlee era. Wilson's aim was to capture the support of 'the young, the new technical workers, and that vast body of voters who were not regular party supporters but who counted themselves as patriots'.[57] This strategy of emphasising dynamic industrialism in the national interest was to prove effective, at least for several years, securing a landslide victory in 1966. However, the travails of office and the paralysis of the British economy inevitably caused explosive conflicts to burst into the open once again. In subsequent decades, new fronts in Labour's civil war were exposed.

4

The Bennite Revolt and the Birth of the Social Democratic Party: Healey, Benn, and Jenkins 1964–87

In the twenty-seven years from the end of the first Wilson government in 1970 to New Labour's victory in 1997, the party won just two general elections. From 1979 to 1990 this poor record was due to the formidable personality and popularity of the Conservative leader, Margaret Thatcher. Before that, both Wilson and Callaghan, moderate leaders who helped keep the Labour Party together, nevertheless made significant mistakes. Tactical errors occurred over matters such as election timing, but the leadership's inability to contain inter-party conflict was another major factor. Labour's centre-right was in turn fatally weakened by the splits over Europe and rivalry over the leadership.

In 1981–2, the party was then almost destroyed by the SDP breakaway. The left had been greatly invigorated, above all by the dynamism of Tony Benn, especially in the period between 1979 and 1982. His drive towards control of the party was only halted when Denis Healey narrowly defeated him in the 1981 deputy leadership election. It took another sixteen years and three more election defeats before Labour returned to power, such was the seismic impact of internecine party warfare, the SDP breakaway, the weakening of the Labour right, and the political ascendency of Mrs Thatcher.

This chapter is organised in the following way. It begins by considering the nature of Labour's defeat in 1970 as a prelude to radicalisation and the shift to the left. The chapter then considers the issue of Europe and Britain's entry to the Common Market, which provoked a major schism within the revisionist centre-right of the party during the early 1970s. The inability to resolve Britain's economic problems in the mid-1970s was a further source of division among ministers in Callaghan's Cabinet. This situation allowed Tony Benn to achieve growing influence in the party. The period of Labour history considered in the chapter is a reminder that Labour's civil wars were never framed by the simplistic contest between left and right. Personality differences played a vital role, as did strategic disagreements about how Labour should respond to a changing society. Crucial too were questions of party organisation, in particular how the leadership should manage its relationship with the trade unions. The key theme throughout the period is the growing divisions within the revisionist tradition itself.

Labour's 1970 Defeat

With hindsight, Labour's unexpected defeat in 1970 marked the beginning of the party's long-term deterioration and decay. Clearly, it was a painful defeat for the Labour prime minister, Harold Wilson. Wilson had gone into the general election confident of victory. Although the party had been behind in the polls for much of the 1966–70 Parliament against a backdrop of deteriorating economic performance, the local election results had been favourable. After Jenkins' April budget, opinion appeared to be moving in the government's favour. Wilson did not rate the Tory leader, Edward Heath, whom he regularly outscored in parliamentary debates, and believed he could do the same in the coming general election campaign. So, as it turned out unwisely, he called a June election, instead of waiting for October.

Having made this error, Wilson then fought a complacent, almost folksy campaign. As his biographer wrote: 'His style was not so much presidential as that of a stage personality who could share old jokes with his fans.'[1] Curiously for such an astute politician, Wilson failed to provide supporters with many persuasive reasons to vote Labour. Nor did the party offer a compelling programme for the future, other than the promise to sustain the economic recovery. It was a 'play safe' manifesto that sought to depict Labour as the natural party of government. Yet the party failed to retain or expand electoral support outside its core political base in the industrial North and Midlands.

The record of the Labour governments of 1964 to 1970 was, in fact, a creditable one, despite the sense of disappointment on the British left. Wilson had dislodged the incumbent Conservative administration in 1964 by appealing to the rising 'intermediate class' of scientists, engineers, and craftsmen in Britain, making it clear that Labour was best placed to stimulate technological advance because of its commitment to state planning of the national economy. Wilson's meritocratic vision of national renewal contrasted favourably with the 'thirteen wasted years' of Tory rule against which Wilson railed in his speeches.

Wilson's ideas initially surfaced in a statement of party policy published in 1961, entitled *Signposts for the Sixties*. The document referred to the 'scientific revolution' underway in Britain, emphasising planning and public ownership while endorsing the mixed economy with a large private sector.[2] Labour insisted that state intervention was necessary to ensure that 'national resources are wisely allocated and community services humanely planned'. Wilson promised that a Labour government would usher in 100 days of dynamic action to kick-start the ailing British economy. Socialism was now about 'national planning ... directed to national ends'.

After 1964, spending on education, health, and social security each rose as a share of national income. There was a significant improvement in educational opportunities with a steady reduction in pupil–teacher ratios, a decisive move towards comprehensive secondary education, a major expansion of universities, alongside the launch of the Open University. The Wilson government presided over an impressive list of radical social and penal legislation, covering abortion, capital punishment, homosexuality, divorce law, theatre censorship, and complaints against public authorities. Although Labour was seen as a party of state bureaucracy, it took significant steps towards advancing personal freedom in Britain. The 1964–70 governments' modernisation of British society and culture was to prove more effective than their efforts to modernise the British economy.

The problem was that Labour's substantive economic policies after 1964 were in reality a 'flimsy blend' of measures.

Wilson was adept at exploiting public anxiety about British national decline, but Labour had no alternative strategy to tackle the British economy's worsening performance. There was no compelling social democratic model that replaced the Beveridge/Keynes synthesis developed for the 1945 government. Wilson was a skilled party manager whose annual address to the party conference was usually effective in pacifying the rank and file, reassuring the faithful that Labour remained a socialist party. The left invariably rallied around Wilson. Yet by the late 1960s, he had become an increasingly isolated figure surrounding himself with a 'kitchen cabinet' of close advisers, notably Marcia Falkender, Gerald Kaufman, and Joe Haines. Wilson's governments had a reputation for ducking contentious issues, most obviously in abandoning the *In Place of Strife* reforms in 1969. According to one observer, 'they stumbled and prevaricated as they did … because their followers were haunted by the ghosts of Hugh Gaitskell and Aneurin Bevan'.[3]

By 1970, the government's position had deteriorated. Healey's judgement was that 'bad trade figures in the last week [of the campaign] may have given credibility to Heath's final attack on Labour's handling of the economy'.[4] The underlying problem for the party was that, after a long period of unpopularity, its recovery in the polls was only recent, so that it did not take all that much to undermine it. Perhaps if Labour had devalued sterling earlier, by 1966 at the latest, there could have been four years of export-led growth and rising living standards rather than just two, and Labour might have won the 1970 election.

Nonetheless, Wilson was convinced that devaluation in

1964 would have allowed the opposition to portray Labour as the party of a weak pound, undermining foreign confidence in the British economy. Labour's economic strategy was highly orthodox while the government relied on foreign loans and creditors, which meant it must be willing to cut public spending. The government struggled to reconcile its ongoing commitment to the expansion of the welfare state with the imperative of economic efficiency and modernisation. The then chancellor, Jim Callaghan, argued that 'those who had advocated devaluation for so long always underrated the political damage that such a step would cause ... in my view the adverse effects were still being felt at the time of the 1970 election'.[5]

Roy Jenkins and Anthony Crosland believed that Wilson and Callaghan had been profoundly mistaken not to prioritise production and economic growth. The cuts package introduced in July 1966 sought to reduce demand by £500 million, 'the biggest deflationary package that any advanced industrial nation has imposed on itself since Keynesian economics began', according to *The Economist*.[6] In relation to devaluation, the revisionists were almost certainly correct and Wilson and his chancellor, who resisted it until the decision was forced upon them, wrong. Many Labour voters were deeply disillusioned after suffering a squeeze on their consumption and living standards due to the government's commitment to reduce the balance of payments deficit.

The election defeat was a crucial turning point for the party's revisionists. If Labour had won in 1970, it would have demonstrated that the modernising social democratic project shaped by Jenkins, Healey, and Crosland, and indeed

Wilson himself over the previous twenty years, had proved a success. Labour could then have become the natural governing party in British politics (which Wilson claimed it already was). All three revisionists had played leading roles in Wilson's governments after 1964. Jenkins was an outstanding home secretary and a successful chancellor of the exchequer; Healey was a notable defence secretary; and Crosland a reforming education secretary. If Wilson had won, he was planning to make Jenkins foreign secretary and Healey chancellor. He would almost certainly have taken Britain into the European Common Market, thus avoiding the damaging splits which followed in opposition.

In personal terms, defeat was a shattering blow for the three men. Denis Healey wrote of the bewildering shock of going from six years of absorbing work to the limbo of opposition. Tony Crosland felt that the defeat was a 'great humiliation'. Jenkins, whose grand manner by now led him to be labelled 'Smoothiechops' by *Private Eye,* still believed he might, in time, become leader, but he was more disappointed than dismayed. He accepted his share of the blame for the defeat, acknowledging that 'it was broadly my policies on which Wilson had chosen to fight and on which he had lost'.[7] The relative freedom of life in opposition was balanced by 'the lack of familiar props of support'.[8] All at once they appeared to become, in the title of a notorious BBC television programme at the time, 'Yesterday's Men'.

Tony Benn, who in government had proved himself a competent, middle-ranking minister, first as postmaster general, then as minister of technology with a seat in the Cabinet, felt differently. Like the others, he was surprised by the defeat but almost immediately realised that opposition provided the opportunity for new faces and ideas to emerge. At an impromptu party at the Croslands' home in Lansdowne Road in West London on the weekend after the election, Tony and Caroline Benn told the Croslands 'we've never been happier'. When Susan asked Tony Crosland about what on earth they meant, her husband replied: 'He is happier in opposition. There's no other time he can make his move.'[9] Benn could sense that the culture of the party was perceptibly changing: while in 1945–51, institutions such as the NEC, the PLP, and the annual conference remained broadly loyal, the party was becoming more openly critical of the government and the leadership. A newly assertive grassroots politics was emerging.

During the 1970s, Benn began a shift to the left, a move he attributed to his experience as a minister in the Wilson governments (as Wilson later said of Benn: 'he immatures with age'). As chairman of the Labour Party in 1971–2, Benn took the lead in pressing for a more radical programme. The former centrist politician, who had worked closely with both Gaitskell and Wilson, now became one of the leaders of the left.

Some cynics suggested that, while the space on Labour's centre-right was crowded with potential leaders (including Jenkins, Healey, Crosland, and Callaghan), there had been few realistic candidates on the left since the death of Aneurin Bevan. Although not a 'great man' like Bevan, Benn had some of the credentials required of a Labour leader. He was charming, witty, and eloquent; above all, he had enormous reserves of energy. Benn had already displayed the last quality over the Peerage Bill when, almost single-handedly, he had forced through legislation allowing peers to disclaim their titles, thus freeing him (as the son of a Labour peer, Lord Stansgate) to continue to sit in the House of Commons.

The Spectre of Europe

Labour's initial period in opposition was haunted by the issue of Europe. The crisis over Europe threatened to overwhelm the party in 1971–2 as negotiations to enter the EEC were underway. Indeed, it was on the European question that Benn made his first move. In the early summer of 1971, the Common Market issue erupted. The attitude of the Labour opposition was in part shaped by the determination of the new Conservative prime minister to take the United Kingdom into the European Community as soon as he could. The key moment was the Paris summit of May 1971, when Heath convinced the new French president, Georges Pompidou, that the UK was serious about becoming a constructive member of the Community. However, with around forty Tory dissidents, Heath now faced the problem of getting the required legislation through the British Parliament.

Pro-Europeans in the Labour Party, above all Jenkins, argued that Heath's successful application had been foreshadowed and substantially assisted by the preparations for entry which had, with Wilson's support, already taken place under the previous Labour government. Yet anti-European forces, which had been largely quiescent while Labour was in government, grew in strength, especially amongst the trade unions. At party conference in the autumn of 1970, an anti-Common Market motion was only narrowly defeated. In

February 1971, Jenkins, who had become increasingly concerned about the gathering storm over Europe, met Wilson to get his backing for a free vote, a request to which Wilson, at that time, seemed favourably disposed.

However, as hostility to the Common Market within the Labour Party became more apparent, Wilson began to shift his position. The crucial figure in Wilson's calculations was Jim Callaghan. On 25 May, Callaghan, always a shrewd judge of party opinion, made an anti-European speech in which he set out his opposition to British membership. He argued that joining the Common Market would mean 'a complete rupture of our identity' and would pose a threat 'to the language of Chaucer, Shakespeare, and Milton'. He concluded: 'If we are to prove our Europeanism by accepting that French is the dominant language in the community, then the answer is quite clear, and I will say it in French to prevent any misunderstanding: "Non, merci beaucoup".' Callaghan's biographer, Lord Morgan, admitted it was not 'his finest hour'. Yet there can be no doubt that Callaghan's declaration influenced the position on Europe taken by Wilson, Healey, and Crosland.

In July, at a special party conference, Wilson came out publicly against entry on Heath's terms, declaring: 'I reject the assertion that the terms this Conservative government obtained are the terms the Labour government asked for.'[10] Wilson and Jenkins saw the issue of Europe quite differently. For Jenkins, Europe was an article of faith: membership of the Common Market was vital for Britain's economic future and to maintain its role in the world. It was unacceptable to Jenkins that Labour would take a tactical position on Europe in opposition that was different to its policy in government.

Wilson, in contrast, had a style of leadership that gave priority to holding his party together, maintaining the unity of the PLP, which he believed was more important than solving the European question.

Consequently, the events of 1971 leading up to the parliamentary vote on the principle of entry in October, in which the Tory government had an impressive majority of 112 (including sixty-nine Labour MPs), proved disastrous for the unity of Labour's centre-right. If Jenkins, Crosland, and Healey had been able to agree on a 'modus operandi' over Europe, the history of the Labour Party in the 1970s and 1980s might have been very different. As it was, the right of the party itself was split.

Any lasting agreement would have required Jenkins to adopt a less strident position, while Crosland and Healey would have needed to adopt a more consistent pro-European stance. Yet Jenkins insisted on defying a Labour three-line whip and backing the Tory government's terms. Crosland, who had been a committed pro-European in the 1960s, was now non-committal, telling his local party that Europe was a second-order issue (in the end, with nineteen other Labour MPs, he abstained in October 1971). Ultimately Crosland struggled to take the issue of Europe seriously. One of Wilson's key advisers said of Crosland: 'There is always something of the detached amused Oxford don about him.'[11]

Healey changed his position on Europe twice, finally voting with the official Labour opposition having previously been converted to the cause of Common Market entry by the German SPD chancellor, Willy Brandt. He changed his position again following Callaghan's 'Non, merci beaucoup' intervention. No wonder Healey was accused of flagrant opportunism. In fairness to both Healey and Crosland, they faced an acute dilemma: if pro-Europeans were regarded as supporting the Conservative government unconditionally, they risked alienating mainstream party opinion. If the three men had abstained together (as was permitted under the party rules), then the European issue might have been negotiated without alienating the Jenkinsites and fatally undermining the long-term cohesion of the centre-right within the Labour Party.

Benn made his own contribution to the fracturing of the centre-right, first by advocating and then persuading the Labour Party to back a referendum on Europe. Although anti-Common Market in the early 1960s, he had taken a pro-European position by the mid-1960s, supporting Labour's application for British entry. He argued that the UK had to cut Queen Victoria's umbilical cord and appealed for technological cooperation with Europe. In opposition, as part of his move to the left, he swung back again. Speaking in the October 1971 House of Commons debate he said: 'I make no apology in the course of having thought about this issue, for having changed the emphasis of my view at different stages.'

The new element in Benn's strategy was the referendum, which, in typical fashion, he began to espouse with great fervour both on constitutional grounds and as a means of 'uniting the Labour Party'. In April 1971, he was unable to get a seconder when he put forward his proposal for a referendum to Labour's NEC. However, as the row inside the Labour Party over the Common Market intensified, support for the idea among the leadership grew. Earlier, Jim Callaghan, a former naval officer, had presciently remarked: 'Tony may be launching a little rubber life raft which we will all be glad of in a year's time.'[12] By 22 March 1972, Benn had exploited his position as chairman of the party to create a narrow majority for supporting amendments to the European Community Bill in favour of a referendum in the UK. A week later, the shadow cabinet, this time led by Wilson, who may have been looking for a mechanism to get a divided party off the hook, voted in favour of a referendum. Indeed, Wilson appeared to positively welcome a focus on Europe in the early 1970s, since it diverted attention from the more fundamental ideological divisions over domestic policy now afflicting the party.

After a lot of brooding during the Easter recess, Roy Jenkins took the fatal step of resigning from the front bench, together with several colleagues, complaining about the constant shifting of position by the NEC and the shadow cabinet. Yet it was not only the referendum issue that led to Jenkins' resignation. His underlying position inside the Labour Party felt increasingly uncomfortable: 'I was convinced that Foot, Shore, and Benn were resolved to go on and on raising any issue they could think of which would embarrass the Labour Europeans. And with Wilson having apparently committed himself to go along with them their majority was not in doubt.'[13]

The resignation of Roy Jenkins as deputy leader in 1972 was a turning point. For Jenkins, it was a major setback in his chances of succeeding Wilson. As an impressive home secretary and an effective chancellor and deputy leader, Roy had been the front runner in the succession stakes. Now he dropped back behind Jim Callaghan and Denis Healey as well. As Wilson's biographer accurately put it, 'Jenkins was signalling by his self-removal that he was no longer a party man'.[14] Jenkins' resignation led to a scramble for position among the revisionists. Healey took over from Jenkins as chancellor, while the Jenkinsites unwisely blocked Crosland from becoming deputy leader. After the 28 October 1971 vote, relations between Jenkins, Crosland, and Healey, reasonably good for much of the 1960s, were never the same again. Conflicting ambitions, personal pique, and vanity, as much as differing approaches to the European question, kept them apart. The fracturing of the old Gaitskellite coalition was to have momentous consequences, leading to a dramatic increase in the power of the left in the 1970s and early 1980s and, arguably, in 1981 to the SDP breakaway.

After 1970, the damaging splits over Europe were exacerbated by the widening gulf between revisionists and fundamentalists within the party over Labour's doctrine and ideological purpose. The new generation of fundamentalists were more aggressive and confrontational than their Bevanite predecessors – and they coalesced around their new-found guru, the charismatic young minister Tony Benn.[15] Benn could sense that the period of social order and domestic consensus that characterised the post-war years in Britain was being shattered by the breakdown of the established economic system. He advocated a new style of participatory politics, as traditional forms of deference and hierarchy were breaking down. In an influential Fabian pamphlet published in 1970, Benn argued that political leaders would have to draw their power 'less from the executive authority they have acquired by election and more from influence, helping people to see what they can achieve for themselves'.[16] Yet Benn's enthusiasm for democratic citizenship sat incongruously with his demand for greater state control of the economy through public ownership. His plans to advance workers' rights were heavily influenced by the radical University of Sussex economist and former Wilson adviser Stuart Holland.

Benn used his powerful position on Labour's National Executive and his post as shadow secretary of state for industry to put forward sweeping plans for nationalisation and large-scale industrial intervention. The most far-reaching proposal was for a National Enterprise Board (NEB), which was Holland's brainchild. Taking a public stake in different kinds of businesses would, it was argued, transform the economy. The growth rate would be raised by sustaining investment in technology while assisting employment creation in the regions. As well as establishing an 'across the board' system of compulsory planning agreements with private industry, Benn came forward with a controversial scheme for the NEB to take a controlling interest in the twenty leading companies.

Crosland and Healey, the Labour revisionists still in the shadow cabinet, strongly opposed Benn's ideas. At a joint meeting of the shadow cabinet and the NEC in May 1973, Crosland derided Benn's proposals as 'half baked' and pointed out that public ownership did not appear to have led to greater equality since the Second World War. That was one of the major themes of the *Future of Socialism*, Crosland's celebrated revisionist work. When the NEC met later that month, the new shadow chancellor, Denis Healey, recommended that the reference to nationalising the top twenty companies be dropped immediately. However, Healey's amendment was defeated by seven votes to six. In a mood of self-congratulation, Benn wrote in his diary: 'The party is firmly launched on a left-wing policy.'[17] Wilson, however, said it was inconceivable that the party would go into a general election supporting Benn's position, while Jack Jones, leader of the Transport and General Workers, advised Benn to stick to issues of real concern to his members, notably prices and pensions.

As it turned out, Labour did not win the February 1974 election. The Tories lost it. The election was held against a background of the quadrupling of oil prices and an all-out miners' strike. Heath put the country on a three-day week and appeared to have the voters behind him. If he had gone for an immediate poll, he might have won. But Heath dithered, choosing a date three weeks later before deciding on a 'who runs the country' election on 28 February 1974.

The Labour Party (including Harold Wilson) had not expected to win the election, which it fought on a manifesto that was not much more than a collection of slogans. Labour's campaign consisted almost entirely of attacks on the Heath government's competence. The so-called 'social contract' with the unions committed the government to expensive measures, without an equivalent commitment to wage restraint by the unions, even though inflation was high and rising rapidly. As well as moving further to the left, over the previous four years the Labour Party had become more dependent on the unions. At the February election, although Labour polled fewer votes, it won more seats than the Tories due to the first-past-the-post system. Labour was greatly assisted by a speech in Birmingham given by the former Treasury minister Enoch Powell, calling on Tory supporters to vote Labour in order to prevent Heath from taking Britain into Europe, costing the Conservatives marginal seats in the Midlands. The weekend after the election, Heath tried and failed to stitch up a coalition with Jeremy Thorpe's Liberal Party. The queen sent for the Labour leader, who proceeded to form a minority administration, though it was clear that there would have to be another election very soon.

The new Wilson government was highly experienced; no fewer than fourteen ministers were Cabinet veterans. The centre-right trio of Callaghan as foreign secretary, Healey as chancellor, and Jenkins as home secretary were balanced by three middle-ranking left-wing Cabinet ministers: Michael Foot at employment, Tony Benn at industry, and Barbara Castle at social services. Wilson declared that he would eschew the presidential style of the 1964–70 period. According to his senior policy adviser, Bernard Donoughue: 'He would leave the main ministers to get on with it ... how lucky he was to have such a good and experienced team.'[18]

In the period leading up to the subsequent October 1974 election, the two most independent-minded Cabinet ministers came from different wings of party: Roy Jenkins from the right and Tony Benn from the left. Jenkins was an increasingly detached figure. There had been some talk in the Wilson camp that Jenkins might become chancellor of the exchequer. But he was instead given his old position as home secretary, a portfolio which, though he performed competently, no longer stimulated a highly gifted politician. Jenkins was less than impressed by Healey's July economic statement, which reduced VAT and increased subsidies on rates, rent, and food. In a widely reported and controversial speech, Jenkins then issued a warning about Labour's shift to the left. Jenkins commented:

I could be accused of merely pontificating platitudes, but at a time when Benn was threatening most of industry, when Foot was running before the trade unions as well as bringing in unilateralism into the heart of government, when half the Cabinet was in favour of coming out of Europe and when even Crosland was putting the Clay Cross councillors above the law, they were not so platitudinous.[19]

For his part, Benn saw himself as the National Executive representative in the Cabinet, fighting for the manifesto and his radical industrial policies, rather than a loyal member of the government, bound by collective responsibility. He felt free to make speeches which could be interpreted by a hostile press as being against private enterprise and big business. As his diaries show, his cavalier behaviour led to clashes with some of his Cabinet colleagues, especially the prime minister and his chancellor, as well as the senior civil service.

However, despite conflict inside the Cabinet and the party, Wilson, assisted by another very poor Tory campaign, managed to win the second 1974 election (held on 10 October) with a narrow three seat majority. The period leading up to and immediately after the referendum of 1975 turned out to be the most productive of Wilson's 1974–6 administration. Preparing for the referendum gave direction to an otherwise directionless government. The result of the referendum then provided an impetus that enabled Wilson to curb the influence of the left, while Healey was able to impose a more effective counter-inflationary policy, including a flat-rate pay limit of £6 a week.

The irony of the referendum result, which produced a two-to-one majority for staying in, was that Benn, who campaigned so hard for a referendum, was on the losing side. Jenkins, who had resigned over the issue thus fatally weakening his chances of the succession to Wilson, had, as president of the all-party umbrella organisation Britain in Europe, led the pro-Europeans to a decisive victory. During the campaign, Roy Jenkins had several clashes with Tony Benn, who as a dissenting minister had been given licence to speak against the terms negotiated by the Labour government. Jenkins dismissed Benn's claim that entry had already cost half a million jobs with the crushing remark that he found it increasingly difficult to take Benn seriously as an economic minister. Then in the final week of the campaign, the two Cabinet ministers met in a forty-minute *Panorama* programme watched by nine million people. Although both men were polite to one another, it was unprecedented for ministers from the same government to argue publicly over such a thorny issue as Europe, yet remain in the same Cabinet.

If the referendum was a triumph for Roy Jenkins, it was a vindication of Harold Wilson's party management strategy. Pro-Europeans could insist that Wilson's behaviour in opposition helped create the situation in which a referendum had become necessary. But, in government, he skilfully used the referendum 'to keep his party in power and in one piece and Britain in Europe'.[20] After all, Labour had been in the bizarre position in 1975 of recommending to the country a deal that it was party policy to oppose (a special Labour Party conference had voted two to one against acceptance of the renegotiated terms of EC entry). In these circumstances, Wilson provided an object lesson in skilfully managing internal party differences.

The Jenkinsites may have sought to use the referendum to boost their hero's chances of leading the Labour Party. Although Wilson's fears that Jenkins was about to form a coalition with left-wing Tories were unfounded, it was undoubtedly true that Jenkins had found working with moderate Tories and Liberals in the referendum campaign 'a considerable liberation of spirit'. It was still the case that as Callaghan had warned Jenkins, leading a cross-party organisation had done him little good among most of his Labour colleagues. With respect to Benn, Wilson was able to use the referendum result to switch 'the darling of the left' from the department of industry to energy. In that department, Benn would have less opportunity to make speeches embarrassing to the Labour government. Another left-wing minister, Barbara Castle, who had been irritated by Benn's populism, called it 'the cleverest move that Harold could make'.[21]

On 16 March 1976, to the surprise of nearly everyone in politics, Harold Wilson told his Cabinet that he was resigning as prime minister and party leader. There is no evidence for later theories that Wilson was being hounded by the Secret Service or blackmailed into resignation. Ben Pimlott concluded, after examining the evidence, that there was no need for any explanation 'other than waning of the appetite for a physically and mentally exhausting office of a Prime Minister who had held the post for a very long time'.[22]

Significantly, the first of the potential candidates to whom Wilson spoke personally about his intentions was Jim Callaghan when they were passengers together in the prime minister's car on the way to the 10 p.m. vote on the night of Wilson's birthday. Callaghan, although nearly four years older than Wilson, was clearly going to run. Most Labour MPs, whose votes alone then decided the issue, expected him to win. Although he had wide ministerial experience (including serving at the Treasury, the Home Office, and the Foreign Office), Callaghan's advantage was his acceptability to Labour MPs and the party. He was the natural unity candidate, 'more so than either Foot on the left, or Jenkins on the pro-market right, more personally approachable than Healey and with more weight than Crosland'.[23]

The key issue of the first ballot was to decide which candidate of the centre-right, almost certainly Callaghan or Jenkins, would take on Michael Foot (although Benn had thrown his hat in the ring 'to fight on the issues', he was not yet a serious leadership candidate) in the second or third ballot. The fact that both Healey and Crosland had also decided to stand was likely to hurt Jenkins (who still thought he had an outside chance of victory) more than Callaghan. The candidatures of Healey and Crosland, neither of whom had a hope of winning, took out of play votes that might otherwise have gone to Jenkins on the first ballot. Equally serious for the Jenkins cause was that many pro-European MPs who would have voted for him four years before now went to Callaghan. They included Roy Hattersley, future deputy leader; John Smith, future leader; Cledwyn Hughes, chairman of the PLP; and Ernest Armstrong, future deputy speaker. Armstrong, who had admired Jenkins for many years, told him that 'the party was in such a fragile state that it needed Callaghan's more mollifying bedside manner'.[24]

When the first ballot was announced on 25 March, Foot topped the poll with ninety votes; Callaghan was next with eighty-four; Jenkins had fifty-six; Benn thirty-seven; Healey thirty; and Crosland a paltry seventeen. Crosland was automatically eliminated. Benn then announced that he was withdrawing, while Jenkins told a meeting of his supporters that he had decided to exit the race. Jenkins wrote later: 'The country, I thought, needed a new Prime Minister quickly and from fifty-six votes that Prime Minister was not going to be me.'[25] Barbara Castle wrote in her diary: 'This further display of political daintiness proves conclusively what I have always known; that Jenkins will never lead the Labour Party.'[26]

On the third and final ballot (Healey stood in the second ballot but only gained an extra eight votes) Callaghan beat Foot by 176 to 137. The composition of the Labour Party in the 1974–9 Parliament ensured that, in most circumstances, whoever was the standard bearer of the centre-right in the final ballot would win. In this context, it is intriguing to note that the combined Jenkins/Healey/Crosland vote on the first ballot came to 103, nineteen votes more than Callaghan's eighty-four. But in contrast to what happened in the 1994 leadership election when Gordon Brown stood down in favour of Tony Blair, in 1976 there was little prospect of any two of them standing down for the third. The intense rivalry of the three most prominent revisionist figures in the party made it certain that the least controversial candidate of the centre-right was the one who became leader of the party and prime minister. The 1976 leadership election merely highlighted the inability of the modernisers in the party to work together effectively.

As Callaghan remarked to an aide on entering Number 10: 'There are many cleverer people than me in the Labour party, but they're there and I'm here.'[27] Healey wrote of Callaghan: 'When Wilson's resignation offered him the unexpected opportunity, Callaghan pursued it with resolution. Once Prime Minister, he had no ambition except to serve his country well.'[28]

Even so, Callaghan acted decisively in the making of his first Cabinet. Michael Foot, representing the left, became leader of the house and effectively deputy prime minister. Denis Healey remained chancellor of the exchequer and was by 1976 increasingly formidable in his post. The surprise appointment was Tony Crosland, who was made foreign secretary (he was personally close to Callaghan). There was no promotion for Tony Benn. Even so, as well as keeping him at the Department of Energy, Callaghan diplomatically held out the hand of friendship to him.

Roy Jenkins had expected to be offered the Foreign Office but when the new prime minister met him on the morning of 6 April, he made it clear to Jenkins that the Foreign Office was not on offer. Callaghan told him that the Home Office was still available and there might be the prospect of the exchequer in the future. There was also the possibility of Jenkins going to Brussels as president of the European Commission. Callaghan pointed out to Jenkins that if he went to Brussels, he might find it difficult to get back into a Labour seat. Significantly, Jenkins replied that he did not want a future in British politics in its existing shape. In the event, Jenkins chose Brussels, a decision which was to represent not only a parting of the ways for both Jenkins and the Labour Party, but later was to have a significant impact on the future of British politics.

The new prime minister recorded in his autobiography

his first conversation with his chancellor, Denis Healey: 'I was shocked when he told me how much had been spent by the Bank of England to support the sterling exchange rate since January 1976. Denis added that we might need to make an approach to the IMF during the summer to replace the reserves we had spent.'[29] It was a prescient warning that 1976 was to be a year dominated by the weakness of sterling and the Labour government's request for a loan from the International Monetary Fund. The IMF crisis, as it came to be known, shook the Labour government to its foundations and called into question the post-war consensus over economic policy. It was also the occasion of a long, drawn-out struggle between the two leading contenders for the succession to Callaghan, between Denis Healey, the pragmatic realist, and Tony Crosland, the intellectual Keynesian.

In 1976, Healey was in his fifty-ninth year and at the height of his powers. He needed to be because he came under intense pressure from the markets, the IMF, foreign governments, especially the United States, the Cabinet, his parliamentary and party colleagues, and his trade union allies. Only Healey's great intellectual ability, endurance, and sheer force of will and personality enabled him to survive the crisis.

By the mid-1970s, Healey had become increasingly confident of his judgement. As chancellor learning to run the economy in the new world of floating exchange rates, he had lost faith in the Keynesian orthodoxy of demand management that many of his advisers and officials still espoused. In his autobiography he wrote: 'I abandoned Keynesianism in 1975 ... his theory had two important weaknesses. It ignored the impact of social institutions, particularly the trade unions.

And it ignored the outside world.'[30] Healey experienced at first hand the enormous power of financial markets to influence exchange rates, while he came to understand the brutal reality that economies in substantial deficit, like the UK, were liable to be punished by the markets. In economics, as in the rest of his politics, he developed into an eclectic pragmatist who believed, above all, in the importance of judgement based on the ascertainable facts of any given situation. In many ways, Healey was the first modern chancellor of the exchequer.

The IMF crisis began in March with a loss of confidence in sterling. For the next nine months, Healey tried in vain to satisfy the markets that the British economy was back under control. But despite cuts of just under £1 billion of public spending in 1977–8 and the negotiation of a three-month standby credit of £5.3 billion (including £2 billion from the USA), by 27 September (the first day of the Labour conference at Blackpool) sterling was in free fall. Two days later, Healey announced that the UK government would make a formal application to the IMF for long-term support amounting to £3.9 billion.

In his memoirs, the normally ebullient Healey added: 'For the first time and the last time in my life I was close to demoralisation.'[31] However, with remarkable resilience, he bounced back, courageously telling a rowdy party conference that he would be negotiating with the IMF based on existing policies, including the pay policy and cuts in public spending. As Edmund Dell, secretary of state for trade, said: 'He was fighting for the country, for the government, and indeed his own career.'[32]

Over the next two and half months, Healey tried to

persuade his Cabinet and parliamentary colleagues that there would have to be further cuts in public spending, enough to satisfy the IMF and win back market confidence. The prime minister, determined to avoid another 1930s disaster and a collapse of the Labour government, played it long by allowing exhaustive and exhausting discussions, including nine Cabinet meetings in three weeks. In the end, Healey comprehensively won the argument. According to Dell: 'Throughout the long debate in Cabinet ... Healey remain determined, eloquent and persuasive. He allowed no argument to pass unanswered.'[33]

The crucial meetings took place on the 1st and 2nd of December. First into bat was Tony Benn, who put forward the case for the so-called 'alternative economy strategy', based on import and exchange controls and the establishment of a siege economy. This policy was rejected by most members of the Cabinet. Crosland, who led the Keynesian dissidents, put forward his proposal of sticking to existing policies with the addition of purely cosmetic cuts. But he had no answer to Healey's pointed question as to what would happen if the IMF rejected the Crosland plan.

On the next day, the chancellor opened with a bravura performance. He pointed out that the Cabinet the day before had rejected the alternative protectionist strategy, while the Crosland plan was totally unsustainable because it would not convince the markets. On the other hand, if the Cabinet accepted Healey's recommendation of £1 billion of cuts in 1977–8 and £1.5 billion the following year, and if (as expected) the IMF agreed, then the government would be able to borrow again, while market confidence would be restored.

The prime minister then followed Healey and made it clear that he supported his chancellor. Crosland immediately fell into line, declaring: 'The unity of the party depends on supporting the Prime Minister.' In these circumstances, it was all over bar the shouting: Healey's proposals were eventually agreed by the Labour Cabinet.

What Healey understood, and Crosland refused to accept, was the fundamental issue of international confidence. In the conditions of 1976, with the pound having fallen in value by over 20 per cent since March and with a loan to repay in December, Healey was right and Crosland was wrong – although as it turned out, the cuts were not actually needed. Healey put it with typical bluntness: 'The trouble with theoretical economists is that they don't understand that when you have a deficit you can only finance it by borrowing, and you've got to persuade people that it's worth lending to you and that they'll get their money back.'[34]

The restoration of confidence in the British economy following the IMF agreement proved Healey's point. Almost immediately, the indicators moved in the right direction. The pound strengthened, interest rates fell, and the current account improved. The real economy then quickly recovered. Inflation continued to decline, and by 1978 the number of unemployed was also coming down, while economic growth had returned to 3 per cent. When Healey attended the IMF annual meeting in October 1977, the British correspondents described him as 'walking on water'. Even the Labour Party conference, which had treated him so cruelly in 1976, gave him a standing ovation the following year.

The IMF's seal of good housekeeping, for which Healey

had argued so forcefully, had proved to have beneficial economic results. Even so, there was still a feeling that, in being forced to go to the IMF, the Labour government had suffered a psychological setback. The Conservatives, with some justice, criticised the chancellor for his earlier policies which had led to the IMF bailout, while the Labour left (led by Benn, who, despite his criticism, did not resign from the Cabinet) promoted the myth of a right-wing 'sell out' to the IMF and the bankers. The Callaghan administration appeared to have lost its intellectual and moral authority. The revisionist belief that a growing economy would produce a fiscal surplus enabling increased public expenditure now lay in tatters. The IMF crisis brought into question the key elements of the post-war consensus: the Keynesian assumption that priority should always be given to full employment alongside the welfare state commitment to high levels of public spending – doubts which helped prepare the way for Thatcherism.

The economic rebound in 1977 and 1978 led to Labour's political recovery, following the agreement with the Liberals (in March 1977) to support the government in Parliament. This ought to have given Labour a realistic chance of victory at the next election. Victory would have made Healey, the architect of the economic recovery, the odds-on favourite to succeed Callaghan as party leader and prime minister, especially as Crosland had tragically died of a stroke in February 1977, while Roy Jenkins was in continental 'exile' in Brussels. Yet Callaghan's blunder in delaying the election beyond the autumn of 1978 led to the 'winter of discontent' defeat in the spring of 1979 and, arguably, to the existential crisis that then beset Labour in opposition from 1980.

In July 1978, Labour had certainly appeared to stand a good chance of winning a forthcoming general election if one was called in the autumn. Inflation, which had reached 23 per cent in 1975, was down to 8 per cent by midsummer 1978. Steady growth had been resumed and unemployment was falling. Living standards were rising again, while the less well-off were protected by increases in benefits. Jim Callaghan had a major advantage over Mrs Thatcher in the public opinion polls, while the Tory lead was down to low single figures; indeed, by the autumn, Labour was nudging ahead.

The case for an autumn election was strengthened by the decision of the Liberals to withdraw from the Lib-Lab pact when the new session began in November. Trade union leaders, who had given strong backing to the government's successful incomes policy, had also warned the prime minister that they could not guarantee continuing support. Much of the Cabinet, above all its younger members, were in favour of the autumn option, as were most Labour MPs. But Callaghan in a mixture of caution (he was not certain of victory) and hubris (he thought he could rely on his personal popularity to swing trade union members behind another stage of incomes policy) decided to delay. According to Dell, Healey preferred an autumn election. If so, he did not argue very hard for it.

All in all, it was a disastrous decision. Several interest groups (including Ford car workers and lorry drivers) broke through the 5 per cent policy. In addition, there were numerous highly publicized public sector strikes, with the dead being left unburied, dirty sheets piling up in the hospitals, and rubbish spilling over into the streets. The breakdown of incomes policy and the disruptive disputes that followed undermined Labour's most effective political card – its claim to be able to manage the trade unions more effectively than the Conservatives. On 29 March, Parliament put the government out of its misery when it was defeated by one vote on a confidence motion. The result of the ensuing election was never in doubt, with the Conservatives under Margaret Thatcher winning a decisive victory: an overall majority of forty-four. Towards the end of a long campaign, Callaghan confided in his aide Bernard Donoughue: 'You know there are times, perhaps once every thirty years, when there is a sea-change in politics. It then does not matter what you say or do … I suspect there is now such a sea-change – and it is for Mrs Thatcher.' For Healey, the Labour Party's 1979 defeat was a personal setback. If Labour had won, he would almost certainly have succeeded Callaghan. In opposition, with the party now deeply divided and incapable of modernising itself, his prospects were far less certain.

Crosland's untimely death had symbolised the demise of post-war social democracy and the marginalisation of the revisionist position within the Labour Party. At root, Labour was now riven with conflict because of basic disagreement as to its fundamental purpose. Healey and Crosland spearheaded the effort to ensure Labour adhered to a parliamentary strategy based on moderation and compromise. Yet the new forces on the left inspired by Tony Benn wanted Labour to confront the power of capital and the political establishment to democratise British society. The stage was set for major confrontation in the party following its 1979 defeat.

The Wilderness Years

The next few years, especially from 1979–81, were amongst the most tumultuous in the party's history. During this period, Labour's very existence was brought into question. After Labour's defeat, Callaghan decided to stay on; rather like Attlee in 1951, he intended to use his authority to try to keep the party on an even keel. This was another disastrous misjudgement: by the time he decided to resign, following the 1980 party conference, the left was in full cry and the odds on a Healey victory had lengthened considerably.

In September 1979, Healey, after visits to Japan and Greece, delivered an eloquent lecture in which he set out his social democratic vision. He warned party activists against believing their views represented those of Labour voters. He explained how his experience as chancellor was still relevant to Labour's economic policies. He could offer no New Jerusalem, 'simply a country with stable prices, jobs for those who wanted them and help to those who need it'. He concluded his remarks with the words of Leszek Kolakowski, the Polish philosopher and historian, who described the social democratic idea as 'an obstinate will to erode by inches the conditions which produce avoidable suffering, oppression, hunger, wars, racial and national hatred, insatiable greed and vindictive envy'. It was a fine speech, but sadly it was a one off. For most of 1980, Healey kept his head down and his mouth shut, hoping to take over from Callaghan as quickly and smoothly as possible. It was a mistaken strategy which allowed Tony Benn to make all the running inside the Labour Party.

Benn was determined to get the maximum political benefit from the 1979 defeat as he had in 1970. Telling Callaghan that he wished to retire to the backbenches, he launched a powerful campaign to take over the party. Benn was then at the height of his powers – charming, witty, and eloquent, he was effective on television, able to command both Parliament and Labour Party conference, while he filled halls with big audiences of activists. His energy was almost demonic, as his diaries from Labour's defeat in May 1979 to the narrow failure of his deputy leadership bid in October 1980 testify.

The Bennite cocktail was a heady brew, part economic and part constitutional. He put together all the left-wing nostrums of the last decade: import controls, a massive extension of public ownership, compulsory planning agreements, so-called 'workers control', and (despite his previous support for the referendum) withdrawal from EEC without a referendum. He labelled this programme 'the alternative strategy'. To this superficially plausible, if wrongheaded, set of policies, Benn added the commitment to internal party democracy. In a breathtaking speech for a minister who had served throughout the Wilson and Callaghan administrations without resignation, he accused those governments of ignoring conference decisions and manifesto commitments. Benn argued that to prevent this happening again the Labour leadership and members of Parliament needed to be made more accountable. Hence the case for giving the extra-parliamentary party (the trade unions and constituency parties) a predominant say in electing the leadership, for giving constituency parties the mandatory right to reselect members of Parliament, and for taking control of the manifesto away from the leadership and giving it to the National Executive.

The Bennite agenda appealed not only to the hard left and

Trotskyite fringe groups (which, following the abandonment of the proscribed left in 1972, had grown more influential within the party) but also to idealistic younger members, drawn mainly from the new salariat of teachers, local government employees, and social workers who felt Labour governments and mainstream social democracy had failed and were looking for an alternative. The new membership helped to promote a cultural revolution within the Labour Party. They wanted a more participatory organisation based on grassroots activism and genuine democracy in making policy.

At the 1979 party conference which followed Labour's defeat, speaker after speaker, including, to his shame, even the party's general secretary, Ron Hayward, accused the leadership and Labour MPs of treachery and betrayal. Both mandatory reselection and the principle of exclusive NEC control over the manifesto were won. The wind was with the Bennites, and Callaghan, like a latter-day Canute, seemed powerless to stop them.

It was against this background of Labour convulsions (as well as an unpopular and right-wing Tory government) that a siren voice from the continent made itself heard. In November 1979, Roy Jenkins was invited to give the Dimbleby lecture. As a successful and innovative president of the European Commission, he was expected to speak on European issues, but he decided to talk about the future of British politics under the title of 'Home thoughts from abroad'.

The question for Jenkins was what kind of politics it was to be. He had departed for Brussels at the end of 1976 disillusioned by the Labour Party. What had happened since had not made him any more enthusiastic. Meanwhile his

European experience had attracted him towards a continental 'power-sharing' model. Though he remained nominally a member of the Labour Party, he had not voted at the 1979 election, while his wife, Jennifer, had voted Liberal. However, his relations with Callaghan, who twice offered him a peerage, remained cordial, and a few months after he had delivered the Dimbleby lecture, he received a warm message from Denis Healey offering him the foreign secretaryship if he became prime minister. This was an indication of the high regard that Healey continued to have for Jenkins' ability, but Jenkins was unattracted by the offer. One of the reasons given by Jenkins was revealing: 'I did not feel that I could bear dealing with foreign affairs under Healey which was a subject about which, apart from Europe, he genuinely knew more than me.'[35] The truth was that Jenkins and Healey simply rubbed each other up the wrong way, an instinctive reaction that both their wives thought foolish. It was certainly a tragedy for the Labour Party.

In any case, Jenkins genuinely believed a new political strategy was now required. Using a military analogy, he argued in his Dimbleby lecture that what was required was 'not to slog through an unending war of attrition stubbornly defending as much of the old citadel as you can hold, but to break out and mount a battle of movement on new and higher ground'. With much of what Jenkins said, Healey would have agreed, as it was the stuff of mainstream European social democracy, which both Jenkins and Healey admired. Where they differed was that Jenkins no longer believed these desirable objectives could be achieved within the Labour Party. Without advocating the creation of a new party, he argued for the 'strengthening of the radical centre'. A few months later, however, Jenkins was more specific, calling for a break-out from the out-of-date 'mould' in which the politics of the left and centre in Britain was frozen.

This was a bold move for a politician who had been born into the Labour Party and, until then, had spent all his life in it. But if Jenkins' project was to get off the ground, it would need the support of as many centre-right Labour MPs as possible, especially the three former Cabinet ministers Shirley Williams, Bill Rodgers, and David Owen, who were amongst the brightest and best of the next generation of potential Labour leaders. Dick Taverne, former MP and one of Jenkins' closest advisers, put it bluntly: 'Unless he [Jenkins] got leading parliamentarians, it wasn't likely to be a very successful break.'[36]

For the moment, the three former Cabinet ministers remained cautious. But as the Bennites swept all before them during 1980, including launching an anti-EEC, pro-unilateralist policy statement at a special one-day conference in May in which David Owen was booed, the three Cabinet ministers issued an 'open letter'. They stated that if the Labour Party 'abandoned its democratic and internationalist principles, the argument may grow for a new Democratic Socialist party to establish itself as a party of conscience and reform committed to these principles'. The prospect of a split was, for the first time, out in the open.

The 'Gang of Three' were also alarmed by what they saw as the feeble resistance of Callaghan and Healey to the left's constitutional proposals. Today the idea of reselection and extending the franchise for the election of a leader beyond the parliamentary party, provided it is based on one person, one vote (procedures which they, in any case, came to support), does not seem particularly controversial. But, at the time, it was obvious to most Labour MPs that the Bennite proposals were as much motivated by the left's drive for power as by democratic considerations.

The so-called Rank-and-File Mobilizing Committee, a Bennite hard-left umbrella organisation that included the Trotskyist group Militant Tendency, made it clear that their game plan was to back constituency general management committees in order to replace right-wing MPs with hard-left ones. The growing presence of the Militant Tendency raised a question that was to haunt the party for the next decade: who ought to be considered a legitimate member of the Labour Party? As Eric Shaw pointed out, Militant was a problem for Labour throughout the 1970s and 1980s because it employed its own organisational staff.[37] The body was a threat to Labour's internal cohesion since its values and principles were outside the party's 'mainstream tradition'. The presence of Militant gave the impression of extremism, which blunted Labour's electoral appeal.

The purpose of the Rank-and-File Mobilising Committee's electoral college proposal (combining MPs, unions, and constituency parties) for electing the leader was to block Healey and, if possible, elect Benn. If not Benn immediately, an interim leader such as Michael Foot would be elected. After the failure of the Bishop's Stortford meeting to arrive at an acceptable compromise, the next event was the September party conference, which proved to be another disaster for the centre-right.

At this point, Benn was at the zenith of his influence inside the Labour Party. He seemed to be everywhere, addressing innumerable fringe meetings and electrifying the main conference by his platform speeches. In an extraordinary burst of sheer demagoguery, Benn wound up Monday's economic debate by promising three Bills as soon as the next Labour government took power: the first, an act to nationalise industry, to control capital, and to introduce industrial democracy 'within days'; the second, to restore all powers from Brussels to Westminster 'within weeks'; the third, to immediately create a thousand peers to be followed by the abolition of the House of Lords. Conference delegates roared their approval but many of Benn's parliamentary colleagues thought he had taken leave of his senses. At a fringe meeting, Shirley Williams, who had served in Labour Cabinets with Benn, repeated his three legislative commitments; she went on mockingly: 'and all this would be done in a couple of weeks. I wonder why Tony was so unambitious, after all, it took God only six days to make the world.'

The right, however, suffered defeat after defeat that week, including withdrawal from the European Community without a referendum and the removal of all nuclear bases, as well as American ones, from the United Kingdom. In a reversal of the vote the previous year, the right succeeded in keeping the drafting of the manifesto away from the NEC. But the other constitutional proposals were lost. Mandatory reselection was ratified. The principle of an electoral college was carried, though only after considerable confusion following rejection of the specific voting proportions. If it was a heady triumph for the left-wing delegates who flooded the conference, it was a horrendous experience for the beleaguered right, especially the Gang of Three, who were on the brink of leaving the party.

A few weeks after the Blackpool conference, Callaghan resigned. In normal circumstances, Healey would have won the ensuing leadership contest. With his experience as defence secretary and as chancellor of the exchequer, he was by far the best equipped of the four candidates (John Silkin, Peter Shore, Michael Foot, and himself). Foot, his most serious rival, had many qualities but the ability to lead the country was not one of them. In October 1980, Healey was comfortably the most popular politician in the country, with Foot scarcely registering in the polls. But these were not normal times. Even if the leadership election was still being decided by Labour MPs under the old rules, the Blackpool conference had changed the atmosphere. It was true that Healey suffered from obvious disadvantages as a candidate. He was a 'loner' without a large network of political friends. There were also the MPs who had been offended at some time or other by his well-known abrasiveness. Those handicaps were minor compared with the two post-Blackpool pressures with which he had to contend.

The first was from demoralised and alienated politicians on the centre-right of the Labour Party, several of whom were already considering leaving the party. They wanted Healey to act as their champion, which he refused to do, at least until he was elected. Equally important were centre-left MPs who were worried about their reselection prospects. The election of Foot, they hoped, would solve their reselection problems. In this sense, as Roy Hattersley put it, 'Michael Foot was the candidate of the quiet life', although, once elected, Foot comprehensively failed to deliver. While Healey led by 112 votes to

Foot's 83 in the first round, Foot defeated Healey by 139 votes to 129 on the second ballot following the elimination of John Silkin and Peter Shore.

Afterwards it was revealed that certainly five and probably more potential defectors had voted for Foot in order to make a split in the Labour Party more likely, while at least a dozen uncommitted MPs succumbed to constituency pressure and voted for Foot to save their skins (though some lost their seats at the subsequent general election). Faced with a critical test in the last purely parliamentary leadership election, the PLP lost their collective nerve and voted for what amounted to a prolonged spell in opposition.

A Healey leadership was one of the might-have-beens of Labour Party history. It would certainly have prevented the SDP breakaway. Even if Margaret Thatcher had won in 1983, it would have been by a much narrower margin, leaving Labour well-placed to modernise and then to stage a political comeback at least one, if not two, elections before it finally took place. Yet Healey himself, because of poor tactics following Labour's defeat in 1979, must take some of the blame for the Foot victory and the subsequent rupture leading to the formation of the SDP.

The SDP Breakaway

In reality, the defeat of Denis Healey for the Labour leadership greatly strengthened Roy Jenkins' position and his argument for establishing a new party. But Roy Jenkins had still to wait, like a patient angler, for the Gang of Three to make up their minds about whether to leave the Labour Party. David Owen was the first to go. After Jenkins' Dimbleby lecture, Owen dismissed it, saying, 'we will not be tempted by siren voices from outside by those who have given up the fight from within'. But after Foot's election as leader, on 29 November, Owen told Jenkins that he had decided to leave the Labour Party and that he believed Shirley Williams would come over as well; he was less sure about Bill Rodgers. However, Rodgers, although successfully standing for the shadow cabinet, eventually agreed to join the Gang of Three, writing in his autobiography that 'leaving the Labour Party was the only course open to me consistent with what my life in politics had been'.[38]

Once the Gang of Three had decided to leave the Labour Party and join Jenkins in a 'Gang of Four' to create a new party, the chaotic Wembley conference, held on 24 January to decide the mechanics of Labour's electoral college, provided the ideal launch pad for the *Limehouse Declaration*, the 500-word document issued the next day by the Gang of Four. The declaration was, in the main, an unexceptional 'revisionist' statement that many social democrats in Europe and most centre-right members of the Labour Party, including Blair and Brown's New Labour, would have had little trouble in supporting. The dynamite was not in the declaration's principles and policies but in its politics. The call to establish a Council of Social Democracy was clearly a staging post in a journey out of the Labour Party. If there was any doubt about their message, the last two sentences made the position of the Gang of Four very clear: 'We recognise that for those people who have given much of their lives to the Labour Party the choice that lies ahead will be deeply painful. But we believe that the need for a realignment must now be faced.'[39]

The launch (on 26 March) of the new national party, the SDP, initially aroused much public enthusiasm. It was a wonderful time to start such a political movement. During 1981, the Conservative government, faced with both rising inflation and rising unemployment, became increasingly unpopular, with Mrs Thatcher herself the least well-regarded prime minister since polling began. Labour, led by the clearly incompetent Michael Foot and racked by a divisive deputy leadership election, slipped from 46 per cent in the January Gallup poll to 23 per cent by the end of the year, the biggest fall by any party in a single year. Following the well-organised SDP launch, the SDP and the Liberals combined as 'the Alliance' moved into second place and, by the end of the 1981 conference season, went top at 50 per cent in the polls. A third-party surge on such scale and duration had never been seen before.

Although Jenkins wanted the SDP to appeal beyond the Labour Party, the party's initial strategy was to persuade as many Labour MPs as possible to join it. Thirteen MPs left the Labour Party to become founder members of the SDP, while fifteen more came over during 1981 or at the beginning of 1982. The departure of twenty-eight Labour MPs was the biggest break away from any party for nearly a century and helped give the new party momentum. Yet, crucially, the twenty-eight defectors represented only just over a third of the centre-right Manifesto group, and under a quarter of the 129 members of the PLP who had voted for Healey in the second ballot of Labour's 1980 leadership election. In fact, most of the SDP's ordinary members had never previously joined a political party, and it drew as much support from the Conservatives as Labour.

If the centre-right was to sustain its position and begin the fight back inside the Labour Party against 'the fundamentalists' corralled by Tony Benn, the crucial figure was Denis Healey. Peter Jenkins, the *Guardian* columnist who was, at the time, close to Healey, claimed that, after Wembley's disastrous conference and the impressive SDP launch, Healey had seriously considered putting himself at the head of the new party.

But if Healey saw the attraction of the SDP as a way of achieving what Labour revisionists had failed to achieve inside the Labour Party, his loyalty to Labour, especially in his own constituency and to its working-class and trade union roots, held him back. His deep knowledge of international politics also made him sceptical about the long-term prospects for the breakaway party, though he was only too aware of the short- and medium-term damage that the SDP could inflict on Labour. In early April 1981, Healey was officially approached in Bonn, Germany, to see if he would accept a nomination as secretary-general of NATO, but he turned down the offer because he saw it as his duty to stay and fight for the future of the Labour Party, not only to stop Tony Benn and the hard left but also to prevent the trickle of defecting Labour MPs becoming an avalanche.

Michael Foot and a majority of the Tribune group tried to prevent Benn from challenging Healey for the deputy leadership. However, Benn was persuaded by his hard-left advisers and supporters to run, ostensibly to try out the new electoral rules but in reality to consolidate the hard-left gains and to attempt to replace Healey, who many of Benn's associates regarded as beatable, as a first step to toppling Foot.

On April Fools' Day 1981, Healey was speaking in Hamburg when he heard the unwelcome news that Benn had decided to run against him for the deputy leadership. Healey had been elected deputy leader by the acclamation of the PLP, immediately following the announcement of his defeat by Foot. Healey now found himself having to fight with all his might for a position that he did not really want, as deputy to a man who he knew was not cut out to be the leader of the Labour Party, in a contest in which the PLP would only hold 30 per cent of the votes (the rest being held by the trade unions and the constituency parties). While Benn was on a permanent high, Healey described six months of electioneering as 'the busiest and least agreeable of his life'.[40]

On top of his duties in Parliament (as well as being deputy leader, he was shadow foreign secretary in the shadow cabinet and on the NEC of the party), he now had to travel the length and breadth of the country, speaking to constituency and trade union meetings and giving daily radio and television interviews. His public meetings were often disrupted by groups of Trotskyites and other extremists whom Benn, to his discredit, did nothing to discourage or condemn. Yet Healey ploughed doggedly on, determined to prevent Benn becoming deputy leader.

If his leadership campaign had been a disaster, Healey was at his most impressive when he had his back to the wall during the deputy leadership contest. He criticised the left for its intolerance and sectarianism, deploring its assault on the authority and integrity of Labour MPs. He compared the approach of the democratic socialist to that of a gardener: 'You have to respect the nature of the soil. You must know that certain plants will grow in certain places and not others and you've got to be prepared for a plague of rabbits to eat them all up before they grow.' Above all, he put with dignity and courage the then unfashionable case for an ideologically broad-based Labour Party, in touch with the concerns of voters and prepared to take on the responsibilities of government.

Instantly recognised by his bulky frame, florid complexion, and bushy eyebrows, Healey would be warmly welcomed on trains, and at marketplaces and meeting halls, up-and-down the country. Shamelessly trading on impersonations of him by the television performer Mike Yarwood, he would go into a comic routine that gave great pleasure to all those he met. To his campaign team, Healey revealed aspects of his personality which those who had thought of him only as an arrogant bully had never seen. Nursing a gin and tonic, he would apply his formidable mind to books, photography, travel, marriage, and children as well as to politics and international affairs.

Meeting on the evening before the count (which took place on 27 September 1981), Healey and his campaign managers agreed that the contest was too close to call. In the end, the deputy leadership was decided by one or two unions (a survey of the Transport and General Workers' Union regions had revealed a big pro-Healey consensus, which, disgracefully, the executive decided to ignore); and by a handful of brave left-wing MPs, led by the future leader Neil Kinnock, who preferred to abstain rather than vote for Benn. Healey won by 50.426 per cent to Benn's 49.574 per cent – or by four-fifths of 1 per cent (although he took 137 of the PLP votes, to Benn's 71).

That evening Giles Radice wrote in his personal diary: 'By beating Benn, however narrowly, Denis Healey has saved the

Labour Party.' This instant judgement may have looked over optimistic in late 1981. But though it took another sixteen years and four general elections before Labour got back to power, Healey's victory was nevertheless a turning point. Benn, who subsequently lost his seat at the 1983 election, was stopped in his tracks. Later that week, the hard left's stranglehold on the NDC was broken. And, despite the subsequent defection of a few more Labour MPs to the SDP, the size of the breakaway was effectively curtailed by Healey's victory. In that sense, Healey really did save the Labour Party.

In 1983, Kinnock was elected to succeed Foot as Labour Party leader. Kinnock set about energetically reforming the party. Although it was again defeated at the general election of 1987, Labour was beginning to make progress towards eventual electoral recovery.

Conclusion

The year 1983 was the end of the road for both Healey and Jenkins at the very top of British politics, though they remained influential and respected figures. The major blame for Labour's disastrous electoral performance in 1983 lay with Michael Foot for his poor leadership, and Tony Benn for his irresponsible and destructive behaviour between 1979 and 1982. Yet Healey had to share some of the responsibility, above all for keeping his head down after the 1979 defeat and for his complacent response in 1980 to the dangers of a breakaway by the Gang of Three. He could, however, take consolation from his narrow victory in the 1981 deputy leadership election, which helped the Labour Party to survive.

The 1960s and 1970s were nonetheless the prelude to the civil wars that consumed the Labour Party in the early 1980s. It was not a matter of a simple left/right divide. As we have seen, differences over Labour's policy on Europe created divisions among the revisionist centre-right. Similarly, Healey and Crosland were at odds in Cabinet over how to manage the economy during the extraordinary turbulence of the mid-1970s. In reality, the core assumptions of British social democracy were breaking down. As the political historian Geoffrey Foote has written: 'The crisis in revisionist thought came to the surface. The promise of higher social spending and greater social equality had always been dependent on a high economic growth rate … The deep schism which emerged over the Common Market was the most dramatic demonstration of its crisis.'[41] The post-war revisionists in these circumstances were unable to produce a new ideological synthesis as they had done after the 1951 defeat. This fundamental weakness combined with growing disillusionment with the governments of the 1960s and 1970s paved the way for Tony Benn to launch his energetic bid for the leadership from the left.

For nearly a year after the formation of the SDP, it seemed a real possibility that it might in fact be the means of 'breaking the mould' of British politics. But although the performance of the two 'Alliance' parties (the SDP and the Liberals) in the 1983 election was the best third-party result for forty years, the harsh reality was that it was not the breakthrough for which its leaders had hoped. Jenkins, partly due to health reasons, did not prove to be the vigorous campaigning leader which his initial efforts at the Warrington and Hillhead by-elections had promised.

Yet there was a more fundamental sense in which the revisionists such as Healey and Jenkins had failed. The split in the Labour Party and the SDP breakaway to which they both, in various ways, contributed led to the weakening of the social democratic ideas in which, despite different views and styles, they still believed. The reality was that the centre-right was badly split over the issue of Europe. While all the leading revisionists believed in the European project, Crosland and Healey had growing doubts. They did not believe that the issue of entering the Common Market was important enough to split the Labour Party. Jenkins, in contrast, saw Europe as a matter of fundamental belief and was unwilling to compromise. As a consequence of the divide, revitalisation of the social democratic project proved virtually impossible. Later on, the SDP was not the source of new thinking that its founders had hoped. The German academic Ralf Dahrendorf remarked that the SDP stood for 'a better yesterday', a promise to recreate the domestic post-war consensus that was becoming increasingly anachronistic in Thatcher's Britain.

The reasons for the long-term failure of the revisionist project inside the Labour Party are complex. The best chance of a breakthrough came under the Wilson administrations of the 1960s when Jenkins, as chancellor, was in the ascendant, Healey and Crosland were powerful ministers, and Wilson himself was a convert to the cause of modernisation. But after the 1970 defeat, which was a crucial turning point, both the left and the unions became more powerful. Tony Benn was the most energetic leader of the left since Nye Bevan and his ability to put the revisionists on the defensive grew during the 1970s. With the defeat of *In Place of Strife* and the successful assault on the Conservative's Industrial Relations Act, the unions' political clout increased substantially, which made governing, especially for a Labour administration, more difficult. Labour ministers knew that economic modernisation required the regulation of wage-bargaining and industrial disputes in the public interest but found compromise with organised labour almost impossible.[42] In this atmosphere, the party was unable to revisit its core theoretical assumptions, devising a new 'social democratic perspective' for late twentieth-century Britain.

It was already apparent by the mid-1980s that the version of social democracy espoused by Crosland, Healey, and Jenkins was badly in need of revision, and that a new radical thrust would be required if the party was to return to power. Healey sought to develop a corporatist model of social democracy with some success. His approach took account of recent developments, especially the impact of global markets and capital flows. But like the Callaghan government, Healey's ideas had been fatally undermined by the so-called 'winter of discontent' of 1978–9. Callaghan himself was a conservative 'safety first' leader who had no intention or desire to transform the country.

The cleavage inside the party between ministers who wanted to modernise Britain and the trade unions who sought to defend their members' interests was becoming unsustainable. Healey's defeat by Michael Foot in the 1980 leadership election was the final nail in the coffin for leading social democrats. In 1981 Jenkins made a bold but unsuccessful attempt at a social democratic breakout. But Jenkins' cavalry charge ended in defeat at the 1983 election, when the

Alliance party failed to overcome the virtually insuperable handicap of the first-past-the-post electoral system. Healey blamed the SDP for Mrs Thatcher's victories and the long delay in Labour's recovery. Jenkins argued that, without the SDP, Labour would never have been dragged back from what he called 'the wilder shores of lunacy and arrogance'. Both contentions are in fact plausible.

It is highly probable, however, that Labour's decisive rejection by the voters in 1983 and 1987 would have taken place even without the existence of the SDP. Successive defeats by Margaret Thatcher were the main reason why Neil Kinnock and then John Smith set out to overhaul the party, initially by returning to the revisionist politics of the 1950s and 1960s. They were followed by Tony Blair and Gordon Brown in the 1990s who were able to transform Labour into a modernised social democratic party capable of winning power, albeit by overhauling the party's doctrine and ethos to create New Labour. In this sense, liberal democracy produced its own remedy by forcing Labour to return to the centre ground of British politics – from where elections are invariably won.

5

New Labour at War: Blair and Brown's
Dual Premiership 1997–2010

On the face of it, Tony Blair and Gordon Brown's 'dual premiership' was the most successful political marriage in the Labour Party's history. Indeed, Blair and Brown were the joint architects of the New Labour project. Their partnership enabled the party to win two successive landslide victories, followed by a decisive third election. They governed for three full terms, by far the longest period in the party's history. In office, Labour was able to reshape the British political landscape, tackling child and pensioner poverty, reforming the constitution, transforming public services, and establishing a new relationship with the European Union (EU). Without doubt, Blair and Brown were a successful combination that not only created and sustained New Labour, but gave the party the longest period of power in its history.

What is so striking in retrospect is the complementary political gifts of the two men. Blair was charming, stylish, and charismatic, the best political communicator of his age, who could dominate the House of Commons, set party conference alight with his speeches, while speaking directly to voters on television. Yet initially he had little interest in the detail of policy or the machinery of government. Brown, on the other hand, was a heavyweight thinker on policy matters, the party's master political strategist, steeped in the traditions of the Scottish Labour Party. He was an incisive and stimulating companion, although not always an effective communicator or interpreter of the public mood.

The political commentator Andrew Rawnsley describes the Blair–Brown partnership as 'the rock on which New Labour was built and the rock on which it so often threatened to break apart. When they were working together, their complementary skills created a synergy which made the Government pretty much unstoppable.' Much of the discussion of the post-1997 Labour governments focused on the rows between the two principals and their respective courtiers. While Blair and Brown's 'dual premiership' was unquestionably successful in recasting British politics, it provoked considerable tension and instability inside the Labour Party.

From the outset, there were explosive rows that no doubt undermined the Labour government and blunted its impact. Although these arguments can be dismissed as superficial, resulting from personality differences which are inevitable in day-to-day high politics, their tone became increasingly strident and ideological as Brown and Blair battled over the future of their political project. The disputes began in the highest echelons of the leadership, but soon filtered down into the wider party. The PLP was increasingly defined by the fault line between 'Blairites' and 'Brownites', encouraged by the media, who loved to rake over the latest battles between Number 10 and the Treasury. The trade unions then felt compelled to take sides, particularly following disagreements with Blair over public sector reform. The longer that Labour remained in office after 1997, the more prone it became to bitter arguments that divided the entire party, pushing it inevitably towards internal conflict, if not outright civil war.

Commentators have depicted the Blair–Brown 'wars' as a form of rivalry concerned with patronage and personality, a contemporary version of the court politics that afflicts all political dynasties. Certainly, there was a battle of egos in which two great political rivals jostled for position and dominance. The press reporting of the conflict wallowed in its 'soap opera' qualities, the melodrama of the 'TBs–GBs' as civil servants liked to describe them. There were endless opportunities for the Sunday newspapers to expose the battles between Number 10 and Number 11.

Without question, the appetite for power played an important role in these disputes. Blair and Brown were surrounded by personal entourages and rival courts who believed it was necessary to emphasise the substantive divisions between them. Brown's advisers sought to portray him as the true heir of the social democratic tradition on the British left; while Blair's team defined Brown as an opponent of reform, a message designed to cultivate support among the Murdoch press. The most provocative charge was that of Blair's director of communications, Alastair Campbell, who labelled Brown 'psychologically flawed'. Brown's supporters genuinely felt he would have been a more heavyweight prime minister than Blair, an authentic carrier of the Labour Party's ambitions as a socialist party committed to a more equal society.

The difficulty for Brown was that the longer Blair clung

on in Number 10, the less valuable the premiership became, increasing his risk of ending up a 'fag end' prime minister. Nevertheless, the divide between the men was not only about career and position. Ultimately, it was about how to *use* power for the public good, while advancing social democracy in British society. There were significant ideological and policy differences that fuelled the growing chasm between the Blair and Brown camps. When defeated at the general election in 2010, Labour appeared to be an increasingly divided party. It spent the next decade in the political doldrums. This chapter will examine the nature of Blair and Brown's relationship, the ideological differences that emerged as Labour entered government, and the underlying causes of the growing enmity between them. As in the previous chapter, the core theme is of a divided centre-right within the Labour Party, which created the space for a resurgent left to emerge following the 2010 and 2015 general election defeats.

The Rivals

Tony Blair, born in 1953, was raised in a prosperous middle-class family in County Durham.[1] His father, Leo Blair, was a successful university law academic and barrister. His mother, Hazel Corscaden, came from County Donegal in the Republic of Ireland. The family spent two years living in Adelaide, Australia, where Leo took up a lectureship in administrative law. Blair was educated at the Durham Chorister School, then joined his brother, Bill, at Fettes College, a well-known Scottish public school in Edinburgh. Blair loathed the experience, despite a promising beginning which included winning a competitive scholarship. Although he heartily disliked the school and became increasingly rebellious, Blair learned how to act on the stage, how to hold a public audience, and how to think for himself. He grew more confident in his views, and by the sixth form was a success academically. Blair attained good A-levels, winning a place at St John's College, Oxford to read law (he later regretted the decision, wishing he had read history).

As an undergraduate, Blair largely avoided politics, especially the bear pit of the Oxford Union debating chamber. Instead, as an undergraduate he socialised actively with fellow students, becoming immersed in discussion of theological questions as part of a reading group led by an Australian, Peter Thomson, a priest in the Anglican Church of Australia. Thomson introduced him to the teachings of the Scottish philosopher, John Macmurray. Blair learned a great deal from Christian socialism, particularly its emphasis on fraternity and duty, and its insistence that socialism was not about public or private ownership but rather using ethical ideals to consistently address social problems. 'Social-ism' was first and foremost a politics of conscience rather than class. Blair also sang in a rock band, the Ugly Rumours, and tried to launch a career as a rock promoter. A friend of Blair's at Oxford later recalled that he had 'an aura about him even then; people noticed him; he stood out; [he] was already deploying the sort of trendiness and charm – which have been in evidence ever since'.

After Oxford, Blair trained to become a barrister, and was taken on in the chambers of an influential lawyer, Derry Irvine, where he also met his wife, Cherie Booth. Irvine, who was well-connected inside the Labour Party, gave Blair a foot on the political ladder. Having fought a hopeless by-election in the safe Conservative seat of Beaconsfield in 1982, Blair was selected to fight the constituency of Sedgefield, County Durham, only weeks before the 1983 election – a remarkable achievement for an outsider with minimal trade union support. He won over local party members by speaking with passion and conviction at the selection meeting. What was unusual about Blair was that he was not obviously part of the Labour tradition, a consequence of his rootless middle-class upbringing. He told *The Observer* in 1994: 'I never felt myself anchored in a parliamentary setting or class.' This background gave Blair the priceless ability to appeal to voters outside the Labour heartlands in the Midlands and southern England. In 1993, *Private Eye* declared that Blair was 'the only member of the Labour Party a normal person could ever vote for'.

Gordon Brown's upbringing was very different to Blair's. He was very much a Scot, rooted in the Scottish Church, in Scottish public institutions, and of course, the Scottish Labour Party. Brown was raised by his parents in Kirkcaldy, Scotland, a town on the northern shore of the Firth of Forth. Brown's father, Dr John Brown, was a highly respected minister in the Church of Scotland. Gordon Brown grew up living in the 'manse' (the local vicarage) where he 'learned a great deal from what my father managed to do for other people. He taught me to treat everyone equally.' Being raised in the centre of social action in the local community inevitably shaped Brown's politics. He was a precocious talent at school, admitted to the University of Edinburgh at the age of sixteen where he secured a brilliant first in modern history.

He was far more active than Blair in student politics, elected rector of the university and increasingly involved in the Labour Party. At the age of twenty-four he edited *The Red Papers on Scotland*, a book that set out a radical agenda for the 1970s. Three years later, he was chosen to chair the Scottish Labour Party's committee on devolution. The celebrated journalist Neal Ascherson judged Brown to be 'the outstanding Scot of his generation'. At the 1979 election, Brown was defeated in the marginal seat of Edinburgh South, and had to wait four years to be selected for the newly created 'safe' constituency of Dunfermline East in the Fife coalfields. He entered the House of Commons in 1983 alongside Blair in the aftermath of Labour's disastrous general election defeat. From there, the arduous task of rebuilding Labour as a credible contender for power began.

The Opposition Years: 1983–1997

As two new boys in Parliament, Blair and Brown forged a close political friendship, sharing a small windowless office off the main committee corridor of the House of Commons, little more than a cupboard with two desks. Brown immediately emerged as the senior partner in the relationship. He was already chairman of the Scottish Labour Party, the author of several published books, and knew his way around the media as a former television producer. In the despair that engulfed the party after the 1983 defeat, Blair and Brown stood out as bright, energetic, and charming, bringing a fresh, more up-to-date outlook to the outdated labourism that had contributed to Labour's defeat in 1979. Both made accomplished maiden speeches in the House. The following year, Blair was appointed as a shadow Treasury spokesman under Roy Hattersley. Having initially turned down the job of Scottish spokesman, Brown joined the front bench a year later, working on regional policy for John Smith.

At the 1987 election, Labour suffered a further devastating defeat. Despite Neil Kinnock's efforts to modernise the party, its policies on tax and unilateralism cost it millions of votes. In the aftermath of the defeat, Brown won election to the shadow cabinet on the *Tribune Group* slate. Blair followed a year later. They made an outstanding contribution to the opposition team. Brown stepped in as shadow chancellor after John Smith's first heart attack, winning plaudits for his response to Nigel Lawson in the 1988 budget debate, while Blair led the opposition to electricity privatisation as shadow energy secretary. As shadow employment spokesman, Blair then updated Labour's industrial relations policy, persuading union general secretaries to abandon their long-standing support for the closed shop.

Despite the policy changes driven by the modernisers surrounding Kinnock, Labour was defeated once again at the 1992 general election, finishing seven points behind the Conservatives. Blair hit the airwaves the morning after the result, insisting in a television debate with the left-wing MP Ken Livingstone that Labour had lost not because it modernised too much, but because it had not changed enough. Kinnock immediately resigned as party leader. That weekend, the two modernisers held a series of meetings to decide on tactics for the forthcoming leadership election. Blair urged Brown to run, yet Brown was understandably reluctant given he was a close ally and friend of the front runner, John Smith. Blair was keen to stand as Smith's deputy to advance the modernisers' cause, but Brown was less than enthusiastic. In any case, Smith had already chosen Margaret Beckett as his running mate.

Smith's twenty-two months as Labour leader were frustrating for Blair and Brown (as well as Peter Mandelson, newly elected to represent the constituency of Hartlepool but playing no meaningful role in advising the leadership). Smith had many qualities. He was masterful as a debater in the House of Commons, and soon established his dominance in the party. Smith initiated important reforms such as 'one member, one vote' for selecting parliamentary candidates, and began to win the trust of voters. Yet the modernisers did not feel that Smith was moving rapidly enough to remake the party. Philip Gould, the party's leading political strategist, told a meeting of the party's NEC shortly after the 1992 defeat: 'In the end, it comes down to this. Voters do not trust us with the economy. They do not trust us to spend their money. They do not trust us with their taxes.'[2]

It was in this period that Blair established himself as the leadership front runner. Brown was appointed to the powerful position of shadow chancellor, but his role in enforcing strict control of spending commitments, his 'mechanical delivery of soundbites', and his somewhat monotonous television performances undermined his status as Smith's natural heir. In the meantime, Blair's reputation was growing as an able communicator who was busily repositioning Labour as the party of law and order. Indeed, he was now acknowledged to be the party's leading modernising politician.

When Smith died suddenly of a heart attack on 12 May

1994, Blair quickly became the hot favourite to succeed him. Brown reminded Blair they had an agreement that as the 'senior partner', Brown would have the first call on the leadership. Blair argued that things had moved on, and he was being strongly pressured to run by fellow MPs. Over the next three weeks, a tortuous round of discussions took place between the camps to broker an agreed position. In return for a shot at the leadership, Blair accepted Brown ought to be given a 'super chancellorship' where he would effectively control economic and social policy; Brown would then succeed him as leader when Blair eventually stood down. The deal was believed to have been agreed at the infamous (and now closed) Granita restaurant in Islington. Blair later regretted making so many concessions to Brown, particularly when policy differences began to emerge in government. He also denied making precise commitments about the leadership, despite Brown being convinced that Blair had agreed to step aside during the second term of a Labour government. Brown was left embittered, convinced he would have made a more successful leader and prime minister. In 1994, it was feared that if Blair and Brown ran against each other, the modernising camp would have been divided, allowing Margaret Beckett or John Prescott to come through the middle. Other figures including Kinnock's former chief of staff Charles Clarke argue that Brown ought to have been allowed to run against Blair, in order to settle the issue of the leadership decisively. The long-term consequence of 'the deal' was the festering of mistrust. From once being a close political partnership, the Blair–Brown relationship became more unstable and antagonistic.

In 1994, Blair won the leadership contest convincingly

in all sections of the electoral college. He began to assert Labour's political dominance immediately. The Conservative administration under John Major was by now extremely unpopular following the UK's chaotic exit from the Exchange Rate Mechanism (ERM), having been in office for thirteen years. Nevertheless, Blair and his team recognised that governments do not simply lose elections. There has to be a viable governing alternative. Labour must be trusted by voters and win the battle of ideas. As well as setting out new positions on economic management, welfare, law and order, constitutional reform, and Europe, Blair believed Labour's policies needed intellectual coherence. At the party conference in 1994, the new leader set out his intention to revise Clause IV of the party's constitution. The clause was originally drafted by Sidney Webb immediately after the First World War, committing the party 'to secure for the workers by hand or by brain the full fruits of their industry ... upon the basis of common ownership of the means of production, distribution, and exchange'. While previous Labour leaders, notably Harold Wilson, Neil Kinnock, and John Smith, believed that rewriting Clause IV was not worth the trouble, Blair concluded that Labour must demonstrate it was willing to change fundamentally. He argued that individuals prospered best in a strong and cohesive society, 'where opportunity and obligation go hand in hand'. From then on, the party became known as 'New' Labour. Although their bond had been damaged by the leadership election after Smith's death, Blair and Brown continued to work closely together up until the 1997 election. Blair needed Brown's economic and tactical advice, while Brown depended on Blair to maintain discipline on economic policy and public spending in the shadow cabinet, and for his appeal to voters in Middle England.

In the run up to the election, Labour's approach was understandably cautious. Brown announced that for the first two years of the Labour government, ministers would retain the spending limits set by their Conservative predecessors. There would be no increase in the basic rate of income tax, nor in the top tax rate. Brown was determined to restore Labour's reputation for fiscal discipline and economic competence. As the political commentator Steve Richards has noted, Brown and his young adviser Ed Balls, a former leader-writer on *The Financial Times*, were effectively rewriting centre-left economic policy following a period in which the economy had emerged as Labour's Achilles heel. The five commitments on Labour's symbolic pre-election 'pledge card' were deliberately modest in ambition, notably small class sizes for primary school pupils and shorter NHS waiting lists, but they symbolised Labour's commitment to improving the lives of ordinary families. The key idea at the core of Blair's modernisation of the party's doctrine was the belief that rights must always be accompanied by duties. He insisted: 'duty is the cornerstone of a decent society', while 'the rights we receive should reflect the duties we owe'.[3]

The 1997 election campaign was a six-week marathon. But Labour now had a highly effective and professional campaign team bridging the Blair and Brown camps, which was run from Millbank Tower. In a well-organised campaign, the Conservatives' divisions over Europe and sleaze were successfully exploited by Labour. In the end, Blair's party won a landslide victory with a parliamentary majority of 179 seats. His election campaign had targeted what his campaign strategist Philip Gould called 'the new middle class': 'the aspirational working class in manual occupations and the increasingly insecure white-collar workers with middle-to-low-level incomes'.[4]

The New Labour machine was able to eat directly into the Conservative heartlands of the Midlands and the South of England. Remarkably, even the Cabinet minister Michael Portillo was ousted from the 'true blue' suburban constituency of Enfield Southgate. After eighteen years in the electoral wilderness, it seemed the modernisers had brought the Labour Party back to power. Without the political partnership of Blair and Brown, victory would have been much harder to achieve. In government, however, tensions and misgivings that had been festering in opposition soon surfaced, with unpredictable consequences for the Labour government's stability and cohesion.

The First Term 1997–2001: Ruling Out the Euro

Blair and Brown dominated the first Labour Cabinet, bringing the habits of opposition into government. Major strategic questions were settled by the prime minister and his chancellor through bilateral negotiation, so-called 'sofa government', rather than exhaustive Cabinet discussion – a stark contrast to the last time Labour had been in power under Wilson and Callaghan. In practice, there was a 'dual premiership' with two centres of power in 10 Downing Street and the Treasury. The approach was designed to compensate for the political inexperience of Labour's new prime minister, augmented by tight control from the centre.

As Blair reflected in his memoir, *A Journey*: 'On 2 May

1997, I walked into Downing Street as Prime Minister for the first time. I had never held office, not even as the most junior of junior ministers. It was my first and only job in government.' On the government's first major decision to transfer the power to set interest rates to an independent Monetary Policy Committee (MPC) of the Bank of England, the rest of the Cabinet were not even consulted, even if it provided the stability in monetary policy that was the bedrock of the government's reputation for economic competence. Andrew Graham, a special adviser in the Number 10 Policy Unit in the 1970s, told a Fabian Society Conference shortly before the 1997 election that the most significant achievement of a Labour government would be 'not to mess up the economy'.[5] The National Minimum Wage, the New Deal for the young unemployed, alongside tax credits for low-income families strengthened the administration's social democratic credentials. Elsewhere, New Labour had early successes. Blair helped to negotiate the Good Friday Agreement (GFA) in Northern Ireland, which finally brought thirty years of bloody political violence to an end. Power was devolved to an assembly in Wales, a parliament in Scotland, and a strategic authority and mayor for London. The Human Rights Act enshrined the fundamental liberties of citizens in law.

Although the new Labour administration was demonstrating its dynamism and reforming élan, even in the first term divisions between Blair and Brown became evident. In 1998, the journalist Paul Routledge published a biography of the chancellor which claimed that Brown still believed Blair had betrayed him over the leadership following John Smith's death. A briefing war between the two camps ensued. The

chancellor had been assiduous in maintaining his own independent political operation. His team included his political
fixer, Nick Brown, now a departmental minister; his spin
doctor, Charlie Whelan; and his schoolboy friend Murray
Elder. On matters of policy in the Treasury, Brown relied on
his economic advisers, Ed Balls and Ed Miliband. The consequence was an increasingly toxic atmosphere around the
government centred on daily briefings to journalists. Brown's
team were enraged when the prime minister's chief spokesman attacked the chancellor's psychological stability. Blair
was apologetic, but told Brown that he should never have
co-operated with Routledge's book.

Despite growing divisions, in 2001 Labour won a second
landslide victory, first and foremost by demonstrating its economic competence. Regardless of the tensions between 10 and
11 Downing Street, it was a remarkably popular government
that maintained a consistent poll lead throughout the first
four years, never losing a by-election. Yet even if the second
landslide victory was a shared achievement, the state of the
Blair–Brown relationship did not bode well for the future.
Even during the 2001 campaign, divisions were becoming
more evident. The atmosphere inside the Labour headquarters in Millbank Tower was venomous. Brown wanted to fight
the election on the relatively cautious agenda of economic
stability, with additional funding for health and education.
Blair's camp sought to advance a 'post-Thatcherite' reform
programme, focusing on social mobility and opportunity, and
putting Britain at the heart of Europe, potentially even by
joining the single currency.

After four years in office, the prime minister felt that despite maintaining political popularity, the government had wasted too much of the first term. It had to pursue major reforms decisively if New Labour was to fashion a political legacy as lasting as that of the Attlee governments after 1945. Many of his aides in Number 10 tried to persuade Blair to move his chancellor to the Foreign Office, believing that having a rival at the centre of power in the Treasury was not sustainable. Yet Blair baulked at the decision. He recognised that Brown did not want to leave the Treasury. As the most successful Labour chancellor in history, Brown was in a very strong position. Blair respected Brown's political acumen, but also feared him, as well as feeling guilty about the supposed betrayal in 1994. The difficulty was that the second term became much more fraught as the underlying tensions between Blair and Brown became increasingly explosive, and the travails of governing grew more acute. The differences between them were now focused as much on personality as on policy.

Second-Term Blues 2001–5: Reforming Public Services

The main priority of the Blair–Brown governments was to improve the quality of Britain's public services, notably the National Health Service (NHS) and schools. British social democracy had long emphasised using the fruits of economic growth to strengthen the welfare state and the public realm. During the Labour governments, unprecedented sums were invested in the NHS and education after an initial phase of prudence in managing the public finances. By 2000, it was recognised there ought to be a sustained period of public investment after two decades of relative stagnation. When

Blair went on the BBC *Frost Programme* to announce that Labour would increase NHS spending as a share of national income to the European average, Brown was incensed, screaming: 'You've stolen my fucking budget!' The Treasury believed that the NHS had already received a large cash injection, and the government ought to be cautious about committing to extra spending.

The question of how to improve public services proved to be the key battleground of Labour's second term, leading to escalating tensions between the Treasury and Number 10. As Blair's 'delivery' guru, Michael Barber argued that public sector reform was not only about money, but systems, management, and personnel. Moreover, both Blair and Brown accepted that the electorate would be reluctant to countenance additional resources for health and education without serious structural reform. In Brown's terms, money had to be accompanied by modernisation. The difficulty lay in determining a credible strategy for improving public services. Initially, the government's focus was on centralised management, using performance indicators such as targets to drive up standards. The 'flog the system' strategy yielded improvements. In the NHS, waiting lists fell dramatically, mortality rates declined, while care for those with cancer and coronary disease improved significantly. In primary schools, basic standards of literacy and numeracy also progressed. British children scored well in reading and maths compared to other industrialised countries. The crime rate fell dramatically.

However, it soon became apparent that the approach would only have a short-term impact. Increasingly, Blair was persuaded of the virtues of a market-orientated strategy where competition was used as the lever to drive improved public sector performance. He averred that Labour should embrace diversity of provision using market forces to raise the quality of public services, while they remained free at the point of use, funded by general taxation. The prime minister's public service reform agenda became increasingly controversial, embracing academy schools, top-up fees in universities, foundation hospitals, and five-year plans to significantly increase choice and competition. Consequently, domestic policymaking in New Labour's second and third term was dominated by 'a bitter battle between Blairites and Brownites over the shape, boundaries and governing philosophy of public services'.[6]

Certainly, Brown remained wary, embracing a more cautious, less market-driven approach. At his core, Brown was a 'democratic collectivist' who believed that the central state had the capacity to create a more efficient economy and a more just society. He did not believe that markets had much of a role to play in public services given the likelihood of unequal access to information alongside pre-existing social inequalities. In 2003, Brown gave a widely reported lecture to the Social Market Foundation (SMF) think tank where he signalled his discomfort with the 'Blairite model' of reform. Blair later wrote that, 'though Gordon resisted many of the reforms and slowed some of them, he didn't prevent them. By the time I left, choice and competition were embedded in the NHS; academies were powering ahead; tuition fees were in place; and welfare and pension reforms were formulated, if not introduced.'

Blair and Brown both spearheaded efforts to radically overhaul British social democracy in the early 1990s. They accepted that Labour could not simply revert to the corporatist policies of the post-war consensus in economic and social policy. The party had to acknowledge that the economy and society were altered profoundly after a decade of Thatcherism. There were fewer trade union members. The manual working class was shrinking as a proportion of the workforce. British industry was declining relative to the service sector. Nationalisation had largely been discredited in the post-war decades. It seems clear that the shadow chancellor agreed with Blair in 1994 that Clause IV of the party constitution ought to be rewritten, discarding the commitment to public ownership.

Nonetheless, there were emerging ideological differences between Brown and Blair that sowed the seeds of subsequent conflict beyond the reform of public services. The key fault line concerned the role of equality in Labour's ideological vision. The prime minister favoured the commitment to equality of opportunity where the state invests in provision such as education to ensure individuals can advance as far as their talents take them. Blair believed that 'Croslandite' equality of outcome, in which the government redistributes resources to the least well-off in society by taxing the wealthy, had been thoroughly discredited during the 1970s.

Brown was more circumspect about such ideological repositioning. He certainly favoured equal opportunity, using the Treasury as a base to invest in skills and training. However, Brown was more reluctant to discard the commitment to equality of outcome. He recognised that voters were sceptical about redistribution, but he used tax credits and tax allowances to redistribute cash 'by stealth' from the relatively affluent to the poorest, particularly households with children and pensioners. Brown still believed in egalitarian redistribution. By the end of the second term, Blair was becoming increasingly impatient with the Treasury's approach, insisting that too much was being spent on tax credits rather than public services, particularly education.

The Euro

Without question, the biggest 'non-decision' of the Blair–Brown era was the choice not to join the euro. Immediately after the 1997 election, Blair made it clear that Britain was very unlikely to enter the single currency in the first wave in 1999. But ministers still had to decide whether to rule out joining the euro for the entire Parliament. Brown, once an enthusiastic pro-European advocating British entry to the Exchange Rate Mechanism (ERM) in 1990, then changed his mind. In October 1997, in an interview with *The Times* newspaper, Brown ruled out joining a single currency 'for the lifetime of this Parliament'. The intervention shocked Blair and his close ally Peter Mandelson, as well as angering pro-European Labour MPs and trade unions. What followed was a hasty round of meetings to clarify the government's position. The following week, Brown told the House of Commons that Britain would not participate in monetary union until after another general election unless there was 'a fundamental or unforeseen change in economic circumstances'. However, the chancellor conceded that if the euro was shown to have worked, it was in Britain's national interest to join.

Even so, Blair regarded UK entry to the single currency as a crucial pillar of his political legacy. In December 2001, he allegedly told Brown that he would stand down as prime minister in return for being able to take Britain into the euro. The difficulty was that Brown did not believe a referendum on the single currency could be won, particularly as the British economy was outperforming its continental competitors. In April 2003, Brown presented the first Treasury analysis of the case for joining against the 'five tests', which, not surprisingly, ruled out entry. Blair refused to accept this judgement, believing that the decision was about politics as well as economics. After a stormy meeting in which the two men clashed repeatedly, Blair told Brown: 'You will have to consider your position.' Brown told the prime minister: 'I'll do just that.' Yet the chancellor ultimately got his way, and entry was ruled out without any proper discussion in Cabinet. Both men pulled back from the brink when it was in their interests to do so. By the summer of 2003, relations had soured considerably.

The Twilight of the Blair Premiership 2005–7

There is little doubt that Blair's political authority was damaged irretrievably by the Iraq War. He had taken Britain to war in Iraq because he believed it was morally the right thing to do. He had great confidence in his own judgement after relatively successful military interventions in Sierra Leone and Kosovo. Blair never conceived of the damage that might be done either to the standing of his government at home, or to Britain's position in Europe, given French and German opposition to the Iraq invasion. The Iraq War inflicted substantial damage, most importantly through loss of life in Iraq and the British military, but also in undermining Blair's political reputation.

A large section of the British public, particularly the liberal intelligentsia, lost trust in the prime minister, believing he had lied and behaved improperly. Labour's opinion poll ratings fell sharply, and its long-term electoral prospects were damaged as Blair's 'big tent' began to collapse.

The Iraq invasion was viewed as 'Blair's war'. He later told the Chilcot Inquiry that despite everything that had happened subsequently, he would take the same decision again. Brown played no direct role in planning for the conflict, although he was regularly consulted by Blair. In public, Brown gave Blair his full backing. However, in the aftermath of the conflict, Brown signalled his disagreement with how the invasion had been handled. He subsequently brought in the War Powers Act as prime minister that required a vote of Parliament to agree on any future military action by British armed forces.

By the time of the party conference in 2003, around half of British voters wanted the prime minister to resign, according to a poll published in *The Financial Times*, as the post-invasion situation on the ground in Iraq deteriorated sharply. As Blair faltered, Brown, who was waiting in the wings, began pressing the prime minister to stand down so he could take over. Blair came close to quitting in the spring of 2004, but his close supporters, notably his wife, Cherie, persuaded him to stay on. The day after the 2004 party conference, Blair announced that he would fight the next general election, serve a third term, and then leave 10 Downing Street. Brown and his team, who were attending the annual International Monetary Fund (IMF) meeting in Washington DC, likened Blair's surprise announcement to 'an African coup'.

Blair and Brown managed to hold their political

partnership together to fight the 2005 election. But by this stage, the infighting was becoming unbearable. In the end, the two men knew they needed one another. The prime minister relied on his popular chancellor to reinforce Labour's credentials for economic competence. Brown still depended on Blair to shore up Labour's support in Middle England. Yet the dual premiership arrangement was breaking down. The two camps fought bitterly over the content of the 2005 election manifesto. The Blair team wanted to push their vision of radical reform in public services, casting their opponents in the Treasury as 'consolidators'. The chancellor sought to emphasise Labour's credentials in managing the economy and ensuring a fairer distribution of income.

Despite the difficult and tough campaign, Labour still won an unprecedented third-term majority of sixty-six seats, although it had the lowest share of the vote for a winning party since the 1832 Reform Act. Dozens of seats were lost to the resurgent Liberal Democrats, who capitalised on opposition to the Iraq War and on university tuition fees. In the aftermath of the election, Blair reassured the PLP that there would be a 'stable and orderly' transition of power once he stepped down, and that Labour was more than capable of winning a fourth term. But his influence as prime minister was clearly draining away, despite the 2005 summer successes of bringing the Olympics to Britain, hosting a successful G8 meeting in Scotland, and rallying the nation after the terrible 7/7 bombings.

In Parliament, Blair was defeated over the '90-day clause' for detention of terrorist suspects without trial, while an Education Bill weakening the role of local education authorities

(LEAs) only just scraped through. An inquiry into 'cash for honours' further damaged Blair's reputation and standing in the eyes of the electorate. His refusal to condemn the Israeli shelling of Lebanese territory then provoked outrage in the PLP, and open revolt among the Brownites. At this point, the Brown camp decided to move decisively. Two junior ministers and a group of parliamentary private secretaries duly resigned, a plot allegedly hatched in a Birmingham curry house. Following a series of frantic meetings between Blair and Brown, the prime minister announced that he would step down in the summer of 2007. Blair felt he had little choice but to endorse Brown as the next Labour leader and prime minister. But relations between them had become deeply embittered.

Brown in Power 2007–10: Governing in the Financial Crisis

The new prime minister entered Number 10 in exceptionally difficult circumstances. Voters were becoming disillusioned with New Labour after a long period in government. Moreover, one half of the Blair–Brown partnership had now departed the scene, leaving the prime minister increasingly exposed. Brown had certainly done the heaviest lifting on policy since the early 1990s. But Blair was the most effective political communicator of his generation. The fallout of the long, drawn-out battle between Brown and Blair had also damaged the government's reputation. Brown's chancellor, Alistair Darling, later wrote that, 'from a ringside seat, I saw the slowly dripping poison of their relationship damage our government ... Tony and Gordon dominated the Labour Party for more than ten years, and were an overwhelming force for good, but by the end their feud allowed a cancer to grow which, I believe, contributed to our defeat in 2010.'[7]

From day one as prime minister, Brown struggled to position himself ideologically. Did he represent continuity or a break with New Labour? Moreover, the newly installed premier was painfully aware that he did not have his own mandate, and always had one eye on the next election. His aim was to reconstruct New Labour's election-winning coalitions of 1997 and 2001, while attracting back liberal middle-class voters who had deserted the party in droves following the debacle of Iraq.

Consequently, Brown was one of New Labour's founding figures who then sought to distance himself from the Blair agenda and legacy. When Brown became prime minister, the measures he initially proposed (such as cutting university tuition fees) were designed to emphasise his distance from Blair. Yet as Steve Richards notes, Brown's 'nightmare inheritance' was that 'he had to keep the Blairites on board while seeking to move on from Blair'.[8] This was a recipe for confusion; Brown never properly defined what he stood for. He ended up introducing superficial changes in policy that did not actually make his government work more effectively. For example, Brown agreed that Blair had been operating a 'sofa' style of government. In 2007, he curtailed the role of special advisers in 10 Downing Street, making greater use of formal decision-making structures to co-ordinate departmental ministers, notably through Cabinet committees. Yet there was little evidence it became easier to get policy through Whitehall.

The major achievement of Brown's administration was the effectiveness of its response to the international economic crisis. The British approach to recapitalising the banks was emulated around the world. At the G20 meeting in April 2009, Brown brought together the leaders of the advanced economies to agree a plan for global economic stimulus. The US economist Paul Krugman gushed that Brown had 'saved the world'. Yet Brown's economic record, once his key political strength, came under scrutiny. He was criticised for allowing public borrowing to rise, based on over-optimistic Treasury forecasts of economic growth. The Treasury's 'light touch' approach to regulating the City led to an unhealthy expansion of financial services, leaving the UK exposed in the wake of the crash. By 2009, Brown had become personally estranged from his chancellor, Alistair Darling, who he believed was too beholden to Treasury orthodoxy in dealing with the fallout of the financial crash. The prime minister made no secret of the fact that he wished to appoint Ed Balls as his chancellor, further exacerbating the tensions between Number 10 and 11 Downing Street. Brown's misfortune was that his premiership was to be defined by the 2008–9 financial crisis, the most serious economic collapse since the early 1930s.

Electoral Defeat and the Rise of Corbynism 2010–20

Against the backdrop of economic turmoil and political conflict, Brown struggled to get his premiership back on track. Without the charismatic presence of Blair, Labour's 2010 election campaign lacked its usual verve and sparkle. Labour's central political message was less than coherent. Alistair Darling wanted to emphasise that a future Labour government would be compelled to take tough public expenditure decisions, but would do so fairly, refusing to cut 'too far, too fast'. Brown, on the other hand, would not utter the word 'cuts' and sought to make the dividing line in the election 'investment versus cuts', as he had done in the two previous election campaigns. As a result, Labour's campaign suffered from the absence of fiscal credibility. The party was consequently defeated, although not as severely as many in Labour had feared, underlining the possibility that Brown and Blair could have won a fourth term had they been willing to work together more effectively.

What was the legacy that the dual premiership bequeathed to the Labour Party? Critics claimed that Blair and Brown left behind a hollowed-out shell of a party depleted of members and morale. The compromises that Blair had forced the party to make exhausted it. Moreover, Blair's and Brown's actions (particularly Blair's over the conduct of Britain's role in the Iraq War) helped to fuel a contemporary betrayal myth. It was alleged that the 'real' Labour Party had been taken over by a narrow cabal of zealous modernisers who abandoned the party's democratic socialist roots in 1994. Of course, it ought to be remembered that in 2010, the majority of party members (54 to 46 per cent) still voted for the 'Blairite' leadership candidate David Miliband, as did the majority of Labour MPs (53 to 47 per cent).

Yet by electing Ed Miliband in 2010 and then Jeremy Corbyn to the leadership in 2015, the grassroots membership and the major trade unions (the GMB, Unite, and Unison) were able to 'get their party back'. Ed Miliband's period as leader from 2010 to 2015 focused on repudiating New Labour's acquiescence to neo-liberalism. He sought to chart a fresh policy prospectus focused on shaping a new model of productive capitalism for Britain. However, Miliband was unable to assuage voters' fears about Labour as a governing party. In 2015, he was defeated heavily. Jeremy Corbyn, who then won the leadership entirely against the odds, was focused on a moral rejection of the Blair era, notably the war in Iraq and the alleged embrace of financial capitalism. The legacy and achievements of the 1997–2010 governments were repudiated. Despite his enthusiastic following on the left of the Labour party, Corbyn's poll ratings remained weak throughout his leadership, dogged by his association with anti-Semitism and Middle Eastern terrorist organisations. In 2017, Labour did better than many feared in the general election against the hapless Theresa May. But two years later, the party was heavily defeated in the 2019 election.

Of course, Blair and Brown cannot be blamed entirely for the decade of political failure that defined Labour in the aftermath of their leadership. In previous periods of Labour history, the party's ejection from government resulted in a protracted phase of ideological conflict and bitter doctrinal dispute. The period since 2010 was no exception. The Labour Party, as we have seen, is constitutionally prone to internal strife and civil wars. What was unusual about the last decade was the extent of the swing to the left. The flood of activists who joined during Corbyn's ascendency were intent on reshaping Labour into a very different kind of political party, shorn of its roots in parliamentary politics. In the wake of the 2019 general election, it appears that they have not succeeded. The leadership will have to do its best to negotiate this troubled legacy in restoring Labour as a serious contender for power.

Conclusion

At their zenith, Blair and Brown were an incredibly powerful political partnership and leadership combination. In opposition, they were unbeatable. In the first and second terms of the Labour governments, they worked together constructively despite growing mutual mistrust, bequeathing a legacy of substantive governing achievement. The sustained growth in the British economy until 2008 made it possible to inject substantial investment into public services, particularly health, education, and policing. There were 89,000 more nurses and 44,000 more doctors in the NHS than in 1997; waiting lists were at their lowest level since the founding of the health service. Over 4,000 schools were either rebuilt or refurbished, while exam results at the ages of eleven and sixteen improved dramatically. The British constitution was fundamentally reformed, resulting in the most radical shift of power to Scotland, Wales, and Northern Ireland since the Great Reform Act of 1832. Britain did not join the euro, but the UK became a more committed member of the European Union (EU). Overall, by working together and combining effectively, Blair and Brown bequeathed a substantive social democratic legacy.

Even so, by the third term, the conflict in the political relationship had brought the Labour Party to the brink of civil war. This is not to suggest that conflict is always unnecessary or detrimental to political success. At times, the underlying tensions between Blair and Brown led to periods of real creativity in politics and policymaking. Blair appealed skilfully to English middle-class voters, while Brown shored up Labour's traditional support and maintained links to the liberal intelligentsia. As Blair's chief polling strategist, Philip Gould, pointed out:

> As became clear in the 2010 election, having two of them campaign together was better than only one. I lost count of the number of times that campaign staff – from all camps – would say in 2010: if only we had Tony. Not because they necessarily wanted him back as leader, but because the pairing of Tony and Gordon in an election campaign was so much stronger than one alone.[9]

Neither figure believed in promoting party unity for its own sake. While both recognised that voters punish divided parties, they understood that the Labour Party had to confront and attempt to resolve ideological conflict, rather than papering over the cracks of doctrinal dispute. In contrast to leadership figures such as Harold Wilson, Blair and Brown, having learned the painful lesson of the 1992 election defeat, pursued the cause of modernisation with vigour and determination.

Yet the chancellor's unceasing quest for the power of the premiership was to become relentless and, ultimately, destabilising. By 2005, Blair as prime minister was a depleted force who had lost trust both with Brown, and among British voters. Yet he remained Labour's most effective and eloquent communicator. The perpetual struggle for power between Blair and Brown did not have the ideological qualities of previous disputes in Labour's history, notably the bitter internal war between Bevan and Gaitskell in the 1950s. Yet the dispute cannot be explained by personality and political rivalry alone.

The divisions over policy and ideology within Labour's centre-right intensified throughout the party's first and second terms of office.

6

The Left Insurgency, Corbyn's Leadership, and the Succession of Keir Starmer

The Rise and Fall of Jeremy Corbyn

With the exception of George Lansbury in the 1930s, Jeremy Corbyn was arguably the most ill-equipped leader in Labour's history. An obscure backbencher who was known largely for backing extreme left-wing positions and for voting against his own government after 1997 (it is said over 400 times), he became leader of the party almost by accident following the imprudence of the MPs who nominated him to ensure a 'real debate' in the leadership contest. The impetus for Corbyn's victory was provided by the thousands of younger, mainly middle-class activists who swelled Labour's ranks in 2015, buoyed by his message of radical change and angered by nearly a decade of austerity.

Significantly, although Corbyn won the overwhelming support of party members and supporters in the leadership election following the resignation of the previous leader, Ed Miliband, after the 2015 election defeat, only fifteen out of 232 Labour MPs cast their first vote for him. More than half the MPs who nominated Corbyn did not actually vote for him. From the beginning, he had little legitimacy within the

Parliamentary Labour Party (PLP), most of whom believed Corbyn was unelectable as prime minister. Following his insipid and unconvincing performance in the 2016 referendum on the United Kingdom's membership of the European Union (Peter Mandelson decried him as being 'for most of the time absent from the fight'), Corbyn had to beat off a challenge to his leadership from the Welsh MP and shadow cabinet minister Owen Smith. With the backing of a growing number of grassroots party activists, Corbyn won easily. Corbyn was fortunate in his opponents: the right and centre of the Labour Party had little distinctive to offer after 2010 and appeared intellectually bereft. Yet the crucial problem of Corbyn's lack of core support in the PLP remained. During his tenure, Labour remained badly split and at key moments appeared on the brink of civil war. The party was unable to offer a viable governing alternative, nor did it make any discernible impression on the national debate underway about Britain's future relationship with Europe in the wake of the referendum.

Nonetheless, the 2017 election was a high point of Corbyn's period as leader. Encouraged by opinion polls reflecting Labour's deep unpopularity, the Tory prime minister, Theresa May, called a snap general election. Untested on the national political stage, she proved to be a wooden and robotic campaigner. Corbyn, by contrast, came across as warm and energetic, offering a message of hope to enthusiastic crowds of grassroots activists around the country. Instead of gaining the sixty or so seats they expected, the Conservatives lost thirteen and, more importantly, their overall majority in the House of Commons. Labour, despite experiencing its third successive defeat, actually gained thirty seats, increasing its share of the vote to over 40 per cent. The party's support had improved more than at any general election since 1945.

In the post-election euphoria, Corbyn and his advisers believed they were on the cusp of entering 10 Downing Street. However, May managed to cobble together a minority government by negotiating a 'confidence and supply' arrangement with the Northern Irish Democratic Unionist Party (DUP). Over the next two years, as May struggled to forge a parliamentary consensus for an agreement over Brexit, Corbyn's weaknesses as a leader were glaringly exposed. On the issue of Brexit, the Labour Party was admittedly split. The majority of members backed Remain and a second referendum (the Economic and Social Research Council [ESRC] Party Members Project estimate the figure was 83 per cent). But a minority in key Northern and Midlands' marginals strongly supported Leave, and were opposed to a 'People's Vote'. Corbyn chose to sit on the fence, announcing that he would remain neutral in any referendum campaign. The strategy of 'constructive ambiguity' worked well for Labour in 2017, but over the next two years it made the party appear weak and indecisive. Pro-European voters began to drift away towards the Liberal Democrats and the Green Party.

Corbyn in turn failed to give any lead over the highly damaging anti-Semitism crisis which threatened to engulf the party. A review into institutional anti-Semitism in the party was established in 2016, led by Shami Chakrabarti, the former director of the campaign group Liberty. But the investigation was derided as a whitewash which cleared the party leadership of any wrongdoing. Shortly afterwards, Chakrabarti was rewarded by Corbyn with a peerage.

Then, when May resigned in the early summer of 2019 and was succeeded by Boris Johnson, the new Tory leader ran rings around the hapless Corbyn, trapping Labour into an election which it was almost certain to lose. In the event, Labour went down to an epic defeat, suffering its worst election result since 1935, losing many seats in its traditional heartlands, and returning only 202 MPs. The overwhelming factor in Labour's defeat was the unpopularity of the leadership and the perception the party was riven by conflict. Opinion polls showed that Corbyn was the most unpopular leader in British political history. He was perceived as an unpatriotic and weak leader, unable to manage a divided party – who would make a disastrous prime minister. Decisively rejected by voters, Corbyn then resigned. The Corbyn era in British politics was already over.

This chapter will examine how the period of Corbyn's leadership relates to previous civil wars that have engulfed the Labour Party. A perennial tension in Labour's history concerns the authority and legitimacy of the PLP. MPs assume an inevitable importance within a parliamentary democracy, yet they are ultimately accountable to their constituents rather than party members. Their views are often perceived as small-c conservative, inviting a clash with the grassroots members who invariably favour greater radicalism. As we have seen, Tony Benn's rise to power after 1979 relied on encouraging animosity towards MPs who were depicted as blocking implementation of socialist measures in Labour's 1974 manifesto. These conflicts re-emerged after 2015 because, like Tony Benn, Corbyn believed in the 'betrayal myth' that Labour failed to emerge as a radical socialist party due to the caution and deference of its MPs. The stage was set for perpetual conflict, but there was also deadlock. The MPs could not easily remove Corbyn, given his overwhelming grassroots support. Similarly, although moves were afoot by 2019 to deselect errant Labour MPs and replace them with left-wingers, it was unrealistic for the Corbynites to seek to reconstruct the entire PLP. The Labour Party in these years became a cauldron of seething animosity.

The Accidental Leader

Jeremy Corbyn was born in 1949, part of the baby boomer generation in post-war Britain. He was the fourth son of two middle-class professionals who were members of the Labour Party. Corbyn attended a private preparatory school followed by a selective grammar school, at which he passed two A-levels (with a grade E), failing a third. He then spent nearly two years in Jamaica as a Voluntary Service Overseas (VSO) cadet teacher, later travelling for a time in Latin America. Returning to Britain, he enrolled at the North London Polytechnic to study trade unionism, although he never completed his degree. Indeed, there is little evidence in Corbyn's education of much studying or reading. Unlike his close colleague John McDonnell, Corbyn's 'leftism' was based more on a rebellion against 'capitalism', and the Establishment in general, than on intellectual Marxism.

In the early 1970s, Corbyn got a job as a trade union researcher for the Tailor and Garment Workers, and afterwards in the Amalgamated Engineering Union. He subsequently became a National Union of Public Employees (NUPE) organiser. He joined the Hornsey Labour Party where he threw himself into political work, becoming chairman of the local Young Socialists (then under the control of the Trotskyist group Militant Tendency). In May 1974, after acting as agent for the Hornsey Labour candidate in the February general election, he and his first wife were elected as local councillors. During the 1970s and early 1980s, Corbyn became part of the London 'hard left' scene, along with Ken Livingstone, John McDonnell, Ted Knight, and Diane Abbott. He edited the far-left newspaper *London Labour Briefing*. Corbyn also became a devoted acolyte of Tony Benn, giving him fervent support in Benn's failed 1981 deputy leadership campaign. At the 1983 general election, which Margaret Thatcher won in a landslide, Corbyn was returned as MP for Islington North with a majority of 5,607.

Entering Parliament as a new MP, he is said to have told left-wing friends that he considered the institution 'a waste of time'.[1] That judgement could well give an insight to Corbyn's subsequent record in the House of Commons. Although he was (and still is) a conscientious constituency member, in Parliament he made little contribution or impact. Unlike his friend (and former lover) Diane Abbott, he was never a member of a select committee, while his speeches in the chamber were undistinguished. When Labour returned to power in 1997 under Blair and Brown, Corbyn gained an unenviable reputation as a serial rebel, voting frequently against his own government. In contrast, former supporters of Tony Benn, notably Chris Mullin, became loyal ministers. Backing left-wing causes, he travelled extensively in the Middle East and Latin America. For Corbyn, politics was ultimately a form of protest, reinforcing his commitment to unilateralism, Cuba, Hamas, and Hezbollah, alongside the Provisional IRA. The idea that he would end up as leader of the Labour Party would have been dismissed by his parliamentary colleagues of the time, including those on the left, as fanciful.

Corbyn's rise was all the more remarkable because, for the previous twenty years, Labour's left was widely regarded as a busted flush. There were occasional victories, notably Ken Livingstone's effort to capture the London mayoralty, eventually as the Labour candidate. But ever since Benn's defeat in the early 1980s, the organised left had been on the back foot in the party, placed in a 'sealed tomb' according to Peter Mandelson. It lacked organisational muscle, and no longer had the capacity to shape the debate about ideas within the Labour Party.

However, a series of unexpected events helped pave the way for Corbyn's rise. The first was the victory of Ed Miliband over the former foreign secretary, his elder brother David, in the leadership election which followed Labour's 2010 election defeat. In the electoral college, David won the support of both Labour MPs and the constituencies but trailed behind his brother in the trade union section. Ed Miliband positioned himself as the anti-New Labour candidate, somewhat implausibly given that he had served as an adviser and minister in the governments of both Blair and Brown, helping to draft Labour's manifesto in the 2010 election. Although highly intelligent, as leader of the opposition Miliband failed to stamp his authority on either his party or the country.

When the Conservative prime minister David Cameron called an election to take place on 7 May 2015, Labour was defeated decisively, despite five years of fiscal austerity and the collapse of the Liberal Democrats, who were punished for entering a coalition with the Tories. Labour ended up with a net loss of twenty-six seats, losing all but one of Labour's Scottish seats.

To the astonishment of the political world, the ensuing leadership election was won by Corbyn. The left searched desperately for a candidate. In 2007 and 2010, first John McDonnell and then Diane Abbott failed even to reach the required number of nominations to get on to the ballot. Corbyn was very much a third choice but, against the advice of McDonnell, he decided to run: 'It was my turn. A few weeds are going to be springing up in my allotment, but I will be able to get back to it shortly,' he told *The Guardian* newspaper.

The problem confronting Corbyn was how to get nominated. To prevent a candidate without a minimum level of support getting on the ballot, there was a 15 per cent barrier (for this election, thirty-five MPs). Most of the MPs who nominated Corbyn had no intention of voting for him, but thought that he was an amiable maverick with no chance of winning. However, they believed that there ought to be a real debate about Labour's future which should include a hard-left candidate. Figures such as Sadiq Khan thought that nominating Corbyn would help them in their own internal selection contests, in Khan's case his run for mayor of London. Even Margaret Beckett, a former foreign secretary in Blair's government, decided to nominate Corbyn. She later said: 'I probably regard it as one of the biggest political mistakes I ever made.'[2] With minutes to go, Corbyn scraped on to the ballot with thirty-six nominations.

Corbyn told *The Guardian* in June 2015 that he believed his chances of victory were slim:

> We had a discussion among a group of us on the Left about how we might influence future developments of the party. All of us felt the leadership contest was not a good idea – there should have been a policy debate first. There wasn't so we decided somebody should put their hat in the ring to promote that debate. And, unfortunately, it's my hat in the ring.

Indeed, the odds on Corbyn becoming leader started at 200 to 1.

However, the problem for the other three candidates in the race (Andy Burnham, Yvette Cooper, and Liz Kendall) was that having been government ministers and special advisers, they still spoke with the caution of office. In contrast, Corbyn gave the kind of left-wing backbench speech he had been making for years. At meetings up and down the country, it became increasingly clear that his pitch of a decisive end to austerity, while rejecting the politics of the Blair era, was receiving a positive response. One of his few parliamentary allies, Clive Lewis, said: 'Jeremy is Jeremy. He isn't a rock star politician, he doesn't have the looks, he doesn't wear slick clothes, but in a way, he is an anti-hero. He is genuine, authentic, and he just seems to have resonated with people.'

Corbyn's unexpected victory was assisted by Ed Miliband's reform of Labour's internal selection procedures. In addition to introducing one member, one vote, anyone who paid a £3 supporter's fee could vote. The left saw their opportunity, signing up new members in droves, while creating a new grassroots organisation with the catchy title of Momentum. Its leaders were mostly veterans of Tony Benn's campaigns, notably Jon Lansman, as well as old-style Trotskyites and communists. But, significantly for the future, many of Corbyn's supporters were new to politics: baby boomers who had grown increasingly disillusioned with New Labour; the under-thirties alienated by the Conservative government's austerity policies, the sharp rise in tuition fees, and the difficulties of getting into the housing market; and white-collar employees in the public sector who stood to lose most from the retrenchment of the state.

Assembling such a coalition was at first glance a political triumph. But as the polling organisation YouGov ominously pointed out, Corbyn's new activists were not representative of the country, nor even of Labour voters. Partly as a result of Miliband's reforms, more than two-thirds of the Labour Party membership were now classified as middle class: 56 per cent were university graduates; 44 per cent were employed in the public sector. Long-term changes in the social composition of the party had been underway since the early 1970s, but Labour was no longer seen as a party with working-class roots. This reality came back to haunt the Labour Party in the 2019 general election.

Corbyn versus the PLP

Corbyn won a convincing victory in the leadership election, gaining over 59 per cent of the vote. He almost won a simple majority in all three sections of the electoral college: 84 per cent of newly registered supporters voted for him, as did 57.6 per cent of the affiliated trade unions, and 49.6 per cent of party members. But the question posed by anxious Labour MPs was what kind of leader this hard-left former backbench rebel would make. Seumas Milne, the former *Guardian* journalist, who was to be appointed Corbyn's director of communications and strategy, told a victory party: 'The challenge is to translate the insurgency into political power.'[3]

In the event, Corbyn was to prove far more of an insurgent than an inclusive party leader. At the outset, he did try to accommodate a range of views. His first shadow cabinet retained prominent Blairites, notably Lord Charles Falconer and Pat McFadden, who was appointed shadow Europe minister. Yet he appeared much more interested in capturing the party for the hard left, the historical goal of the Bennite wing, than winning a general election for the Labour Party. In ideological direction, style, and disposition, he was far removed not only from the New Labour politics of Brown and Blair, but from the moderate social democracy of previous leaders, notably John Smith, Neil Kinnock, James Callaghan, and Harold Wilson. The Oxford historian Ross McKibbin concludes that Corbyn was 'probably unique in his lack of conventional qualifications for the job'.[4]

The fault line throughout the Corbyn ascendancy was his failure to win the support of the overwhelming majority of his MPs. His first reshuffle in January 2016 was a reminder of the constraints under which he was compelled to operate. Having briefed the press that the shadow foreign secretary, Hilary Benn, and the shadow chief whip, Rosie Winterton, would be removed from their posts, Corbyn's team were forced to retreat following the hostile reaction of the PLP. As a body, they continued to mistrust his judgement, were unimpressed by his parliamentary and media competence, and did not believe he was capable of leading the Labour Party to victory. Indeed, many feared for their seats. Except for a brief period following Labour's relatively strong performance at the 2017 general election, MPs continually plotted his downfall. As the left-wing journalist Owen Jones commented: 'The parliamentary party ... mostly believed that Corbynism was a hideous aberration which needed to be brought to a swift termination.'[5]

The first major rebellion (at the end of 2015) was on the issue of bombing Isis in its Syrian redoubt, and was led by the shadow foreign secretary, Hilary Benn, the son of Corbyn's former mentor. Following an emotional ten-and-a-half-hour debate in the House of Commons, sixty-six Labour MPs voted against Corbyn and with the Tory government in favour of bombing. In a rousing finale to his speech in the debate, Benn told the House:

> We are here faced by fascists – not just their calculated brutality, but their belief that they are superior to every single one of us in the chamber tonight, and the people we represent. They hold us in contempt. They hold our values in contempt. They hold our belief in tolerance and decency in contempt. They hold our democracy, the means by which we will make our decision tonight, in contempt. And what we know about fascists is that they need to be defeated.

However, the Corbynites within the party steadfastly opposed what for them amounted to the killing of innocent civilians.

In the aftermath of the 2016 EU referendum in which Corbyn played such an inglorious role, an even more serious rebellion took place. Once again triggered by Hilary Benn, twenty-three out of thirty-one shadow cabinet ministers resigned, and 173 MPs then backed a motion of no confidence in the leader. Corbyn's position now appeared perilously weak. However, supported by his shadow chancellor, John McDonnell, and by Diane Abbott, who Corbyn subsequently made shadow home secretary, he refused to quit. When Owen Smith, a former shadow cabinet member, challenged him for the leadership, Corbyn put his trust in the party membership, now swollen to more than 500,000 (the largest left-wing party in Europe). He won easily. Corbyn had survived but the highly damaging split between the Labour leader and Labour MPs was as wide as ever.

Corbyn managed to pull together a ramshackle shadow cabinet in the aftermath of the resignations, but the Labour parliamentary opposition to Theresa May's government was weak, so much so that the Tories were able to open a big lead in the opinion polls. By April 2017, according to the polling organisation YouGov, the Conservatives were eighteen points ahead of Labour, while Corbyn's personal ratings were catastrophic, with only 13 per cent favouring Corbyn as prime minister, compared with 51 per cent for May.

Corbyn's Hour of Glory

On 18 April 2017, an opportunistic prime minister called a snap election for 8 June, sensing that she would secure a big majority. The political class was certain that the Tories were going to win – and win big. In the event, the election proved much closer than the pundits expected. Corbyn, running on the slogan 'For the many, not the few' (borrowing, though without acknowledgement, Blair's rubric from the 1997 election), threw himself into the arena which he enjoyed most – campaigning. He went on public walkabouts, met and talked to voters, and addressed mass rallies of his own supporters. Even his television appearances were more effective than anticipated. Corbyn managed to exude calm authority in contrast to the cold and robotic prime minster, while inspiring voters, especially the young. Using social media with great skill, the left-wing grassroots organisation Momentum backed Labour's campaign with drive and enthusiasm.

By contrast the Conservative campaign, like Theresa May, was wooden and uninspiring. The Tories' campaign slogan was 'strong and stable' leadership. In practice, Mrs May was reluctant to engage directly with voters. While Corbyn obviously enjoyed meeting people, the prime minister was unwilling to take part in spontaneous encounters or unscripted debates. Her performances on television were uninspiring. The *Guardian* journalist John Crace called her 'the Maybot', a description which had resonance and soon caught on.

Impressively, Labour won the battle of the manifestos. The media commentators were expecting a Labour manifesto red in tooth and claw. Though open to criticism, it was not quite like that. Jeremy Paxman, the renowned TV interviewer, asked why, given Corbyn's republican views, abolishing the monarchy was not in the manifesto. Corbyn calmly replied, 'Look there's nothing in there, as we are not going to do it.'

Labour's 2017 manifesto was certainly a radical document,

based on commitments to end austerity and tackle inequality. It promised extra resources for public services, a hike in income tax on those earning more than £80,000 a year, abolishing tuition fees, and bringing utilities into public ownership. One Momentum activist described the manifesto as 'a series of ten-second policies'.[6] Martin Wolf, the *Financial Times* commentator, believed that Labour under Corbyn was right to confront 'outworn shibboleths', devising policies that improved the rate of economic growth through an entrepreneurial state.[7] As the recovery in the British economy stagnated because of the global slowdown and fear of an impending Brexit, Corbyn's radical economic alternative started to gain traction. Labour's shadow chancellor, John McDonnell, claimed that the party's programme, unlike that of the Tories, was prudent and carefully costed. Even so, the independent Institute for Fiscal Studies (IFS) estimated that, despite the higher taxes it would impose, there was a black hole of £30 billion in Labour's financial plans. Yet the Conservatives were similarly accused of not being honest with voters about the cost of their programme. Neither of the main parties were regarded as fiscally credible, which helped Labour.

Over the Tories, Labour had the advantage that they appeared to be offering idealism and hope. In contrast, the Tory manifesto seemed stodgy and uninspiring. It included proposals to means test pensioners' winter fuel allowance, and to abandon the 'triple lock' guaranteeing sustained rises in the state pension. This was a risky move given the importance of older voters to the Tory electoral coalition. The key measure in the Conservative manifesto was to make adults pay for social care by levying a tax on the value of their assets above

£10,000. Labour cleverly attacked the proposal as a 'dementia tax'. Four days later, May was forced to abandon the policy due to hostility from her own MPs and candidates who were being hammered on the doorstep, unconvincingly denying that she was shifting position.

The result of the 2017 election confounded political commentators. The Conservatives, who had been hoping to smash Labour, instead lost thirteen seats and their overall majority. Labour gained thirty-two seats from the Tories, winning 3.6 million more votes than in 2015, with over 40 per cent of the popular vote. Corbyn was the hero of the hour, given a standing ovation at the PLP and then a rock star welcome from fans at Glastonbury Festival, who sang 'Oh Jeremy Corbyn!' in celebration. There was a growing belief that the Labour Party was about to experience another '1945 moment' in which the mood of the nation shifted decisively towards socialism. The left, it appeared, was back as a major force in British politics, with Corbyn at the helm.

Corbyn's Descent

In their excitement, the Corbynites believed that they were on the brink of power. The reality was very different. Though Labour had performed well in 2017, the party had still suffered its third successive defeat. The Conservatives won the most seats in 2017, securing their highest share of the vote since the 1983 general election. In fact, the result in 2017 was the largest swing to an incumbent government since 1832. It is telling that in neither 2017 nor 2019 did Labour make any significant net gains among former Tory voters. The party's victories were achieved by squeezing the Green and Liberal Democrat vote. Despite the abysmal campaign, the Conservative vote held up remarkably well, ending roughly where it had been in the polls when the prime minister called the election – at 43 per cent. In fact, Labour gained fewer parliamentary seats in 2017 than it had under Neil Kinnock in 1992.

There were also ominous signs that the Labour coalition was beginning to unravel. The Tories had failed in their strategy of capturing Labour seats that backed Leave, but they had substantially reduced Labour majorities in such former strongholds as Ashfield, Bolsover, Sedgefield, and West Bromwich East. May, despite her inept election campaign, and her failure to show any instinctive human sympathy following the Grenfell Tower tragedy in west London, was then able with the backing of the DUP to cobble together a minority government. Above all, the focus of politics returned from campaigning in the streets to two and a half years of parliamentary wrangling and deadlock at Westminster. While Brexit had not been the major issue at the 2017 election, the question of Brexit now began to dominate British politics. It revealed only too clearly Corbyn's inherent weakness as a leader.

When May became prime minister in July 2016, she announced that her main objective was to take the UK out of the EU. That was no easy task. The UK had voted to leave, but how this was to be done and what the future trading relationship with Europe should look like had not been on the ballot paper. As *The Observer* commentator Andrew Rawnsley pointed out, Mrs May was dealt a bad hand which she played spectacularly badly.[8] From the first, she failed to reach out to the whole nation, instead concentrating her energies on trying to placate the Brexiteers in her own party. Her Lancaster House speech put down negotiating 'red lines' that limited her room for manoeuvre, especially over the issue of the border in Northern Ireland. When she lost her majority in the 2017 election, May was forced to rely not only on the narrow-minded and obdurate Democratic Unionist Party (DUP), but also on the so-called European Research Group (ERG) of hard-line Brexiteers.

Corbyn's attitude towards the negotiations was ambivalent. Personally agnostic about British membership of the EU, which he had previously disparaged as a capitalist club (he voted against joining in 1975), he hoped to seize advantage of May's difficulties. However, faced with a split inside his own party between a majority of Remain voters and a minority of Leavers in Labour seats in the North and the Midlands, Corbyn sat uncomfortably on the fence. For far too long, Labour failed to take up a firm and clear position on Brexit. As the pro-Remain movement both within and without the party gathered strength during 2018, 'the divided Labour leadership sat tight and waited, refusing to reveal its non-existent hand'.[9] Eventually at the 2018 party conference, Labour, led by Keir Starmer, passed a wide-ranging motion leaving open the option of a confirmatory referendum.

As Theresa May twisted and turned in the wind, vainly attempting to reach a settlement acceptable not only to the Brexiteers but to a majority in Parliament, Corbyn failed to adopt a clear position, coming across as a weak and indecisive leader. On 2 April 2019, May made a despairing switch in strategy – a move she arguably should have made when she became prime minister, and certainly when she lost her overall majority following the 2017 election. She announced that she was opening negotiations with the Labour Party to try to agree on a joint Brexit plan. Wisely, Corbyn accepted the invitation immediately.

However, although both sides said that talks were being held in a constructive spirit, there remained crucial sticking points, including May's so-called red lines and Labour's support for a 'confirmatory public vote'. Most commentators thought it unlikely that two politicians who so far had shown little sign of statesman-like qualities would be able to produce a deal which was in the interests of the nation as a whole. So it proved. After six weeks, the talks were abandoned. It was an opportunity lost, possibly the last one which could have produced a sensible Brexit agreement.

In 2018, Corbyn's mishandling of the crisis over anti-Semitism in the Labour Party provided another indication that he was not suited to being leader. Corbyn vehemently denied that he was personally anti-Semitic. There were, however, two incidents in his career before he became leader that raise questions about his position. In 2012, local government officials at Tower Hamlets had threatened to paint over a mural by Mear One, a Los Angeles street artist, depicting hook-nosed bankers (obviously Jews) playing Monopoly on the backs of the poor. Corbyn, apparently on free speech grounds, offered his support to this anti-Semitic artwork. Photos also emerged from 2014 that showed Corbyn laying a wreath at a Tunis cemetery for dead members of the terrorist group Black September. The group had been responsible for the murder of the Israeli Olympic team in Munich in 1972. There were other examples of anti-Semitism, or tolerance of anti-Semitism, by

Labour Party figures and NEC members, notably Ken Living-stone, Christine Shawcroft, Pam Bromley, and Pete Willsman.

The extremely hostile response of the British Jewish com-munity and leading Jewish MPs such as Luciana Berger, Louise Ellman (both of whom eventually left the Labour Party, although Louise Ellman has now returned), and Margaret Hodge made it abundantly clear that the party under Corbyn would need to demonstrate not only that it was against anti-Semitism in all its forms, but that it was taking concrete steps to root it out of the party. However, as the report of the Equality and Human Rights Commis-sion (published in October 2020) demonstrated, the Labour Party under Corbyn's leadership comprehensively failed these tests. Above all, the Commission (originally set up by the last Labour government) found that there had been a complete failure of leadership. Instead of taking the report seriously, key figures on the left then called for the EHRC to be abolished.

Yet it was Corbyn's reaction to the Salisbury nerve agent poisoning of the former KGB spy turned MI6 informant Sergei Skripal and his daughter that most shocked Labour MPs. When the prime minister told the Commons on 12 March 2018 that samples of the substance given to the Skripals had been identified as the Soviet-era nerve agent Novichok, Corbyn, instead of joining in the condemnation of Russia, called for dialogue, and two days later asked if the govern-ment had sent a sample of the nerve agent to Moscow for testing. The well-regarded MP Pat McFadden, the former European shadow minister whom Corbyn had earlier sacked, rose from the backbenches with a withering rejoinder to

Corbyn: 'Responding with strength and resolve when your country is under threat is an essential component of political leadership. There is a Labour tradition that understands that.'

In the next few months, the PLP was in open rebellion against the Corbyn leadership. On 18 February 2019, the Independent Group of seven Labour MPs led by Luciana Berger and Chuka Umunna left the Labour Party (a miniature version of the SDP breakaway in the early 1980s). On 11 March, the inaugural meeting of the Future Britain Group took place. It was chaired by the deputy leader of the party, Tom Watson, with the support of Peter Mandelson, the guru of New Labour. It comprised 150 Labour MPs who had decided to stay in the party, but on a semi-independent basis.

Swamped by a sea of troubles, the Corbyn leadership began to disintegrate. Corbyn himself was increasingly withdrawn and often absent from his office. At meetings with senior officials he would become distracted, offer garbled responses, and play around with his mobile phone. In Parliament, his performance was inadequate. As even his closest supporters admitted: 'It was all beginning to fall apart.'[10]

On 24 May 2019, May, deserted by her Cabinet, resigned the premiership. On 23 July, Boris Johnson, part cynical opportunist, part outrageous buffoon, won a resounding two-to-one victory in the Tory leadership election and the next day became prime minister, the post he had coveted all his political life. Johnson, advised by Dominic Cummings, then outsmarted Corbyn at every turn. Running as an out-and-out Brexiter, his slogan 'Get Brexit done' was designed to appeal to voters who were fed up with the years of parliamentary shenanigans. Despite the opposition of many Labour MPs, he then tricked the opposition parties into an early election: 'So began the most disastrous Labour campaign since 1935.'[11]

Labour's election machine in 2019 was shambolic. The party put forward its promises as if displayed in an advent calendar. Each day, the party would announce a new policy idea, targeting a different segment of the electorate. But the impact was more confusing than persuasive. Despite trailing far behind in the polls, Corbyn foolishly adopted an offensive strategy, confining most of his visits to marginal or Conservative seats. It was not until the last two weeks of the campaign that the party shifted resources to defend seats which until then were thought to be safe, and started to focus on 'bread and butter' issues which were more likely to attract traditional working-class voters, especially in the so-called Labour 'red wall' areas.

In 2019, Labour's coalition between younger well-educated voters and older working-class supporters, which had already shown signs of disintegration, fell apart. The weaknesses of Corbyn's leadership accentuated these fissures. Indeed, most analyses of Labour's defeat identified Corbyn's performance and poor reputation as the main reason why Labour voters abandoned the party. An illustration of the widespread hostility to Corbyn was demonstrated by the experience of a former Labour whip: 'Door one wouldn't vote for him because he was scruffy; the next person wouldn't vote for him because of the antisemitism in the party; the next because of his connection with Hamas; and the next because he seemed unable to lead.'[12]

The result was a defeat of 'epic proportions'.[13] Labour produced its worst election performance since 1935, obtaining less than one third of the vote, and electing only 202 MPs. Crucially the party lost sixty-one seats, many in its traditional heartlands in the North of England and the Midlands. In much of the South of England, Labour was no longer a serious contender. The party also lost a sizeable number of seats in Scotland and Wales. Its unpopularity was universal, leaving open the question of whether Labour could ever win power again.

The difficulty for the Corbyn project was that the landscape of UK politics was obviously changing: a long-term process of structural realignment was underway. Two major national referendums had unleashed structural aftershocks: the 2014 referendum on Scottish independence, and the 2016 referendum on whether the UK should remain an EU member. New dividing lines were emerging in British politics. In Scotland, whether voters were 'for' or 'against' the union was now the central question. In England and Wales, support for 'leaving' or 'remaining' in the EU decisively shaped political attitudes.

In 2017, as the authors of *The British General Election of 2019* point out, Labour had been successful in shifting the founding premise of the election from achieving Brexit to offering a verdict on the Conservatives' domestic policy agenda, in particular austerity. Yet by the 2019 general election 'the atmosphere was very different': 'Brexit was more urgent … the nation was more divided, and voter frustration at a deadlocked political process was more intense.'[14] Labour's effort in encouraging voters to focus on the state of the cash-starved NHS came to little.

The landscape was further reshaped by long-term social and demographic changes which defined new coalitions in

British politics. Age had become the new dividing line, with older voters significantly more likely to support the Conservatives, as young electors flocked to Labour. The relationship between class and voting was clearly changing. It was not the case that class no longer mattered. Yet Labour was now securing significantly more support among the higher social grades. Conversely, workers on low to middle incomes seem more willing to vote Conservative in recent elections. There is a growing cleavage between those who populate large urban areas and those who live in smaller towns and rural communities. New political identities are emerging across Great Britain.

Meanwhile, post-2010 austerity created new patterns of inequality and precariousness. Pensioners and older voters who had largely been protected from post-2010 austerity remained loyal to the Tories, despite proposals in the manifesto to end the pension 'triple lock' and bring in a so-called 'dementia tax'. Younger voters, even those who were relatively well educated from middle-class backgrounds, revolted against austerity measures that damaged their future economic prospects. Younger and middle-aged voters between the ages of twenty-four and forty-five shifted towards Labour, no doubt concerned that the next generation would, in all likelihood, be materially worse off than their parents.

As a consequence, the electoral map of Britain was being redrawn. Labour lost seats and found itself squeezed by the Tories in northern England and the Midlands but made gains in the cities and the South: Brighton and Hove and Canterbury, overwhelmingly populated by younger, more middle-class, liberal voters, were the symbols of Labour's advance. Mansfield, a former mining town in Derbyshire which leaned heavily towards Leave in the EU referendum, elected a Conservative MP for the first time in its history. The Conservative victory at the Hartlepool by-election in May 2021 underlined the shift in voting patterns.

British politics was increasingly polarised between younger, more liberal, pro-European, and well-educated voters who were more likely to live in cities; and older, more socially conservative, pro-Leave voters who lived in towns and villages. There was some truth in the claim of a growing divide between 'cosmopolitan' and 'communitarian' Britain. That said, the electorate was not comprised of those who thought the world was either 'open' or 'closed'. Neither had the traditional dividing line between left and right on economics disappeared. On key issues, the two 'tribes' of British politics were closer together than we might think. Britain was most certainly not in the grip of an existential culture war. Nevertheless, in the altered political climate where the Conservatives shifted left on economic policy and right on culture, the Corbyn project fared spectacularly badly.

Taken as a whole, Labour suffered a huge defeat in 2019 as negative perceptions of Jeremy Corbyn had become more entrenched, while the Labour campaign was unable to turn them around. In particular, 'indecision and double-speak on Brexit tarnished Corbyn's image as a principled, plain-speaking leader'.[15] The Labour campaign itself was derailed by bitter infighting as senior advisers were unwilling even to communicate with one another. The atmosphere inside Labour HQ had become toxic and dysfunctional.[16] The result was an electoral disaster.

The Starmer Succession

Following the resignation of Jeremy Corbyn in the immediate aftermath of the election, Sir Keir Starmer was elected leader of the Labour Party on 4 April 2020. In contrast to Corbyn, he was extremely well qualified for the post. A brilliant law student, an accomplished public speaker, and a confident performer in the House of Commons, he was one of the outstanding lawyers of his generation.

Keir Rodney Starmer was born on 2 September 1962 and grew up in Surrey. He was the second child of Josephine Baker, a nurse, and Rodney Starmer, a toolmaker. His parents were Labour Party supporters and named him after the party's first parliamentary leader, Keir Hardie. He passed the eleven-plus examination to Reigate Grammar School. Somewhat unusually for a Labour leader, Starmer is the product of a southern English upbringing – although his family were far from wealthy.

As a teenager, Starmer was a member of the East Surrey Young Socialists. He studied Law at the University of Leeds, graduating with first-class honours in 1985. The following year he went on to undertake postgraduate studies at St Edmund Hall, Oxford. He became a bencher at the Middle Temple and from 1990 onwards was a member of Doughty Street Chambers, specialising in human rights law. He was appointed as Queen's Counsel on 9 April 2002, aged only thirty-nine.

In July 2008, Starmer was made head of the Crown Prosecution Service (CPS) and director of public prosecutions. He was widely respected for his work in public office. Leaving the CPS in November 2013, Starmer was selected the following year to be Labour's prospective parliamentary candidate for Holborn and St Pancras. At the following year's election, he was elected with a majority of 17,048. A number of his supporters urged him to stand in the 2015 leadership election following the resignation of Ed Miliband, but wisely he ruled this out, given his obvious lack of political experience.

Corbyn appointed Starmer shadow minister of state for immigration. However, with other members of the front bench he resigned in 2016 in protest at Corbyn's inept style of leadership, arguing that it was 'simply untenable now to suggest we can offer an effective opposition without a change of leader'. When Corbyn was re-elected following the failed leadership challenge of Owen Smith, he persuaded Starmer to accept the role of shadow Brexit secretary with a place in the shadow cabinet.

Starmer became a vocal supporter of a second referendum, and persuaded the party to adopt this position in the 2019 manifesto. Nevertheless, the strongest advocate of the 'hug a remainer' strategy was not Starmer, but Corbyn's closest political ally, John McDonnell. McDonnell was persuaded by opinion poll evidence which demonstrated that Labour's vote would decline in every seat in the country if the party adopted a pro-Brexit policy.[17] According to Pogrund and Maguire, the research showed that Labour's core demographic – younger voters, working-class voters, and Muslim voters – had shifted decisively towards support for Remain since the 2016 referendum.

The polling found that most working-class voters cared more about the impact of austerity than the nature of Brexit. At that stage, internal analysis produced for the party showed that with an anti-Brexit policy, it would lose seventeen seats, but with a pro-Brexit position, Labour would shed more than forty-five seats. McDonnell for one believed that the electoral writing was on the wall. Labour MPs insisted that the second referendum policy was a major contributor to the party's loss of Red Wall seats in northern England and the Midlands, leading to its devastating defeat. Yet it is likely that Labour's losses would have been even greater had it adopted a pro-Brexit policy.

When Corbyn then resigned as party leader following Labour's crushing defeat in December 2019, Starmer threw his hat in the ring at the prompting of close colleagues in the PLP, notably Carolyn Harris and Jenny Chapman. He almost immediately became a hot favourite, winning endorsements from fellow MPs as well as the public sector trade union, Unison. Yet Starmer's victory was by no means assured. There was a widespread belief that Labour was almost certain to choose a woman as its next leader. Yet the leading women candidates, including Lisa Nandy, Rebecca Long-Bailey, Emily Thornberry, and Jess Phillips, failed to make much of an impact on the race. What was remarkable about Starmer's victory was that the party was still believed to be under Corbynite control. Starmer showed that the left's grip could be broken. He went on to win the leadership contest in the first round with 56.2 per cent of the vote.

Starmer's overwhelming victory resulted from the fact he appealed to members and supporters with diametrically opposing political views. 'Corbynistas' such as Laura Parker (Corbyn's former private secretary) and Paul Mason (an ex-BBC journalist and Marxist commentator) endorsed him, believing that Starmer wanted to retain Corbyn's radical policies while presenting a more competent face to the elect-orate. The 'ten pledges' in Starmer's leadership manifesto committed him to nationalisation of rail and mail, no more 'foreign wars' such as Iraq and Afghanistan, while fighting to restore free movement for UK citizens in the EU. On the other hand, for the opponents of Corbynism, Starmer offered the best prospect of winning back the party membership, while reasserting the politics of responsible moderation. He promised to reposition Labour from an activist social move-ment to a credible governing party. In his acceptance speech, Starmer said that he would refrain from scoring party polit-ical points, and that having become opposition leader during the Covid-19 pandemic, he planned to engage constructively with the government. Equally importantly, he made clear that as party leader he would fight to remove the 'stain' of anti-Semitism from Labour. Without doubt, Starmer's rise to the top was meteoric, taking only five years, compared to that of Tony Blair, which had taken eleven years.

Starmer's period in office was initially dominated by the impact of the Covid-19 pandemic, and subsequently the roll-out of the vaccine. In many respects, he delivered a sure-footed performance. Two aspects of his leadership were particularly impressive. The first was his initial handling of the government's response to the pandemic. Starmer out-lined a convincing critique of the Johnson administration's complacent performance from March 2020 on lockdowns, the availability of personal protective equipment, the inad-equate test and trace system, and the shambles in schools. He managed to do so without sounding overly partisan or irrationally critical of the government's track record. Starmer exposed the prime minister's poor judgement, while acknowledging that dealing with a global pandemic would be a hard task for any government.

Secondly, Starmer largely avoided the bear trap set for him on Brexit. He acknowledged that Labour had little choice but to vote for the trade deal agreed with the EU before Christmas 2020. While the deal was clearly inadequate and unlikely to resolve the European question for the long term in British politics, for the Labour Party to have voted against it, effectively supporting 'no deal', would have been a catastrophic political error. Starmer had the political judgement to understand this at the outset. Despite opposition from the Remain wing of the Labour Party, he whipped the PLP to support the deal – and was right to do so. Voting against would have created the impression that Labour wanted to re-open the Brexit question when the mood in the country was for it to be resolved. Moreover, opposing the deal would have damaged Labour irreparably in the so-called 'Red Wall' seats in the North of England where many voters supported Brexit in the 2016 referendum.

Moreover, Starmer has managed his party effectively. He dismissed Rebecca Long-Bailey, his left-wing rival in the leadership contest, from the shadow cabinet for promoting an article referring to anti-Semitic conspiracy theories. He made it clear that dealing with the legacy of anti-Semitism after Jeremy Corbyn's tenure as leader was one of his main priorities. The recommendations made by the Equality and Human Rights Commission (EHRC) to deal with unlawful discrimination in October 2020 were to be implemented in full. When in a TV interview Corbyn implied the EHRC's findings had been exaggerated, Starmer suspended his membership and then removed the party whip. Moreover, Starmer supported the appointment of a new party general secretary, David Evans, who was acting against party members and suspending Constituency Labour Parties where there was evidence of anti-Semitic activity. This was the robust response required if Labour was to regain the trust of the Jewish community and restore its reputation as a party of equality. As a result, Labour appears more united than at any point in the last ten years. The breach between the leadership, the shadow cabinet, and the PLP has largely been healed. There was a recognition that Labour had lost four successive elections since 2010, and needed to get its act together if it was to survive as a serious force in British politics.

In taking on the role of leader of the opposition, the fifty-eight-year-old Starmer certainly has recognisable attributes. He was respected as a senior lawyer and former director of public prosecutions. Starmer had previously run a large public service organisation, and has an understanding of what is required to deliver change. He is a confident performer in the House of Commons, while his skills as a communicator on television are improving. Nonetheless, as leader, Starmer clearly faces serious challenges.

His first problem is that he confronts a proven election winner in Boris Johnson. For all the justified criticism of Johnson as a lazy and dishonest prime minister who breached Covid lockdowns, he has been an electorally successful politician who won support for the Conservative Party in areas of Britain that have been safely Labour since the First World War. The extraordinary success of the UK vaccine roll-out since January 2021 made the prime minister's position appear at the time to be almost impregnable.

Johnson has made cultural identity, alongside the commitment to 'levelling up' the UK, the central divide in British politics, reinforced by his determination to 'get Brexit done'. He united 'Leave Britain' behind the Tory Party while 'Remain Britain' was split between Labour, the Liberal Democrats, the Greens, the SNP, and Plaid Cymru. Starmer has to devise a new electoral strategy if Labour is to win next time. The party has a mountain to climb. It will need a bigger swing than it achieved in 1945 or 1997 to secure an overall parliamentary majority.

The second related challenge is Labour's position in Scotland and the politics of the Union. Labour cannot win power at Westminster unless its position in Scotland significantly improves. Yet Labour is still polling behind the Conservatives. Its position has been dire ever since the 2014 independence referendum. Pro-Union voters have been gravitating towards the Tories, despite their historic unpopularity in Scotland. Labour needs a new political project for Scotland building on the election of its leader, Anas Sarwar, as the SNP administration appears to be running out of steam.

The third task for Starmer is to rebuild trust in Labour on the economy. Labour has been behind on economic management since the financial crisis of 2008. Voters simply do not believe that Labour is a safe pair of hands in managing their money. They fear that in power, the party will spend too much, public debt will balloon, while taxes on ordinary wage earners will rise. The fallout of the Covid-19 pandemic has reinforced the pressure on Labour to prove that it is a competent manager of the economy. The party will have to show that it has a plan to deliver a post-pandemic recovery, and that it will distribute the costs to those able to pay without terrifying the middle classes into thinking there was a hidden 'tax bombshell' to come.

Early in 2021, Starmer endured a difficult few months as opposition leader. Relentless talk of the government's 'vaccine bounce', and Labour's continued electoral weakness in many parts of the UK, contributed to the political narrative turning against him. Following the buoyant approval ratings Starmer enjoyed early in his leadership, dissatisfaction with his performance grew. The loss of the Hartlepool by-election in May and the indifferent 2021 local government election results in England reinforced the rising mood of disquiet in the party (despite strong performances in Wales, and in some English city regions). Unease within Labour, even among those who enthusiastically backed Starmer in 2020, was perceptible. Much of the unhappiness focused on the leader's cautious approach in setting out his priorities while articulating the party's direction following his predecessor's departure.

Nonetheless, Starmer's predicament cannot be fully understood without considering the political context he inherited. The list of vulnerabilities is formidable: a decade of electoral defeats nationally in UK politics; the slow descent into internal party factionalism; the shocks of the 2016 Brexit referendum; the remorseless rise of Scottish nationalism; and the loss of so many Labour seats in Scotland. By the end of the decade, Labour was a party in existential crisis. There was no clear strategy to win a governing majority in the context of the UK's first-past-the-post electoral system. Labour had last won a national election in 2005. In 2019, it had suffered its worst result since 1935. Particularly troubling was the long-term erosion of working-class support, a demographic trend underway since the 1970s. After the 2019 election was so clearly dominated by the agenda of 'Vote Leave', there was an effort to refocus on developing ideas for Labour among think tanks and the party's intelligentsia. Yet no clear direction has so far emerged.

As such, Starmer decided that his mission was not to heal the divide within the Labour Party but to win a forthcoming general election. There is nothing disreputable about wanting to end the bitter conflict that engulfed Labour over the last decade. This book has demonstrated throughout that divided parties invariably fail to win elections. Yet the fundamental task for Labour is to establish itself as a credible alternative government. That means having the debate to settle contentious policy issues, rather than waiting until the party is in office. Voters need to know that Labour says what it means and means what it says. They need to be confident that the party has got its act together, particularly on the issue of economic management. Starmer has many of the credentials to be a successful prime minister, but he needed first to be an effective leader of the opposition. That meant setting out a compelling political vision about the purpose of the Labour Party and its aspirations for Britain.

In September 2021, the Fabian Society published Starmer's personal political credo, *The Road Ahead*. This analysis drew on conversations with voters up and down the country during that summer. Starmer wrote: 'I have been struck by the complicated, sometimes contradictory way people are feeling [after Covid]. It is not rare to encounter optimism, worry, joy and reflection all during one chat.' The pamphlet was striking in its enthusiasm to embrace the legacy of past Labour governments and their 'towering achievements'. The Attlee government represented radical change in the aftermath of the Second World War. The Wilson era 'began the modernisation of Britain'. After 1997, 'Labour understood that a more liberal, tolerant country was being born alongside the old one … it set about fixing the gaping holes left by Thatcherism with proper public services, constitutional reform and leadership in Europe'. To be successful in a post-pandemic Britain, Starmer exhorted, Labour had to adapt and update its image and appeal as the party had done before.

The core theme of *The Road Ahead* was 'the contribution society'. Labour's mission was to create opportunity and security, fusing together 'a good society' and a 'strong economy'. There had to be a 'new deal for business and working people'. Labour would tackle the inequalities that have held young people back by transforming state education, removing charitable tax relief from independent schools. A Starmer government would use technology to 'revolutionise' the delivery of public services, particularly healthcare. There would be a new emphasis on law and order.

As Starmer underlined in his speech to the party conference in Brighton, his government would restore the mantle of fiscal responsibility that Labour acquired under Blair and Brown: 'There will be no promises we can't keep or commitments we can't pay for.' Starmer's administration would seek to grow the economy through active industrial policy, while seizing the opportunities of adaptation to climate change through the Green New Deal. Historians may come to judge Starmer's address in Brighton to be among the finest given by a Labour opposition leader, comparable to Hugh Gaitskell in 1960, Harold Wilson in 1963, Neil Kinnock in 1985, and Tony Blair in 1994. Starmer courageously came out fighting after facing a barrage of criticism. He was clear about the tasks facing Labour, refusing to fudge the major issues. But the speech was only the beginning. Starmer will need to show resolution and courage in revitalising his party in the years ahead.

The optimists within Labour believe that like President Biden in the United States, Starmer could yet become the competent, politically 'moderate' agent of a more radical agenda for the UK centre-left. The comeback of the Social Democrats in Germany, who finished as the largest party and in a position to lead the next government, was a signal that the centre-left across Europe is gradually recovering at the ballot box.

From the autumn of 2021, Labour was enjoying significant poll leads while Starmer was beginning to pull ahead of Boris Johnson in voters' perceptions of who would make the best prime minister. The polling company YouGov reported that Labour's consistent lead in the polls was based on solid foundations. For instance, they cut the Conservatives' lead on which party was best placed to manage the economy from twenty-four to six points. The Labour Party was perceived more favourably on issues such as reducing unemployment and dealing with inflation.[18] The party was performing particularly strongly in the northern marginals (the Red Wall seats) that had been lost to the Conservatives in 2019.[19] In his speeches, Starmer has emphasised his patriotism without engaging the Conservatives directly on 'culture war' issues or reopening the question of Brexit. He has brought both experience and new talent into the Labour shadow cabinet. As a result, writing in *The New Statesman* in January 2022, the political commentator Philip Collins noted that, 'The shift in the polls is significant, and feels like an abiding change, not a fleeting verdict.'[20]

Starmer and Labour nonetheless need to be wary of trying to win the next election on the strategy of safety first. As the former Cabinet minister Richard Crossman contended after the Attlee government's defeat, Labour still requires a map – aligned with a positive and optimistic vision of the future – if it is to recast the political landscape, altering the economic and social fabric of Britain. The Labour leader has proved himself to be a highly effective opponent of the current prime minister in the House of Commons, exposing his lying and mendacity during the 'party-gate' scandal in early 2022. But Starmer needs to demonstrate that he has a clear and persuasive vision for the future of the UK.

After all, he is aiming to govern a country struggling to overcome the effects of a devastating pandemic, just as Brexit has left the nation without a coherent view of its role in the world. The political nation of the United Kingdom itself has become increasingly fragmented. In an uncertain and volatile climate, underlined by the Russian invasion of the sovereign territory of Ukraine, greater clarity and precision in setting out Labour's fundamental purpose will be required if Starmer and his party are to emerge as a credible governing force.

Conclusion

This would be a formidable list of problems to overcome for any Labour leader. Starmer has to modernise and transform a party in which the Corbyn legacy still runs deep. This chapter has shown that Corbyn's tenure led to a major reshaping of the party. There was a fundamental shift in its ideology and organisation. Corbyn's supporters were understandably reluctant to sacrifice their newly established political and ideological ascendency. Some passionately believed in the democratisation of the party. Others, particularly the trade unions, understood the task as achieving complete political and ideological control by adopting a left manifesto. The left knew that it had an unprecedented opportunity to refashion the Labour Party in its image, an advantage Corbyn was reluctant to forfeit after decades in the wilderness. The risk for Corbyn, however, was always that efforts to remake the PLP in the leader's image would recreate the historical schism that nearly destroyed Labour in the early 1980s. The party was now perceived to be dangerously divided.

Throughout his leadership, Corbyn was heavily constrained by the shallowness of his support among parliamentarians. The problem that he confronted was that he himself was a serial rebel who voted on many occasions against his own government: how could he plausibly impose discipline on Labour MPs after 2015? Corbyn's supporters fought to transform the PLP's character. Representatives of Momentum were urging mandatory reselection, as they had done in the early 1980s; the left sought to reassert control over party conference. Constituency boundary changes made it possible to apply pressure to sitting MPs. By 2019, a number of long-standing parliamentarians had either stood down or left the party. The fault line between the leadership and the PLP meant Labour was fundamentally divided, contributing to its subsequent election defeats. For many Labour MPs, the situation was untenable. As such, Corbyn's leadership marked an escalation in the civil war without parallel in the party's history.

In these circumstances, Starmer will have to show courage and skill if he is to keep his party together. A major advantage is that, as in the late 1980s and early 1990s, Labour may at last be rediscovering the will to win. Apart from a few disgruntled voices on the hard left, there is a recognition that Labour must be a united force if it is to have any hope of victory at the next election. Above all, Labour must update its ideas and offer a convincing programme for government in a post-pandemic world.

7

Conclusion: The Way Ahead

'When power is imminent, or in the party's possession, a short-term, utilitarian, quantitative socialism of the belly seems to prevail; but out of power the party appears to revert to a socialism of the heart that yearns for the qualities of a fraternal, libertarian, socialist world in the distant future.'[1]

—Frank Bealey

'To find unity of outlook on so important and difficult a matter, is essentially an educational task. It is not something that can be brought about by resolutions to a conference, by majority votes, or even by tactical manoeuvres behind the scenes. There has to be a meeting of minds, an exchange of arguments, long and quiet discussion.'[2]

—Rita Hinden

This book has told the story of a political party which, for all its unquestionable virtues, was prone to bitter dispute and rancorous division throughout its history. Labour has long been 'an unruly and fissiparous coalition with an extraordinary propensity to shoot itself in the foot'.[3] It remains the case that parties embroiled in sectarian strife are unlikely to win voters' trust. In a parliamentary democracy where there is an emphasis on competent government and sound management of the economy, a party that cannot agree among its own leadership, let alone with its rank-and-file members, is unlikely to be trusted with power. The electorate must be confident that faced with a grave economic crisis or unanticipated shock such as a terrorist attack, natural disaster, or foreign war, the government will stick together, providing leadership rather than collapsing into bitter factional infighting – and imploding at the first sign of difficulty.

The civil wars that have engulfed the Labour Party over the last century are a plausible explanation of the party's unimpressive electoral performance. Despite having among its electorate the largest and most politically self-confident industrial working classes in Western Europe, since the party was founded in 1906 the British Labour Party has only ever won clear-cut parliamentary majorities in 1945, 1966, and three times under Tony Blair after 1997. Just six Labour leaders have ever served as prime minister since the initiation of full-franchise mass democracy in Britain. The history of the British Labour Party is a history of electoral and political failure: its short bursts in government have been followed quickly by defeat and further rounds of infighting. Labour has never managed to emulate the achievement of the Social Democratic Party in Sweden, which, in the course of the twentieth century, established itself as the dominant and natural governing party.

The Argument of the Book

Both major parties in Britain have at different times been overcome by serious internal divisions. The issue of European integration led to dispute and recrimination that convulsed the post-Thatcherite Conservative Party for three decades. The reaction against the Franco-German vision of a federal Europe and the UK's chaotic departure from the Exchange Rate Mechanism (ERM) in 1992 amplified that disharmony. The referendum on EU membership in 2016 subsequently destroyed David Cameron's premiership, and, in the years since, the Tories have appeared badly split. Moreover, in the four decades since Margaret Thatcher came to power, the Conservative Party has struggled to reconcile its paternalistic 'one nation' tradition with the emphasis on free markets and the intellectual influence of the American New Right. The Thatcherite legacy has further divided and at points sapped the strength of the party.

Yet despite the schisms influencing modern Conservatism, the history of the last century indicates it is the Labour Party that is most prone to damaging splits. The rancour and bitterness during Corbyn's leadership after 2015 is the most recent episode in a tumultuous century of infighting and ideological discord. Indeed, the last five years of internal conflict have been among the worst in Labour's history. Since 2015, the party has been locked in a protracted existential struggle for its soul: a civil war apparently without end. The divide was not only about the party's doctrine or ideology. After all, the 2017 election manifesto was by historical standards a relatively modest social democratic prospectus, a far cry from the 'suicide note' produced under Michael Foot in the 1983 election that committed Labour to sweeping renationalisation and unilateral disarmament. In the Corbyn era, battles raged over the fundamental question of Labour's purpose and identity: who legitimately owned the title deeds to the party's future? As the historian Ben Jackson has noted, the Labour right viewed the left as inimical to the Labour tradition.[4] The Labour right exhibited a steadfast commitment to parliamentarianism, the imperatives of national security, the rule of law, and established constitutional norms. The right believed that the organised left posed a fundamental threat to Labour's image as a moderate, electable, and competent party in British politics. As the political scientist Henry Drucker pointed out in 1977, respectability and acceptance by orthodox institutions in the name of gradual, evolutionary change was always at the core of Labour's predominantly working-class 'ethos'. The PLP more recently refused to accept Jeremy Corbyn's disavowal of that moderation and denigration of Labour's reputation as a patriotic party.

On the other hand, the party's left believed that the right, particularly the modernisers in the Blair era, were the aberration in Labour's history. In jettisoning the commitment to common ownership of the means of production and by accepting much of the Thatcher inheritance in social and economic policy, it was alleged the right had sought to strip the Labour Party of its socialist beliefs. The Labour left was committed to a transformational agenda that sought to radically restructure the British economy in accordance with socialist ideology.[5] The left argued that the post-1997 governments failed to create a new settlement in British politics which meant shifting the axis of political debate to the left, destroying the 'neo-liberal' pro-market consensus fashioned by successive Conservative administrations after 1979.

Yet Labour's left and right do not simply disagree over the shape of the party's programme. Their core assumptions about the nature of society and how to achieve political change are perceived as diametrically opposing. While the right embraces gradualist, incremental reform, the left envisages a revolutionary transformation of the existing social and economic order. Nonetheless, as this book has shown, the party's divisions do not always fit neatly onto a pre-defined left/right axis. In the 1960s and 1970s, for example, key divisions emerged *within* the centre-right grouping. David Marquand has interpreted Labour's historic divisions as emanating from an unresolvable 'clash of political philosophies' between the social democratic right and the socialist left since the 1950s.[6] But that is only the beginning of the story.

The scope for co-existence, mutual acceptance, and even tacit co-operation between rival factions has, not surprisingly, proved limited for much of the party's history. After 2015, many Labour parliamentarians did not believe that Jeremy Corbyn had a legitimate right to lead the party, despite his popular mandate with party members and trade union affiliates. Factions on the right and left were locked in an eternal struggle, a fight to the political death in which there could only be one victor. That is the true meaning of political civil war.

In this context, it is hardly surprising that many of those seeking to lead Labour preached the virtues of party unity. Labour, it was said, needed to advance as a 'broad church' party where different ideological beliefs were tolerated and respected. Party institutions, notably the National

Executive Committee and shadow cabinet, ought to contain an ideological balance between left and right, revisionist and fundamentalist, an approach that shaped Harold Wilson's and James Callaghan's party management strategies in the 1960s and 1970s. In their view, loyalty to the leadership was important, but in a broad church party it should be possible to dissent honourably from the leadership line.

The dilemma created by the emphasis on unity, however, is that to be an electorally viable political party, Labour must be capable of winning elections. If it faces inwards, focusing on party management and how to contain internal disagreement, the party is unable to look outwards, understanding the changing needs and aspirations of the electorate. And therein lies certain electoral defeat. The fate of Gordon Brown and Ed Miliband as party leaders illustrates the dangers of a compromising approach that allows the Labour Party to feel comfortable about itself again, instead of asking hard questions about its position on society and politics.

This book's central argument, derived from examination of Labour's century-long history of civil wars through the lens of the careers of key figures in the party, is that the goal of unity cannot override the imperative of a viable strategy for winning power. Presenting a united front to voters is insufficient in the absence of a compelling programme and governing agenda. A prospective party of government must not postpone difficult arguments that will inevitably arise, and that are far harder to resolve once in power. It is, of course, tempting to paper over the cracks of ideological discord with clever slogans and political marketing techniques. Yet fundamental differences will be exposed by the harsh glare of scrutiny during an election campaign, and subsequently in office. The party leadership needs to have the political confidence to be clear and honest with its own membership, but above all, with the voters whose support it cannot do without.

The History of Labour's Warring Factions Since 1918

Prior to the outbreak of the First World War, Labour was a delicately constructed alliance of prophets and pragmatists. There was an element who believed in real-world 'practical socialism', alongside a not insignificant number of visionaries who believed passionately in a New Jerusalem on earth. It was against this backdrop that Ramsay MacDonald brought the first Labour governments to power in the 1920s. Although later condemned as a traitor and splitter, MacDonald sought to hold his party together in the face of the economic firestorm unleashed by the Great Depression in 1929. Yet MacDonald's unwillingness to enter into detailed and practical examination of policy, his apparent lack of sympathy for the plight of the unemployed, his loyalty to his austere and economically orthodox chancellor, Philip Snowden, and his inability to effectively manage the rest of his Cabinet meant that MacDonald's premiership was almost destined to end in failure. It took the Labour Party more than a decade to recover from the deep splits which then ensued.

Following the triumphant years of the Attlee administrations, which had unprecedented legislative achievements to their credit, Labour was once again divided between Bevanites and Gaitskellites in the aftermath of the 1951 defeat. Although the split was fuelled by personal conflict between two men centred on differences in class background and personal temperament, the gulf between Gaitskell and Bevan was a more fundamental struggle over Labour's purpose as a political movement in a changing society. The question at stake concerned whether Labour was a class-based party committed to advancing working-class interests through its institutions, notably the trade unions (as Bevan believed); or was Labour a Gaitskellite party of conscience and reform aspiring to represent all classes, creating a more equal, cohesive, and harmonious society?

By the early 1950s, it was apparent the British people sought liberation from the grim 'patriotic egalitarianism' of wartime and the Attlee years. In these circumstances Labour had to embrace 'a socialism of joy and expansive opportunity'.[7] Yet major splits – between left and right, Bevanites and Gaitskellites, revisionists and fundamentalists, parliamentarians and activists – haunted the party for the rest of the decade, enabling the Conservatives to dominate the age of affluence. In these circumstances, Gaitskell emerged as an unquestionably courageous and spirited leader. He recognised that Labour was in danger of appearing to be a nostalgic party out of touch with an emerging new society. Gaitskell did not believe that it was right to say one thing to his members and another to voters. The leadership must advocate feasible and credible policies that ensured Labour was viewed as a viable governing party.

Harold Wilson temporarily succeeded in brokering a truce in Labour's civil war, triumphing at the general elections of 1964 and 1966. The rhetorical appeal of modernisation emphasised the 'white heat' of the technological revolution and economic growth to advance social justice, ending 'thirteen wasted years' of Conservative rule. But against the background of turbulence from the mid-1960s and convulsions in the British economy, alongside rising tensions in industrial relations, traditional divisions soon reasserted themselves. Then when the party lost the 1970 general election, it was haunted by the spectre of Britain's unresolved relationship with Europe. Although Labour unexpectedly won again in 1974, the party had become more bitterly polarised than at any previous point in its history.

The divides became even more intense in the early 1980s as the left was ascendant, and the threat grew of a breakaway by the Labour right who were repulsed by the atmosphere of sectarianism and 'illiberal Labourism'.[8] The formation of the SDP and the defection of the Gang of Four in 1981 marked the most serious split inside the party for fifty years. Although the challenge of the SDP eventually faded, Labour was to lose four successive general elections. It was then out of power for eighteen long years.

By 1997, Labour had triumphantly emerged from the wilderness of opposition, winning the largest majority in its history under the leadership of Tony Blair and Gordon Brown. The party now had an unprecedented opportunity to refashion Britain in the image of modern social democracy. Yet while an impressive array of progressive social, economic, and constitutional reforms were enacted, the growing antagonism between Blair and Brown created a deep fissure within the party. Although these differences at the outset were essentially personality-based, since both men remained committed modernisers, disagreements over policy and the ultimate direction of New Labour's social democratic project soon emerged. The question of Europe, more particularly the UK's prospective membership of the single currency, played a decisive role in deepening the divide. By 2010, the conflict between Blair and Brown had exhausted the party.

Over the next decade, the Labour Party was led by two figures who sought to repudiate New Labour's inheritance: Ed Miliband, and above all Jeremy Corbyn. While the majority of party members had become alienated from the Blair 'project', Corbyn's leadership after 2015 hardly made the party any more united or effective as a contender for power. The difficulty was that the PLP desired a leader who could become prime minister, while the party's grassroots were swelled by thousands of new members who wanted Corbyn to be leader of a social movement. A deep split then emerged between the leadership and the parliamentary wing. The chasm ensured that in 2017 and 2019, Labour suffered two further election defeats. It was haunted by persistent accusations of the leadership's failure to confront growing anti-Semitism at the party grassroots. To be plausibly accused, in effect, of institutional racism demonstrated just how far Labour had lost its moral compass.

It is hard to dispute that Labour as a party has been prone to ruptures and conflicts throughout its history. The age-old divide between revolutionaries and reformers, fundamentalists and revisionists on the left of British politics still runs deep. Throughout the book we offer a historical perspective on the challenges and problems facing Labour – and what should be done to overcome them.

The Revisionist Outlook

As the authors of this book, we come from distinct political generations in the Labour Party. Giles Radice was member of Parliament for Durham North having been elected in a by-election in 1973; a member of the shadow cabinet; and subsequently chair of the Treasury Select Committee. He worked at the heart of the Labour Party for more than half a century, having started his career as an official at the General, Municipal and Boilermakers' Union (GMB) in the 1960s after leaving Oxford and completing his national service. Radice had the advantage of observing closely many of the great leaders of the party: Hugh Gaitskell, Harold Wilson, James Callaghan, Neil Kinnock, John Smith, Tony Blair, and Gordon Brown. As one of Labour's leading revisionists and historians ('a Blairite before Blair'), he has long believed in a party that is both ideologically broad-based, while in touch with the changing aspirations of voters and a radically altered society. As chair of the international think tank Policy Network, Radice continued to build links with social democrats on the European continent and in the US.

Patrick Diamond came of age politically in the early 1990s as the modernisation of the party proceeded apace under John Smith and Tony Blair. After Cambridge University he worked for the Labour Party, and then after a brief spell in consultancy joined the Institute for Public Policy Research (IPPR). Diamond became an adviser to Peter Mandelson, and then worked for Tony Blair, Alan Milburn, and subsequently Gordon Brown in the Number 10 Policy Unit before embarking on an academic career, later succeeding Radice as chair of Policy Network.

Although of different generations, Diamond shares Radice's commitment to an unashamedly pluralist party that is determinedly revisionist. They continue to believe in a politics where ideas are openly debated, where diverse ideological perspectives are welcomed and not merely tolerated, and in which policies are constantly updated to take account of a changing economy and society. The revisionist outlook is that politics is not concerned with destroying a class enemy, but involves patient and constructive debate in the national interest, informed by rigorous analysis of empirical facts and evidence. We should never forget Keir Hardie's exhortation that 'class war ... is harmful to the cause of socialism ... it distracts attention from the real issue and fosters a belief that mere class hatred will transform society'.

Hardie also believed that co-operation with other countries, not least elsewhere in Europe, and an internationalist outlook were essential in achieving the aims of social democracy. So, having considered Labour's long and turbulent history of fratricidal conflict, it would be remiss of us not to address where the party goes next. It is to that essential question that the remainder of this chapter is devoted, mapping the way ahead.

Overcoming Civil Wars: Political Strategy

Following the party's devastating electoral loss in 2019, its worst performance in terms of seats in the House of Commons since 1935, Labour elected a new leader. Keir Starmer came to the helm of the party in the tumultuous circumstances of the outbreak of the Covid-19 pandemic. After four successive defeats in less than a decade, Starmer's principal aim was to launch the Labour Party's political recovery. It was paramount that Labour was again viewed as a credible opposition, able to hold the Conservative government to account, especially given its questionable decision-making during the latter stages of the Brexit process and the outbreak of Covid-19. A period of effective opposition would hopefully transform Labour into a viable party of government heralding a future-facing programme of economic and social reform matching Attlee's scale of ambition in the aftermath of the Second World War.

It is clear that to advance, the party cannot remain locked in the New Labour mindset of the mid-1990s. The starting point for any credible revitalisation is to confront the issues that a Labour government is likely to face in the 2020s, fashioning a convincing national story of optimism and hope. The party has to develop a socialism of self-fulfilment and expansive opportunity for the new century. The condition of Britain is necessarily different to that which confronted Labour in the mid-1990s. After all, it is a quarter of a century since the Blair government came to power. The world has been altered profoundly. The impacts of the coronavirus pandemic threaten to reorder our economy and society. We have witnessed the troubling erosion of trust in the rules-based multilateral order and liberal democracy across the globe. Britain is now outside the European Union. The aftershocks of the 2008 financial crisis and great recession still reverberate. The rise of techno-capitalism and the fourth industrial revolution propelled by automation and digital technology threaten jobs. Huge advances in science, including the invention of life-saving drugs and vaccines during the Covid crisis, are transforming our life prospects. Above all, the looming challenge of climate change and the environmental destruction of the planet are becoming ever more visible.

The Labour Party must face up to the realities of a changing society in a rapidly evolving world. If it is to win the next election, Labour's task is not simply to devise new policies or invent a new campaign catchphrase. It is to confront fundamental weaknesses in the party's political image and identity, while catching the tide of new ideas. The leadership needs to regain the confidence of an electorate that has become alienated and sceptical about politics as a whole. It is not enough for voters to share the party's values of a strong and fair society. There has to be confidence that Labour's leadership team are competent, and that the party's policies are credible; unity and governing purpose are essential. The analysis throughout this book demonstrates that Labour is defeated where it is politically divided, but above all, where it is unable to articulate a convincing vision of the future, and where it abides by a doctrine that has little relevance to the realities of society as it is, only as it is imagined to be.

Resolute political leadership involves reconciling unity with governing direction. Having a trusted leader is crucial for any party's success. An effective leader of a centre-left party must combine empathy and emotional intelligence with political conviction, notably the strength to take tough decisions. Clarity of leadership entails courage, a willingness to be bold and decisive as well as resolute in a crisis. Labour starts from a position of being a party that voters instinctively believe has its heart in the right place, but is perceived to be unwilling to take painful decisions. It therefore needs a leader that can hold the party together while reaching out beyond Labour's 'heartlands' to speak to, and for, the whole nation.

This leadership style acknowledges that Labour is necessarily a broad church. The legitimate left in the party must have its say in internal debates over policy. The left historically has been an important source of creative thinking and fresh ideas. Party members can act as Labour's conscience, willing the parliamentary leadership to embrace radical measures that combat inequality and injustice. All that said, the left does not have the monopoly on political wisdom, morality, or values. The revisionist wing of Labour has an equally strong commitment to a more just society, having been the first to elaborate the politics of 'conscience and reform' in the 1940s and 1950s.

Labour's leadership must have the right mindset. Its goal should be to combine commitment to the party's aims and values with pragmatism about the means of delivery. Labour must accept the reality of Britain as it is today, and look to the future not the past. To win elections, the leadership must be clear about the party's strategy, clarifying its ideological purpose while rejuvenating its institutions and organisation. Above all, Labour must sustain a broad-based electoral alliance.

In its widely read report on the 2019 election, the organisation Labour Together concluded that: 'The institutional and cultural bonds that linked many voters to Labour have become weaker and weaker … the seeds of the [2019] defeat stretch back two decades.'[9] The implicit assumption of the report is that the party's electoral failure is a consequence of the New Labour project, which ruptured its relationship with working people, underlined by its catastrophic performance in Red Wall seats in 2019. The argument is that New Labour politicians believed working-class voters had nowhere else to go, so they focused their message and policies on middle-class voters in affluent Middle England. The working-class electorate responded, by and large staying at home on polling day from 1997 onwards.

Provocative and incisive, the analysis of Labour Together is nonetheless questionable. The report misrepresents Labour's position by resorting to stereotypes, mythologising a past where Labour had a stable and harmonious relationship with the working-class electorate in Britain. Such a time never existed. Even at the zenith of Labour's power after the Second World War, a third of working-class voters still supported the Conservative Party. As the polling expert Peter Kellner points out, the British Tory Party has *always* drawn around half its support from the manual working class.

Recent research demonstrates that in 1997, Labour won a roughly equal number of working-class and middle-class seats, measured by pay levels and housing tenure.[10] It was in 2017 under Jeremy Corbyn that Labour's gains were overwhelmingly skewed towards more middle-class constituencies. Moreover, the image of the Red Wall as being 'left behind' places 'that don't matter', marred by post-industrial decay and despair, is highly misleading. More often, the former industrial towns in the North and the Midlands are invariably surrounded by 'gleaming new suburbs, a British counterpart to the American dream where a couple on a modest income can own a home and two cars and raise a family'.[11] Research conducted for the Resolution Foundation demonstrated that while the living standards of Red Wall seats remain below the national average, they are by no means the poorest or most deprived constituencies. New Labour performed relatively well in these seats after 1997, appealing directly to the material values of the predominantly working-class electorate focused on wages and living standards.[12] It was when the party neglected the core issues of economic competence, law and order, and standards in public services after 2010 that these voters gradually abandoned it.

We are convinced that Labour must remain a national party, representing the widest coalition of interests. Labour should seek to win the support of voters in marginal seats, as well as core supporters in so-called heartland areas. The party must attract votes from every part of the nation, instead of acting as a tribal, class-based force speaking only to the sectional interests of 'our people'. In the earliest years of the Labour Party, its leaders from Keir Hardie to Ramsay MacDonald recognised it was impossible for Labour to win by relying on the votes of industrial workers alone. The sectarian mindset that prevails in some sections of the party inflicts immense harm on Labour's prospects.

Labour will need to appeal to a far wider group of voters than it has in the last decade if it is to win a general election, including many who previously voted Conservative. Like it or not, Britain is becoming a predominantly middle-class society. More voters are employed in middle-class occupations, while more identify as 'middle class'. The proportion of university graduates has risen from 15 per cent of eighteen- to thirty-year-olds in 1997 (the year of Labour's landslide) to almost 50 per cent by 2021. Labour neglects this changing social structure at its peril. It must recognise that the 'middle class' is a diverse social grouping which includes many households that are economically precarious. Not all middle-class voters are highly educated liberal cosmopolitans living in cities and employed in the public sector. There is a large suburban middle class in Britain, often working in small businesses and the private sector, juggling a mortgage and high living costs. They have been crucial in delivering Labour victories in the past. At the same time, the party cannot afford to lose touch with its working-class supporters, as has happened increasingly in recent years. The task is to recreate Labour as a modern, left-of-centre force in British politics, steadfastly a party of community embracing all classes.

The Strange Death of Labour Scotland?

If it is to secure a UK-wide parliamentary majority, Labour must first win back support in Scotland. This will be a difficult task, it will take time, and it will have to begin from the bottom up. Britain is more electorally fragmented than at any point since the dawn of mass suffrage. As Professor Vernon Bogdanor has noted, for the first time in modern political history, a different party won in each of the UK's four constituent nations in recent elections. In Scotland, there were particular factors that explained Labour's seismic loss of votes to the Scottish National Party (SNP). It was not just the politics of the union. As one Labour activist explained in our recent study *Can Labour Win?*:

We have a long-term structural issue. There were decaying parties, constituencies where we were suffering from 'safe-seat-itis', we took them for granted and then we were hit by a tsunami. We didn't challenge the SNP in power properly; we waited for them to implode. We can't outflank the SNP as a nationalist party, we did the right thing in remaining a unionist party, but this provided the SNP with a handy attack in the election.

It is clear the factors underlying Labour's long-term decline in Scotland go beyond the 2014 referendum, but that plebiscite unquestionably accelerated the party's decay. According to the polling expert John Curtice, 35 per cent of those who voted Labour in 2010 voted to leave the UK in 2014. Astonishingly, around half of those who voted to stay in the UK subsequently voted SNP in the 2015 and 2017 general elections. Labour's anaemic performance in the 2019 UK election was driven in part by Scottish pro-European 'remain' voters refusing to support it. 'Identity liberals' in Scotland drifted inexorably to the SNP while unionists sided with the Conservatives.

Curtice emphasised that Labour has been on the back foot in Scottish politics for more than a decade. It failed to develop a compelling national project after the Scottish Parliament was created in 1999. The Blair governments were, in truth, ambivalent about devolution, delegating powers only reluctantly while seeking to control Scottish politics from Westminster. Margaret Thatcher left office long ago in 1990. Thirty years later, Labour was still basing its electoral appeal on not being the 'hated Thatcherite Tories' who inflicted the Poll Tax and public spending cuts on the Scottish people. After a decade in power nationally after 1997, Labour itself was becoming increasingly unpopular. The weakness of its strategy was exposed in the 2007 Scottish parliamentary elections when the SNP made substantial gains.

Increasingly, voters no longer valued the language of 'partnership' between London and Edinburgh. They wanted a party that would stand up resolutely for Scottish interests. These voters were attracted by the SNP's vision of egalitarianism and its commitment to a strong society that Labour allegedly abandoned in the 1990s. According to the British Election Study (BES), SNP voters were, on average, more supportive of higher taxes and redistribution than those who opted to stick with Labour (although there is little evidence Scottish voters are fundamentally to the left of the rest of the UK: the British Social Attitudes [BSA] survey reveals that while 43.8 per cent of Scots favour higher taxes and public spending, the figure in England is 36.4 per cent). The BSA indicates that Scotland is perceived to be more left wing and social democratic than it actually is. Even so, the SNP benefited from being viewed as to the left of the UK Labour Party. In addition, the SNP pioneered methods of participatory democracy that reinforced Labour's image as the last bastion of a closed, even corrupt, old-fashioned bureaucratic culture.

As well as shaping an alternative agenda for governing Scotland, Scottish Labour has to become a campaigning party, capable of taking the argument to the SNP, building up strength and confidence at Holyrood, while striving to win seats at Westminster. It must break with the narrow, insular mindset of political control that too often dominated Labour-run councils in Scotland, recalling that social democracy means giving communities the power to shape their own lives rather than relying on top-down control and faceless bureaucracy. To succeed, Scottish and Welsh Labour must have political autonomy from London. There should be a distinctive English Labour Party emphasising its commitment to city regions and local devolution, and Labour must fight the next election on an English manifesto. It is vital that Labour projects itself as a party capable of speaking up for English political interests given the rising tide of nationalism.

However, the English, Welsh, and Scottish Labour parties must in turn develop a shared social democratic vision for the whole of Britain. Labour should set out a compelling centre-left programme combining economic efficiency with social justice for every part of the UK. The flaws in the SNP's governing approach will eventually be exposed. The SNP has centralised control over Scottish public spending and policy making. Its record in education and law and order is far from impressive. Labour's vision of a progressive *United* Kingdom anchored in a vision of universal economic and social citizenship still has resonance. As Ben Jackson avers, Labour should avoid resorting to a 'declinist' narrative where social democracy is depicted as having been defeated by the forces of global capitalism.[13] Instead, it must revive faith in the UK as four nations where democratic progress ensures that civil and political rights can continue to guarantee economic and social justice for each citizen and community.

Labour's Programme in the Covid Decade: A New Revisionism

The new social democratic programme must reflect Labour's aspiration to unify classes and nations across Britain. The core idea of social democracy according to Leszek Kolakowski, the

Polish philosopher and historian, is 'an obstinate will to erode by inches the conditions which produce avoidable suffering, oppression, hunger, wars, racial and national hatred, insatiable greed and vindictive envy'.[14] Social democrats should marry their belief in social justice with their commitment to economic egalitarianism and prosperity. They aim to forge social and economic institutions that counter inequality, stimulate opportunity, and forge a genuine sense of community. Rather than obsessing about the arcane goal of nationalisation and state ownership, social democracy focuses on equality, the abolition of class snobbery, the fullest expression of democratic citizenship. In Hugh Gaitskell's words, social democracy entails a loathing of social injustice and intolerance, 'of the indefensible differences of status and income that disfigure our society'. The aim is fellowship and fraternity, 'while preserving the liberties we cherish ... not only in our country but all over the world'.[15]

Rather than focusing on detailed policies for its next manifesto, Labour must clarify its ambitions for society. The party must constantly update its ideas as it did after the defeat of the 1945–51 government. In his introduction to *The New Fabian Essays* (1952), Richard Crossman wrote that the renewal of ideas was necessary, 'Partly due to the achievements of the labour movement ... partly due to changing social conditions', and as a result of 'inadequacies in the original analysis'. It was essential to acknowledge the changing condition of Britain. Crossman contended that in the wake of the 1951 defeat, 'The Labour Party has lost its way not only because it lacks a map of the new country it is crossing, but because it thinks maps unnecessary for experienced travellers.'[16]

In new circumstances, Labour must reach out to the most striking sources of political energy in Britain, including the anti-racist movement Black Lives Matter (BLM) and those young people rightly demanding radical action on climate change. Labour should recreate the broad-based movement for political and social reform that helped it to power in the early 1940s, early 1960s, and early 1990s. The purpose is not merely to win an election, but to create a new climate of opinion in Britain that will sustain a Labour government, enabling it to carry through major political, social, and economic reforms. The party should not forget that it is fighting a perpetual battle of ideas against the forces of conservatism. Yet Labour won in 1945, 1964, and 1997 not merely because of the rejection of failed Conservative governments, but because Labour's ideas and values were in tune with the demands of the time, rejecting stagnation in favour of radical modernisation.

To put its values into effect, Labour needs a practical and credible governing programme. It must develop a positive prospectus informed by a coherent theme, not a laundry list of detailed policies. The party's programme must unify the labour movement around a shared social democratic agenda, taking account of the seismic impact of the pandemic. That will require sustained intellectual engagement and rethinking in the aftermath of the Covid crisis. As the British Academy report on the pandemic noted: 'No single metaphor can capture the complexity or ramifications of the societal impact of Covid-19. Its arrival, ever-changing twists and turns, dilemmas it presents, and devastating impacts have demanded practical and policy solutions at a phenomenal pace.'[17] While parallels between the pandemic and the 1945 era may be misplaced, the age of Covid is nevertheless likely to produce far-reaching political change. The following section of the chapter outlines our programme for centre-left reform in the wake of the global pandemic.

Economic Security and Reconstruction: Towards a Green Recovery

It has become conventional wisdom that the central issues in British politics are now fundamentally defined by identity rather than economics. It is said the task for Labour is to reconnect with its working-class 'leave' supporters in Red Wall seats in the North and Midlands. These communities have certainly become more alienated from Labour. As one woman from Darlington told the pollster Deborah Mattinson: 'They thought we'd always vote Labour – we'd always be their little puppets. They just took it for granted that everyone up North would vote Labour. Well, they were wrong.'[18] Even so, as Maria Sobolewska and Robert Ford contend in their book *Brexit Land*, public hostility to immigration and Europe is gradually declining in Britain.[19] These issues are being supplanted on the public agenda by more traditional conflicts over redistribution, living standards, workers versus employers, and the funding of public services in the aftermath of the pandemic. The centrality of the economy to Labour's electoral appeal remains indisputable.

Labour will never win and govern until the party re-establishes its reputation for economic competence. Unfairly or not, Labour was blamed by voters for the financial crash in 2008. It has yet to regain their confidence over a decade later.

Labour needs an economically radical programme, while at the same time demonstrating its commitment to fiscal rectitude and sound economic management. The party needs to make clear that more spending and debt are not the solution to every problem.

The Covid-19 pandemic forced the Johnson government to do 'whatever it takes' to fight the virus and protect the economy. Since the early spring of 2020, there has been a remarkable expansion in the size and scope of the state. The victory of President Joe Biden in the United States demonstrates that the world is not moving against the left, and that the era of Reagan–Thatcher dominance that led to the shrinking of government in favour of the market has come to an end.

Yet it is simplistic to interpret the present juncture as the manifestation of another 1945 moment. There is a yearning for solidarity and social protection. It is clear that the commitment to narrow individualism affords an inadequate governing philosophy. Even so, voters still worry about their jobs, livelihoods, and wages. Many are employed in the private sector. They want a government that supports them. Yet they acknowledge the state can only take on so many burdens and obligations. As Mervyn King and John Kay emphasise, in the aftermath of the pandemic, governments of the future will have to deal with conditions of 'radical uncertainty'.[20]

It is apparent that the pandemic is accelerating structural trends already reshaping Britain's economy and society. Even before the crisis, forecasts indicated that approximately one million jobs in the UK retail sector were in danger of being lost. Meanwhile, the application of Artificial Intelligence (AI) is transforming sectors such as transport and logistics, alongside traditional middle-class professions, notably legal conveyancing and accountancy. Economic insecurity was growing in Britain before the pandemic took hold. Labour must govern in an era where many voters are understandably anxious about their jobs and future living standards, given the cost of living crisis.

The party requires a coherent economic outlook and philosophy. Keynesian ideas still provide insight and inspiration, highlighting the limits to laissez-faire capitalism and market forces. However, these ideas need to be updated for the post-pandemic world. Social democracy acknowledges the fundamental importance of markets, profit, and private ownership. It questions the Marxist assumption that capitalism is destined to collapse under the weight of its own contradictions. Yet social democrats need a critique of global capitalism's failings. They must acknowledge that while the mixed economy is here to stay, there are fundamental problems with the British variety of capitalism. Inequality can only be tamed in a market economy if there are countervailing institutions, including progressive taxation and redistribution by governments. Despite the globalisation of product, labour, and capital markets since the 1970s, nation states retain the capacity to act, protecting livelihoods and upholding the public interest.

As such, the governing principles of Labour's economic strategy should be, first, that UK governments must work to create an international economic architecture that ensures there is necessary scope for domestic policy action. The state should have the capacity to intervene during serious downturns, while international co-operation will help to protect social and economic rights for workers. That was the purpose of European Union (EU) membership, maintaining high social and environmental standards for the UK. That arrangement for Britain is now gone. In a post-Brexit world, the country will have to manage its exchange rate so as not to deter foreign direct investment, to maintain low inflation, and to guard against financial panics and sudden withdrawal of capital.

The second principle acknowledges the negative consequences of global capitalism, particularly its short-termism and monopolistic tendencies that concentrate market rewards. These must be curbed more effectively by government action. The risk of concentration has grown in the era of big tech. Moreover, British business needs a financial and legal constitution that embeds long-term obligations towards customers, workers, and communities, as Will Hutton has long argued. It is clear that private investment is inherently unstable, tending to plummet during downturns. Wages and prices are not flexible enough to reduce unemployment automatically. State intervention can improve the long-term performance of the economy. Moreover, budgetary policy is an important instrument, maintaining economic stability and off-setting contractions in the economic cycle.[21]

Thirdly, the state must play a key role in building a more productive and efficient economy through investment in growth-enhancing sectors alongside public services. The UK requires a post-Brexit industrial policy that has vertical and horizontal elements. The public sector should invest for the long term in education, health, skills, training, infrastructure, research and development, science, and technology. The UK government's share of total investment fell from 47.3 per cent in 1948–76 to 18.4 per cent in the period from 1977 to 2007. It has been anaemic since the 2008 financial crash. It is not enough to rely on the private sector and public–private partnerships (PPPs) to drive economic development. The private sector historically under-invested in public goods because the financial rate of return was so low.[22] Only government can act as investor of last resort.

Industrial policy must tackle soaring regional inequalities in Britain which have been exacerbated by structural changes since the 1970s and 1980s. The Oxford economist Paul Collier demonstrates that even before the global pandemic, the UK was among the most geographically unequal countries in the advanced capitalist world. The Policy Institute at King's College London has shown that in the wake of Covid-19, reducing spatial inequality is a key priority for voters across Britain. The impact of deindustrialisation, particularly the closure of coal mines, steel works, and shipbuilding in former industrial towns in the Midlands and northern England, has had devastating long-term effects. In addressing that legacy, regional policy must focus on creating a transport and digital infrastructure linking the whole of the UK, while ensuring the provision of high-quality affordable housing.

The main priority in economic strategy should be green growth and well-paid, secure jobs that reduce global emissions. The state can play an enabling role, guaranteeing future investment in clean industries. The 'Green New Deal' proposed during Jeremy Corbyn's tenure ought to be the centrepiece of Labour's programme at the next election. The New Economics Foundation (NEF) has observed that while carbon emissions initially declined at the outset of the Covid crisis, they are rebounding as the global economy returns to 'normality'. The climate emergency shows no sign of abating.

The Green New Deal can help to ensure the UK meets its 2030 targets on climate change while tackling the current energy price crisis, reducing the dependence of households on electricity and gas by retrofitting and insulating homes. NEF has calculated that if the resources used for tax cuts from 2010 to 2013 had been invested in residential insulation programmes, emissions would have been 30 per cent lower in the UK by the end of the decade.[23]

The centre-left needs to take seriously NEF's radical proposals including an environmental border tax that raises the price of importing environmentally harmful products. Only government can co-ordinate public and private investment, supporting the long-term transition to a green economy.[24] The Green New Deal channelling the spirit of Franklin Delano Roosevelt must be turned by Labour from a slogan into a detailed programme for government focused on investment in green infrastructure projects that create high-quality skilled jobs throughout the country. The UK government is able to borrow easily for capital investment given negative real interest rates over the long term: it must adopt a 'whatever it takes' approach.[25] The environment and well-being should be at the core of how our economy is organised and run.[26]

Moreover, to create a more egalitarian economy with less regional inequality, university, research, and cultural assets should be moved out of the 'Golden Triangle' of London, Oxford, and Cambridge so they are dispersed across the UK. As Paul Collier notes, 'Government is ridiculously over-centralised in the capital … and so is finance'.[27]

Finally, economic policy must support a new social contract in Britain where individuals and communities are supported to fulfil their responsibilities and obligations. Over the last thirty years, individuals have been forced to cope with the transfer of risk from the state and the private sector to individual workers. While employees should take responsibility for updating their skills through retraining, public investment is necessary to modernise the structure of the economy, delivering more high-skill, high-productivity, high-wage employment throughout the country. Meanwhile, Labour has to fashion a coherent fiscal policy.

The last decade has been marked by economic stagnation and grinding austerity. Living standards for the majority have grown more slowly than for any sustained period since the 1950s. The pressures are most acute for families in work. The squeeze on tax credits since 2010 has hit the poorest families hardest. For the young, wages have fallen in real terms alongside spending power, especially in parts of the country where rents have risen sharply, and large numbers are dependent on the private rental sector for housing. The collapse in owner occupation among young people is a significant development, accompanied by the rise of generational inequalities. Many parents fear that the life prospects of their children will be significantly worse. The impact of the pandemic threatens to exacerbate these trends.

The next Labour government should aim to secure rising living standards, despite the pressures imposed by the pandemic, as part of a more resilient growth model. The party must continue to develop a compelling critique of an economy failing those on middle and lower incomes. Yet by focusing exclusively on exploitative zero-hours contracts and the living wage since the 2010 election, Labour struggled to appeal to more affluent workers – the skilled working class and white-collar occupational groups – who did not believe the party had much to offer voters that were aspiring and upwardly mobile. Research carried out for the think tank Britain Thinks demonstrates that the middle class is growing in Britain, and that while there is pessimism about future opportunities for young people, 'The meritocratic narrative of working hard and "earning it" is deeply embedded in the national psyche.'[28]

The decline of trade unions, particularly in the private sector, is of course concerning. Yet the classic British organisational model of union recognition and industry-wide collective bargaining is unlikely to return in a highly diversified ser-vice-orientated economy. Workers need to be protected from arbitrary abuse and exploitation by employers. New model trade unions are part of the answer to ensuring the rewards of future growth are shared fairly; extending employee owner-ship by redistributing capital and assets is another important reform. In Germany, the new SPD chancellor Olaf Scholz won back votes in the 2021 election by acknowledging that many working-class voters felt they had been blamed for their own failure to advance in the new economy. Scholz told *The Guardian* newspaper in September 2021: 'Merit in society must not be limited to top earners … those who keep the show on the road don't get the respect they deserve. Respect must not be limited to top-earners and those with university degrees.' Scholtz believed that Michael Young's 1958 satire *The Rise of the Meritocracy* 'was an almost prophetic description of the trends of our time'.[29]

The Welfare State and Social Policy

To succeed in office, Labour requires a viable social democratic programme that appeals to the left-leaning half of the
country, including party members, while providing a credible plan for government. Throughout the ages, Labour's core
approach has been to identify workable policies that combine
individual aspiration with social justice. The party's fundamental purpose remains to offer a hand-up to those who want
to get on, while extending a helping hand to those in trouble.
The party must protect the vulnerable, make further progress
in tackling poverty and social deprivation, while remaining a
force for expanding opportunity, breaking down class barriers
that hold people back.

Labour's mission remains to dismantle the obstacles that
restrain the flourishing of individual potential, encouraging
every citizen to make the most of their capacities. Many of the
voters recently interviewed by Deborah Mattinson felt, 'The
Labour Party seemed stuck in the past, failing to understand
or respond to [their] aspirations.'[30] Labour had to understand,
'voters wanted to make something of themselves'. In research
conducted by Penny Bochum for our pamphlet *Can Labour
Win?* in 2015, one voter told us: 'I'm hard-working, I pay my
dues, and I don't seem to get on, while others are getting
benefits and bonuses. The ordinary working people are at the
bottom of the pile.'

At the core of the appeal to economic efficiency and social
justice are well-funded public services. It is apparent that over
the last decade, public services in the UK have been severely
damaged by austerity. The squeeze on health funding has badly
depleted the capacity of the NHS. The decline in public sector

employment has led to deteriorating standards in the courts, prisons, probation, the fire service, the borders agency, tax collection, museums, libraries, and food safety. Local council budgets have declined by more than 40 per cent. In schools, spending per head has fallen dramatically, while pupil/teacher ratios are rising. Scandalously, Sure Start early years centres in deprived neighbourhoods have been closed.

The British Academy has underlined the fundamental importance of investment in education and human capital throughout working life to reduce disparities in socio-economic disadvantage already widened by the pandemic.[31] An incoming Labour government will need to urgently address declining standards in schools by tackling large class sizes, renewing school buildings, and modernising the curriculum. By charging VAT on private school fees and removing charitable tax relief, a new government can channel urgently needed investment into the state education system. Moreover, the last Labour government was right to expand access to both higher and further education, including apprenticeships. The UK is increasingly a highly skilled knowledge economy. It will need more, not fewer graduates over the next twenty years.

It is apparent that Covid-19 has amplified existing health and social inequalities: mortality rates have been highest in areas of overcrowded housing, low-paid service employment, and high social deprivation. There is widespread agreement on the left that Britain needs a sustainable approach to funding public services in the light of growing inequalities. A future government should aim for a tax-to-GDP ratio of 40 per cent across the economic cycle. If Labour wants to reassure voters their money is being spent wisely, it ought to introduce hypothecation, directing taxes towards key areas of spending. Finding a long-term funding mechanism for health and social care is an imperative. The Treasury was traditionally hostile to 'earmarking' taxes since it reduced flexibility to direct resources.

Yet in his 2015 budget, the Conservative chancellor introduced an apprenticeship levy to pay for training, alongside a rise in vehicle excise duty to fund road repairs. The government recently announced a rise in National Insurance (NI) contributions to pay for social care and catch-up funding for the NHS after Covid, but relying on NI means penalising workers on low and middle incomes. The aim of hypothecation is to make citizens feel directly 'connected' to the taxes they pay. There ought to be greater transparency, with citizens receiving information about how their money is spent and its impact. Every household in Britain should be given a 'citizens' statement' that explains how the tax system works and how public spending is allocated.

At the core of the social democratic agenda in Britain since World War Two has been the development of the modern welfare state. Labour's mission should now be to rebuild a 'cradle to grave' welfare system that provides genuine social security in a society radically changed since the Beveridge era. The pandemic and the economic shock it unleashed exposed gaps and vulnerabilities in the structure of social protection. Labour needs innovative social policies, a new Beveridge settlement that restores confidence in the founding principles of social security. As Peter Hennessy suggests, there is a 'duty of care' in which the state owes obligations to its citizens as well as requiring responsibility in return.[32]

After 2010, Labour flirted with the idea of reviving the contributory National Insurance principle. Yet small-c conservatism blocked that policy advance. By the 2015 election, Labour's message on welfare amounted to little more than abolishing the reviled 'bedroom tax'. In 2017 and 2019, Labour's welfare policies were judged by the Institute for Fiscal Studies (IFS) to be less fiscally redistributive than the Liberal Democrats.

British politics over the last decade has been shaped by the acknowledgement among a large segment of the voting population that their children may be less well off than their parents. These sentiments fuelled support for Britain's departure from the European Union (EU), while providing a fertile political base for Corbynism in the Labour Party. Many of the activists who swelled the party's ranks are young graduates dissatisfied with the current economic and social settlement. The immediate promise of mass higher education appears not to have been realised, as graduates struggle to attain professional jobs and middle-class living standards, while the housing market remains out of reach. Consequently, confidence in the meritocratic society and advanced capitalism has been eroding sharply. Labour must address the causes of the malaise.

The Labour Party should also be prepared to confront contentious issues with voters, notably immigration, welfare reform, and crime, particularly the rise in violent offences. Voters throughout the country remain concerned about physical crime that blights local communities: burglary, car theft, drugs-related crime, and vandalism. It is a stark fact that one in five voters fear that they or a close family member will be a victim of violent crime. Scotland has recently experienced a record rise in drugs-related deaths. Meanwhile, lack of amenities for young people has led to escalating anti-social behaviour and knife crime. Citizens want to live in a society and communities where there are duties and responsibilities, as well as rights enshrined in law.

Constitutional and Political Reform

Another cause uniting Labour's values with the needs of the country is political and constitutional reform. Labour's ideological appeal should involve political and democratic re-engagement, not only furthering economic and social justice. Labour must develop a new politics accompanied by the necessary political and constitutional reforms. Covid-19 is a reminder of the fundamental importance of democratic politics. In any society, good governance is the difference between life and death, stability and disorder.

Labour must respond to the growing demand for devolution and control in local communities. The response to the pandemic has demonstrated the limitations of centralised policymaking and implementation, particularly in public health and infection control. The party should build out of the dynamic base it has created in local government. By winning power locally and running councils, particularly in areas of the country where the party does not currently have MPs, Labour will demonstrate its competence. The Cameron government succeeded in stealing the mantle of localism and devolution from Labour with its proposal for a 'Northern Powerhouse', an idea that originated under the Blair and

Brown governments when powers were handed back to local communities after decades of centralisation. The answer for Labour is not to turn its back on devolution, but to demonstrate it is even more determined to give back genuine powers to local people, including tax-raising powers and fiscal autonomy. People should have a greater say in the decisions that affect their lives, whether at work, in housing, or in their locality. Paul Collier is right that, 'Bringing agency and spatial equity together, Labour needs unequivocally to commit to devolution.'[33]

On constitutional questions, Labour must encourage active discussion with other parties, notably the Liberal Democrats and Greens. Labour should advance a new politics in Britain, where necessary seeking an accord with other progressive forces. This is not a matter of an electoral pact or tactical agreement which magically produces a centre-left government. It remains the case, however, that the Conservatives were able to win in 2017 and 2019 against a divided centre-left. As Keynes predicted a century ago, the twentieth century was overwhelmingly a Conservative century as Labour and the Liberals were divided into separate parties. Social democrats and liberals ought to work together on matters of common concern: how to create a genuine partnership between Britain and the EU in the wake of Brexit; how to update Britain's constitutional settlement to create a vibrant federal polity; how to advance social justice while protecting the civil liberties of British citizens.

When faith in politics declines to low levels, constitutional reform can never be a panacea for tackling apathy and disengagement. Politicians urgently need to reconnect with voters.

Britain's political culture will not change, however, until there is reform of its anachronistic institutions. That must include stronger parliamentary scrutiny of decision-making in White-hall and Westminster, modernisation of the House of Lords, radical devolution in England, and further opportunities for citizen engagement in the governing process.

A Pro-European Internationalist Party

Finally, Labour must remain a pro-European, international-ist party. Britain voted to leave the EU, and the party must respect that result. Yet Britain's historic and geographical ties with the continent of Europe will endure. Labour should remember that we will never be able to build social democ-racy in one country. Progressive reform will only arise through alliances and engagement across the borders of nations. The party has long believed that Britain must play a leading role in Europe, and that the EU is still crucial for jobs, growth, and living standards throughout Britain. Growing threats on the borders of the European continent, from the Middle East to the Russian invasion of Ukraine in 2022, must be addressed through a common European security and defence strategy.

Labour rightly remains a patriotic party. That is not incon-sistent with nurturing a close and constructive relationship between the UK and Europe. Britain's interests are best served if it maintains a pro-European disposition, working with our allies to ensure we meet the security and economic challenges of the future which the epoch-defining Ukraine crisis has merely served to emphasise. After all, it was the Labour foreign secretary Ernest Bevin who played a leading role in establishing NATO in 1947. The party must reaffirm its continuing support for the western alliance and liberal democracies around the world. It should be clear that under a Labour government, Britain will retain an independent nuclear deterrent while continuing to meet its defence obligations, working for security and justice at home and abroad.

Reforming the Labour Party and Trade Unions

If it is to remain a united force while providing the viable alternative government the country needs, the Labour Party as an institution must be updated and revitalised. Of course, it is necessary to balance different interests across the labour movement. Above all, it is essential to ensure the party faces outwards and listens to voters. As a movement, Labour must create structures of engagement, participation, and decision-making that genuinely involve party members and supporters in policy formulation and organisation through deliberative democracy. As a matter of priority, Labour should revitalise and modernise the party. It should build up community organisations as a way of strengthening local parties. Labour should champion a new form of community politics where local issues are at the forefront of campaigning. The party should develop the next generation of candidates and councillors, particularly in areas where Labour is still chronically under-represented.

Labour as a party still has a major problem with its image. Even the name is off-putting to large sections of the British public, redolent of heavy industry, male industrial workers, and the cloth cap. 'Labour' gives the impression that the party stands for an interest group rather than a vision of society, in a world where voters see themselves as consumers and citizens, not only as workers and producers. The party ought to learn lessons from the trade unions that have successfully updated their image and appeal.

Labour will need to symbolise its conversion to the new politics by opening the party up to wider society, electing its leaders through open primaries in which supporters can participate. All future parliamentary selection contests should be conducted through primaries to ensure greater openness. Special care must be taken to guard against entryism by those who do not support Labour's aims and values. The policymaking process underpinning the party's next manifesto should be participative, with opportunities through face-to-face meetings and digital technology to join the debate. Labour's annual conference ought to become a two-day event with fewer formal procedures, and more opportunities for direct involvement. Labour must project itself as a dynamic social movement rather than a narrow interest group.

Young people particularly are so often engaged directly in their communities. Yet they are understandably put off by bureaucratic party meetings. There needs to be stronger encouragement of local activity and more community input, harnessing the potential of social media. Youth mayors and youth parliaments have proved effective in involving young people in the democratic process. Labour ought to encourage more of them.

Meanwhile, the Labour Party must re-establish its relationship with the trade unions. Whatever its origins, Labour cannot be viewed as an exclusively union-based party. It must be a broad, one-nation party, pursuing national solutions to national problems. Although the party should respect trade union views and oppose attempts to curtail the right to collective organisation, it must never allow itself to be dominated by an interest group, however influential. For their part, the trade unions cannot afford to be portrayed as partisan organisations. The relationship between a Labour government and the unions should be focused on partnership: an ethos of 'fairness not favours'.

The Collins Review published in 2014 led to the abolition of the electoral college, and the introduction of a system of 'one member, one vote' for electing the party leader and deputy leader. Following the 2015 and 2020 leadership elections, Labour should review how the system is working given widespread concerns about its legitimacy. It was right to raise the threshold of MPs nominations required to stand for the leadership and deputy leadership. Labour must ensure a fairer balance of representation on the National Executive, where the unions currently have two-thirds of the seats. Local councillors should have a stronger voice. At party conference, trade unions still have 50 per cent of the votes. Reform will give ordinary members and registered supporters a stronger voice in the party's policymaking.

Conclusion

The key insight of this book is that Labour must face up to internal differences, embracing a plurality of centre-left traditions to win the battle of ideas in British politics. The party needs to develop a culture of tolerance where honest disagreement is acknowledged rather than feared. We argue that in the New Labour era, in reaction to four consecutive electoral defeats and a largely hostile media, the leadership of the party developed an unhealthy antipathy to internal debate and disagreement. That attitude was ultimately counter-productive since difference is fundamentally healthy and necessary in order to drive forward new ideas while developing domestic and international policy. Too often, the Labour leadership believed that it could govern and re-think the party's strategy single-handedly without drawing on intellectual resources within and outside the party – ultimately an implausible approach.

Of course, Labour needs to be a united party. But it must not sacrifice the capacity for intellectual innovation and dynamism that winning parties need. Where necessary, the leadership has to be willing to challenge the Labour party, as Attlee, Gaitskell, Wilson, and Callaghan were prepared to do, while listening to the plurality of voices across the spectrum of internal opinion. If it merely preaches the virtues of unity, the party is unlikely to ever win power again.

Labour must aim to unify the left and centre vote in Britain, proposing a radical social democratic programme that inspires party members and the grassroots, while addressing the aspirations of the nation. Voters want competent, efficient, and values-driven government. The lesson of history is that Labour wins, as in 1945, 1964, and 1997, when it advances opportunity for all, uniting a diverse sweep of classes and constituencies while projecting its appeal as a national party. If Labour is to recast itself as a national movement representing Britain's progressive majority, it must rediscover its radical roots, not merely defend the institutions and gains of the past.

In recent years, despite its high-flown rhetoric, the party risked becoming a force for conservatism and inertia rather than radical change. Jeremy Corbyn implied he would return Britain to the world of the 1970s, rather than looking forward to the 2020s. Labour's mission is not to consolidate the policies of the Attlee era, or the Blair–Brown era. It is to alter British society to ensure that wealth, power, and opportunity lie in the hands of the whole national community, rather than a narrow and privileged elite. The party can be proud of what it has achieved over the last century. But it needs to stop looking backwards, instead offering a persuasive vision of where Britain needs to be in the future. History demonstrates that Labour wins when it has a confident message of optimism and hope. Politics in the UK remains extraordinarily volatile. It is quite possible that at the next election, Keir Starmer will face a Tory leader other than Boris Johnson. In those circumstances, he will need to define and articulate his political vision with greater clarity against an opponent who may be benefiting from a political honeymoon.

Many so-called experts have in the past written off the Labour Party. They say that the party's historic mission is over: it is now doomed to decline. But how could that be when so many unjustified inequalities still exist in Britain, when individuals lack opportunity, and when communities are under strain? The party must prove its detractors wrong by refusing to waste its period in opposition in sterile bickering that produces a programme irrelevant to Britain's problems. Instead, Labour must take the opportunity to show that its values and policies are in tune with the needs and concerns of the 2020s.

There is unquestionably an appetite for a centre-left political party that faces up to, and strives to address, the long-term challenges confronting Britain, particularly in the light of Covid-19. That can only be done by establishing economic credibility and political trust. Voters are willing to hear a message from Labour which is honest about the difficult choices and trade-offs that lie ahead, instead of promising everything while engaging in the futile politics of protest. The party's case to the nation should be that with a Labour government in the 2020s, Britain can be among the most prosperous, secure, compassionate, *and* environmentally sustainable countries in the world. In embarking on that task of intellectual and practical reconstruction, there is not a moment to lose.

Notes

Foreword
1. B. Pimlott, *Harold Wilson* (London: Harper Collins, 1992).

1. Why Labour is Given to Civil Wars
1. D. Marquand, 'Inquest on a Movement: Labour's Defeat and the Consequences', *Encounter* (July 1979) p. 9.
2. P. Clarke, *A Question of Leadership* (London: Penguin, 1991).
3. D. Marquand, 'Maximum Embarrassment', *London Review of Books*, 9/9, (May 1987) p. 22.
4. B. Pimlott, *Harold Wilson* (London: Harper Collins, 1992) p. 102.
5. Pimlott pp. 157–8.
6. A. Gamble, 'The Progressive Dilemma Revisited', *The Political Quarterly*, 88/1, (2017) pp. 136–43.
7. Pimlott p. 176.
8. Gamble pp. 136–43.
9. D. Marquand, *Ramsay MacDonald: A Biography* (London: Heinemann, 1977) p. 438.

10. A. Bullock, *Ernest Bevin: Foreign Secretary* (London: Heinemann, 1983) p. 738.
11. R. Crossman, ed., *New Fabian Essays* (London: Turnstile Press, 1952) pp. 190–1; A. Crosland, *The Future of Socialism* (London: Jonathan Cape, 1956).
12. D. Howell, *British Social Democracy* (Oxford: OUP, 1976) p. 176.
13. B. Donoughue, *Downing Street Diary: With Harold Wilson in No.10* (London: Jonathan Cape, 2004) p. 139.
14. Howell p. 265.
15. A. Rawnsley, *The End of the Party: The Inside Story of New Labour* (London: Penguin, 2010) p. 165.

2. Government or Opposition: The 1931 Split and the Fall of Ramsay MacDonald

1. The biographical material in this chapter is informed by David Marquand's groundbreaking revisionist biography *Ramsay MacDonald: A Biography* (London: Heinemann, 1977).
2. Marquand (1977) p. 6.
3. Marquand (1977) p. 12.
4. Cited in Marquand (1977) p. 68.
5. Labour Party, 'Labour and the New Social Order' [pamphlet] (London: Labour Party, 1918).
6. F. Bealey, ed., 'Introduction', in *The Social and Political Thought of the British Labour Party* (London: Tinglin, 1970) p. 67.
7. M. Francis, *Ideas and Policies Under Labour 1945–51: Building a New Britain* (Manchester: MUP, 1997) p. 15.
8. Bealey p. 67.

9. D. Howell, *British Social Democracy* (Oxford: OUP, 1976).
10. Cited in Marquand (1977) p. 297.
11. Labour Party, 'Labour and the Nation' (London: Labour Party, 1928).
12. D. Marquand,'England, Our England: The Dilemmas of Revisionist Social Democracy', *Dissent Magazine* (Nov.–Dec., 1969) p. 43.
13. E. Dell, *A Strange, Eventful History: Democratic Socialism in Britain* (London: HarperCollins, 2000) p. 35.
14. B. Webb, *The Diaries of Beatrice Webb* (London: Virago, 1985) p. 182.
15. Marquand (1977) p. 579.
16. P. Clarke, *A Question of Leadership* (London: Penguin, 1991) p. 156.
17. H. Dalton, *The Political Diary 1918–60*, B. Pimlott, ed. (London: Jonathan Cape, 1987) p. 356.
18. Howell.
19. D. Marquand, *Britain Since 1918: The Strange Career of British Democracy* (London: Weidenfeld & Nicholson, 2008) p. 85.
20. Cited in D. Marquand (1977) p. 235.
21. Cited in B. Donoughue & G. Jones, *Herbert Morrison: The Portrait of a Politician* (London: Politicos, 2001) p. 8.
22. Cited in Marquand (1977) p. 653.
23. B. Webb p. 252.
24. R. Skidelsky, *Politicians and the Slump* (London: Penguin, 1970) pp. 31–2.
25. Clarke p. 158.

26. Cited in R. Toye, 'The Labour Party and Keynes', in D. Tanner & E. H. H. Green, eds., *The Strange Survival of Liberal England: Political Leaders, Moral Values and the Reception of Economic Debate* (Cambridge: Cambridge University Press, 2007) pp. 160–1.

27. G. Peden, *Keynes, the Treasury and British Economic Policy* (Basingstoke: Palgrave Macmillan, 1988).

28. Clarke p. 155.

29. Donoughue & Jones (2001) p. 152.

30. Toye pp. 193–4.

31. R. McKibbin, 'The Economic Policy of the Second Labour Government 1929–31', *Past & Present*, 68/1, (Aug. 1975) p. 114.

32. McKibbin (1975) p. 105.

33. Bealey p. 2.

34. K. Morgan, *Labour in Power 1945–51* (Oxford: OUP, 1984) p. 17.

35. Marquand (1977) p. 453.

36. S. Hannah, *A Party With Socialists In it: A History of the Labour Left* (London: Pluto Press, 2018) p. 53.

37. Morgan p. 15.

38. M. Freeden, 'The Ideology of New Labour', *The Political Quarterly*, 70/1, (1998) p. 187.

39. J. Tomlinson, 'Why Wasn't There a "Keynesian Revolution" in Economic Policy Everywhere?", *Economy and Society*, 20/1 (1991).

40. A. Thorpe, *A History of the British Labour Party* (Basingstoke: Palgrave Macmillan, 2015) p. 90.

41. *Ibid.*

42. E. Durbin, *The Politics of Democratic Socialism* (London: George Routledge & Sons, 1940).
43. J. Tomlinson, p. 68.
44. Dell p. 62.
45. Durbin p. 46.
46. Morgan p. 16.
47. McKibbin (1975) p. 140.
48. S. Brooke, 'Evan Durbin: Reassessing a Labour "Revisionist"', *Twentieth Century British History*, 7/1, (1996) pp. 27–52.
49. Cited in Brooke p. 46.
50. Cited in G. Foote, *The Labour Party's Political Thought* (Basingstoke: Palgrave Macmillan, 1985) pp. 192–4.
51. Cited in Brooke p. 43.
52. Morgan p. 135.
53. H. Dalton, *Practical Socialism for Britain* (London: Routledge, 1935) p. 134.
54. R. McKibbin, *Parties and People: England 1914–51* (Oxford: OUP, 2008).
55. Morgan p. 17.
56. R. Crowcroft, *Attlee's War: World War II and the Making of a Labour Leader* (London: IB Tauris, 2011).
57. Howell.
58. R. Tawney, 'The Choice Before the Labour Party', *The Political Quarterly*, 3/3, (1932) pp. 323–45.

3. Revisionists versus Fundamentalists: Gaitskell and Bevan at War 1951–64

1. H. Dalton, *The Political Diary 1918–60*, B. Pimlott, ed. (London: Jonathan Cape, 1987).

2. Dalton p. 3.

3. K. Morgan, *Labour in Power 1945–51* (Oxford: Clarendon Press, 1984) p. 503.

4. P. Hennessy, *Never Again: Britain 1945–51* (London: Penguin Books, 1992) p. 423.

5. D. Marquand, 'Maximum Embarrassment', *The London Review of Books*, 9/9, (1987).

6. Morgan p. 441.

7. Hennessy p. 157.

8. Dalton p. 397.

9. M. Foot, *Aneurin Bevan: A Biography* (London: Scribner, 1974) p. 326.

10. Foot p. 498.

11. K. Harris, *Attlee* (London: Orion, 1995) p. 405.

12. B. Brivati, *Hugh Gaitskell* (London: Politicos, 2006) p. 17.

13. P. Williams, *Hugh Gaitskell: A Political Biography* (London: Jonathan Cape, 1979) p. 25.

14. Williams p. 99.

15. Brivati p. 78.

16. Foot p. 300.

17. Foot p. 295.

18. Foot p. 299.

19. H. Gaitskell, *The Diary of Hugh Gaitskell 1945–56*, P. Williams, ed. (London: Jonathan Cape, 1983) p. 134.

20. Morgan p. 432.

21. Hennessy p. 416.

22. Cited in Foot p. 458.

23. Dalton p. 343.

24. Foot p. 379.

25. Brivati p. 176.
26. S. Haseler, *The Gaitskellites: Revisionism in the British Labour Party 1951–64* (Basingstoke: Macmillan, 1969) p. 76.
27. D. Howell, *British Social Democracy* (Oxford: OUP, 1976).
28. Harris p. 450.
29. Cited in B. Donoughue & G. Jones, *Herbert Morrison: The Portrait of a Politician* (London: Politicos, 2001) p. 456.
30. Foot p. 431.
31. Cited in Marquand (1987) p. 20.
32. Harris pp. 531–2.
33. Gaitskell p. 371.
34. House of Commons, Historic Hansard (27 October 1955) col 408.
35. D. Healey, *The Time of My Life* (London: Methuen Publishing, 2015) p. 169.
36. House of Commons, Historic Hansard (2 August 1956) col 223.
37. Gaitskell pp. 574–5.
38. Gaitksell p. 437.
39. Foot p. 516.
40. M. Abrams & R. Rose, *Must Labour Lose?* (London: Penguin, 1960) p. 100.
41. A. Crosland, *The Conservative Enemy* (London: Jonathan Cape, 1962) p. 57.
42. Brivati p. 332.
43. A. Bevan, *In Place of Fear* (London: William Heinemann, 1952) p. 201.

44. Gaitskell p. 702.
45. Gaitskell p. 763.
46. Howell.
47. J. Callaghan, *Time and Chance* (London: Collins, 1987) p. 149.
48. Healey p. 155.
49. Gaitskell p. 767.
50. Abrams & Rose p. 117.
51. Howell.
52. Callaghan p. 150.
53. H. Morrison, *Herbert Morrison: An Autobiography* (London: Odhams, 1960) p. 238.
54. A. Schlesinger, 'Appraisals of New Fabian Essays', *The Review of Economics and Statistics,* 35/3, (1953) p. 201.
55. S. Hannah, *A Party With Socialists In it: A History of the Labour Left* (London: Pluto Press, 2018).
56. Marquand p. 196.
57. F. Bealey, ed., 'Introduction', in *The Social and Political Thought of the British Labour Party* (London: Littlehampton, 1970) p. 198.

4. The Bennite Revolt and the Birth of the Social Democratic Party: Healey, Benn, and Jenkins 1964–87

1. B. Pimlott, *Harold Wilson: The Authorised Biography* (London: Harper Collins, 1991) p. 553.
2. D. Howell, *British Social Democracy* (Oxford: OUP, 1976) p. 125.
3. D. Marquand, 'Maximum Embarrassment', *The London Review of Books*, 9/9, (1987) p. 18.

4. D. Healey, *The Time of My Life* (London: Methuen Publishing, 2015) p. 345.

5. J. Callaghan, *Time and Chance* (London: Collins, 1987) p. 223.

6. Cited in D. Marquand, *Britain Since 1918: The Strange Career of British Democracy* (London: Weidenfeld & Nicholson, 2008) p. 238.

7. R. Jenkins, *A Life at the Centre* (London: Methuen Publishing, 1987) p. 302.

8. *Ibid.* p. 195.

9. C. A. R. Crosland, *Tony Crosland* (London: Jonathan Cape, 1964) p. 210.

10. Labour Party, *Labour and the Common Market: Report of a Special Conference of the Labour Party, Central Hall, Westminster, 17 July 1971* (London: Labour Party, 1971) pp. 42–9.

11. B. Donoughue, *Downing Street Diary: With Harold Wilson in No.10* (London: Jonathan Cape, 2004) p. 414.

12. Cited in D. Powell, *Tony Benn: A Political Life* (New York: Continuum, 2001) p. 152.

13. R. Jenkins p. 345.

14. Pimlott p. 595.

15. Marquand (2008).

16. A. Benn, *The Benn Diaries: 1940–1990*, R. Winstone, ed. (London: Arrow Publications, 1996) p. 6.

17. A. Benn, *The Benn Diaries: 1940–1990*, R. Winstone, ed. (London: Arrow Publications, 1996) p. 439–60.

18. Donoughue p. 43.

19. R. Jenkins p. 388.

20. P. Jenkins, 'Community and independence', *The Guardian* (7 May 1975).

21. B. Castle, *The Castle Diaries 1964–70* (London: Weidenfeld & Nicolson, 1984) p. 459.

22. Pimlott p. 652.

23. K. Morgan, *Callaghan: A Life* (Oxford: Oxford University Press, 1999) p. 475.

24. R. Jenkins p. 435.

25. R. Jenkins p. 436.

26. Castle p. 159.

27. P. Hennessy, *The Prime Minister: The Office and its Holders Since 1945* (London: Penguin, 1998) p. 379.

28. Healey p. 448.

29. Callaghan p. 414.

30. Healey pp. 378–9.

31. Healey p. 429.

32. E. Dell, *The Chancellors: A History of Chancellors of the Exchequer 1945–90* (London: Harper Collins, 1997) p. 428.

33. Dell p. 439.

34. P. Whitehead, *Writing on the Wall: Britain in the Seventies* (London: Michael Joseph, 1988) pp. 196–97.

35. Healey p. 523.

36. Whitehead pp. 196–97.

37. E. Shaw, *The Labour Party Since 1979: Crisis and Transformation* (London: Routledge, 1996) p. 76.

38. B. Rodgers, *Fourth Among Equals* (London: Politicos, 2000) p. 205.

39. Limehouse Declaration, issued by S. Williams,

D. Owen, B. Rodgers and R. Jenkins to the Press
Association (25 Jan., 1981).

40. Healey p. 481.
41. G. Foote, *The Labour Party's Political Thought*
(Basingstoke: Palgrave Macmillan, 1985) p. 229.
42. Howell pp. 125–6.

5. New Labour at War: Blair and Brown's Dual Premiership 1997–2010

1. This biographical account of the lives of Blair and
Brown draws on: J. Rentoul, *Tony Blair* (London:
Sphere, 2001); J. Sopel, *Tony Blair: The Moderniser*
(London: Bantham Books, 1995).
2. Cited in S. Richards, *Whatever it Takes: The Real Story
of Gordon Brown and New Labour* (London: 4th Estate,
2010) p. 300.
3. Cited in D. Marquand, *Britain Since 1918* (London:
Bantham Press, 2008) p. 376.
4. P. Gould, *The Unfinished Revolution: How New Labour
Changed British Politics Forever* (London: Abacus, 2011)
p. 361.
5. Cited in Rentoul pp. 292–3.
6. Marquand p. 382.
7. A. Darling, *Back from the Brink* (London: Atlantic
Books, 2012) p. 243.
8. Richards p. 304.
9. Gould p. 479.

6. The Left Insurgency, Corbyn's Leadership, and the Succession of Keir Starmer

1. T. Bower, *Dangerous Hero* (London: William Collins, 2019) p. 79.
2. Bower p. 167.
3. Bower p. 186.
4. R. McKibbin, 'Labour Dies Again', *The London Review of Books* (3 June 2015) p. 26.
5. O. Jones, *This Land: The Struggle for the Left* (London: Penguin 2021) p. 71.
6. Jones p. 145.
7. Cited in P. Diamond, 'New Jerusalems? The Labour Party's Economic Policy-Making in Hard Times', *The Political Quarterly*, 92/2, (7 April 2021) p. 270, https://onlinelibrary.wiley.com/doi/10.1111/1467–923X.12988?af=R.
8. A. Rawnsley, 'MPs must seize control of the Brexit calamity. Mrs May has already lost it', *The Observer* (24 March 2019).
9. Jones p. 186.
10. Jones p. 256.
11. G. Pogrund & P. Maguire, *Left Out: The Inside Story of Labour Under Corbyn* (London: Bodley Head, 2020) p. 299.
12. R. Syal, 'Corbyn, antisemitism and Brexit: Labour MPs on why they lost', *The Guardian* (17 Dec. 2019), https://www.theguardian.com/politics/2019/dec/17/corbyn-antisemitism-and-brexit-labour-mps-on-why-they-lost, accessed 14 November 2020.
13. E. Goes, 'The Labour Campaign', in J. Tonge, ed.,

Britain Votes (Oxford: OUP/Hansard Society, 2018) pp. 84–97.

14. R. Ford et al., *The British General Election of 2019* (Basingstoke: Palgrave Macmillan, 2021) p. 558.
15. Ford et al., p. 560.
16. Pogrund & Maguire.
17. *Ibid* p. 112.
18. P. English, 'Are the Public Beginning to Think Labour Could Govern?' (YouGov: January 2022), https://yougov.co.uk/topics/politics/articles-reports/2022/01/27/are-public-beginning-think-labour-could-govern, accessed 2 February 2022.
19. M. Kelly, 'Tories face losing most of their Northern Red Wall MPs say polls', *Newcastle Chronicle* (19 January 2022), https://www.chroniclelive.co.uk/news/north-east-news/tories-red-wall-mps-polls-22800037, accessed 4 February 2022.
20. P. Collins, 'Events have conspired to give Labour another chance', *The New Statesman* (19 January 2022), https://www.newstatesman.com/politics/labour/2022/01/events-have-conspired-to-give-labour-another-chance-will-keir-starmer-seize-it, accessed 25 January. 2022.

7. Conclusion: The Way Ahead

1. F. Bealey, ed., 'Introduction', in *The Social and Political Thought of the British Labour Party* (London: Littlehampton, 1970) p. 146.
2. M. Abrams & R. Rose, *Must Labour Lose?* (London: Penguin, 1960) p. 117.

3. D. Marquand, 'Maximum Embarrassment', *The London Review of Books*, 9/9 (1987) p. 21.

4. B. Jackson, 'Getting Labour Together', *The Political Quarterly*, 91/1, (Jan.–March 2020) pp. 5–6.

5. S. Hannah, *A Party With Socialists In it: A History of the Labour Left*, (London: Pluto Press, 2018).

6. Marquand p. 21.

7. Bealey p. 50.

8. Howell p. 171.

9. Labour Together (London: Labour Together, 2020) p. 9–11.

10. C. Clarke, 'Against Their Interests', *Medium* (May 2016).

11. *The Economist* (2021).

12. C. McCurdy, et al. 'Painting the Towns Blue' [report] (London: The Resolution Foundation, 2020).

13. B. Jackson, 'A Crisis for Devolution?', *The Political Quarterly*, 91/3, (Jan.–March 2020) pp. 499–501.

14. Cited in P. Diamond (ed.), *The Crisis of Globalisation*, p. 183, (London: IB Tauris, 2018).

15. H. Gaitskell, *The Diary of Hugh Gaitskell 1945–56*, P. Williams, ed. (London: Jonathan Cape, 1983) p. 537.

16. R. Crossman, ed., 'Introduction', in *New Fabian Essays* (London: Turnstile Press, 1952) pp. 14–15.

17. D. Abrams, 'The Covid Decade: Understanding the Societal Impact of Covid-19' [report] (London: The British Academy, 2021) p. 4.

18. D. Mattinson, *Beyond the Red Wall* (London: Biteback, 2020) p. 54.

19. M. Sobolewska & R. Ford, *Brexitland: Identity, Diversity*

and the Reshaping of British Politics (Cambridge: CUP, 2020).

20. M. King & J. Kay, *Radical Uncertainty: Decision Making for an Unknowable Future* (London: The Bridge Street Press, 2020) pp. 2–3.

21. R. Skidelsky, 'What Would Keynes Say Now?', *Project Syndicate* (December 2020), https://www.project-syndicate.org/commentary/keynes-how-to-pay-for-war-against-covid19-by-robert-skidelsky-2020–03, accessed 9 February 2022.

22. W. Hutton, 'New Keynesianism and New Labour', *The Political Quarterly*, 70/1, (1995) pp. 97–102.

23. L. Krebel et al., 'Building a Green Stimulus for Covid-19' (London: NEF, 2020), https://neweconomics.org/2020/07/building-a-green-stimulus-for-covid19, accessed 3 December 2021.

24. M. Mazzucato, 'Financing the Green New Deal', *Nature* (December 2021), https://www.nature.com/articles/s41893–021–00828-x, accessed 8 January 2022.

25. M. Wolf, 'The levelling-up white paper is a necessary call to arms', *The Financial Times* (7 February 2022), https://www.ft.com/content/19c28c15-cd88–40b6-bd7a-15115b624ef5, accessed 7 February 2022.

26. C. Kumar et al., 'Building a Resilient Economy' (London: NEF, 2021), https://neweconomics.org/2021/01/building-a-resilient-economy, accessed 15 November 2021.

27. P. Collier, *The Future of Capitalism: Facing the New Anxieties* (London: Harper Collins, 2018).

28. Britain Thinks, 'We're all middle-class now? Social class

in 2021' (London: Britain Thinks), https://britainthinks.
com/wp-content/uploads/2021/03/Social-Class-2021_
Full-report_FINAL-1603211-Read-Only.pdf, accessed 21
November 2021.

29. Cited in interview with Olaf Scholz (September 2021),
https://www.theguardian.com/world/2021/sep/08/
olaf-scholz-merit-society-not-be-limited-top-earners-
germany-election, accessed 18 December 2021.
30. Mattinson p. 57.
31. Abrams.
32. P. Hennessy, *A Duty of Care: Britain Before and After
Covid* (London: Penguin, 2022).
33. Collier pp. 156–7.

Bibliography

Abrams, M. & Rose, R., *Must Labour Lose?* (London: Penguin, 1960).

Adonis, A., *Ernest Bevin: Labour's Churchill* (London: Biteback, 2020).

Bealey, F., *The Social and Political Thought of the British Labour Party: Readings in Politics and Society* (London: Weidenfeld and Nicolson, 1970).

Benn, A., *The New Politics: A Socialist Reconnaissance* (London: The Fabian Society, 1970).

Bevan, A., *In Place of Fear* (London: William Heinemann, 1952).

Bew, J., *Citizen Clem: A Biography of Attlee* (London: Riverrun, 2014).

Bower, T., *Dangerous Hero* (London: William Collins, 2019).

Britain Thinks, 'We're All Middle Class Now? Social Class in 2021' [report] (16 March 2021), https://britainthinks. com/wp-content/uploads/2021/03/Social-Class-2021_Full-report_FINAL-1603211-Read-Only.pdf.

British Academy, 'Shaping the Covid Decade: Addressing the Long-term Societal Impacts of Covid-19' [report] (2021), https://www.thebritishacademy.ac.uk/

publications/shaping-the-covid-decade-addressing-the-long-term-societal-impacts-of-covid-19/.

Brivati, B., *Hugh Gaitskell* (London: Politicos, 2006).

Brooks, L., 'Three things the latest British Social Attitudes Survey tells us about Scotland', *The Guardian* (26 March 2015), http://www.theguardian.com/uk-news/scotland-blog/2015/mar/26/three-things-the-latest-british-social-attitudes-survey-tells-us-about-scotland.

Bullock, A., *Ernest Bevin: A Biography* (London: Politicos, 1960).

Bullock, A., *Ernest Bevin: Foreign Secretary* (London: Heinemann, 1983)

Callaghan, J., *Time and Chance* (London: Collins, 1987).

Castle, B., *The Castle Diaries 1964–70* (London: Weidenfeld & Nicolson, 1984).

Clark, T. and Dilnot, A., 'Long-Term Trends in British Taxation and Spending' [report] (London: Institute for Fiscal Studies, 2002), http://www.ifs.org.uk/bns/bn25.pdf.

Clarke, P., *A Question of Leadership: Gladstone to Thatcher* (London: Penguin, 1991).

Collier, P., 'The new battle of ideas: How an intellectual revolution will reshape society', *The New Statesman* (28 April 2021), https://www.newstatesman.com/politics/2021/04/new-battle-ideas-how-intellectual-revolution-will-reshape-society.

Coughlan, S., 'The taboo about who doesn't go', BBC News (27 Sept. 2020), https://www.bbc.co.uk/news/education-54278727.

Crowcroft, R., *Attlee's War: World War II and the Making of a Labour Leader* (London: IB Tauris, 2011).

Crosland, C. A. R., *The Conservative Enemy: A Programme of Radical Reform for the 1960s* (London: Jonathan Cape, 1962).

Crosland, C. A. R., *Can Labour Win?* [pamphlet] (London: The Fabian Society, 1960).

Crosland, C. A. R., *The Future of Socialism* (London: Jonathan Cape, 1956).

Crossman, R. H. S. (ed.) *New Fabian Essays* (London: Turnstile Press, 1952).

Crossman, R. H. S., *The Diaries of a Cabinet Minister: Volume I-III* (London: Hamish Hamilton, 1975).

Dalton, H., *Memoirs Volume III: High Tide and After* (London: Muller, 1962).

Dalton, H., *The Political Diary 1918–60*, B. Pimlott, ed. (London: Jonathan Cape, 1987).

Dalton, H., *Practical Socialism for Britain* (London: Routledge, 1935).

Dell, E., *A Strange, Eventful History: Democratic Socialism in Britain* (London: HarperCollins, 2000).

Dell, E., *The Chancellors: A History of Chancellors of the Exchequer 1945–90* (London: Harper Collins, 1997).

Diamond, P., *The British Labour Party in Opposition and Power 1979–2019: Forward March Halted?* (London: Routledge, 2021).

Diamond, P., *The Crosland Legacy: The Future of British Social Democracy* (Bristol: Policy Press, 2016).

Diamond, P. and Radice, G., *Can Labour Win?* (London: Policy Network, 2015).

Diamond, P. and Radice, G., *Southern Discomfort Again* (London: Policy Network, 2010).

Donoughue, B., *Downing Street Diary: With Harold Wilson in No.10* (London: Jonathan Cape, 2004).

Donoughue, B., *Prime Minister: The Conduct of Policy Under Harold Wilson and James Callaghan* (London: Jonathan Cape, 1987).

Donoughue, B. & Jones, G., *Herbert Morrison: Portrait of a Politician* (London: Weidenfeld & Nicholson, 2001).

Durbin, E., *The Politics of Democratic Socialism* (London: Taylor & Francis, 1940).

Economist, The, 'The truth behind the Tories' northern strongholds' (3 April 2021).

English, P., 'Are the Public Beginning to Think Labour Could Govern?' (YouGov: January 2022), https://yougov.co.uk/topics/politics/articles-reports/2022/01/27/are-public-beginning-think-labour-could-govern.

Foot, M., *Aneurin Bevan: A Biography* (London: Scribner, 1974).

Foote, G., *The Labour Party's Political Thought* (Basingstoke: Palgrave Macmillan, 1985).

Ford, R., Bale, T., Jennings, W., Surridge, P., *The British General Election of 2019* (Basingstoke: Palgrave Macmillan, 2021).

Furman, J. & Summers, L., 'A Reconsideration of Fiscal Policy in the Era of Low Interest Rates', University of Harvard Discussion Paper (30 November 2020).

Francis, M., *Ideas and Policies Under Labour 1945–51: Building a New Britain* (Manchester: MUP, 1997).

Freeden, M. 'The Ideology of New Labour', *The Political Quarterly*, 70/1 (1999).

Gamble, A., 'The Progressive Dilemma Revisited', *The Political Quarterly*, 88/1 (2017), pp. 136–43.

Goes, E., 'The Labour Campaign', in J. Tonge, ed., *Britain Votes* (Oxford: Oxford University Press/Hansard Society, 2018), pp. 84–97.

Goodway, N., 'A radical sell-off scheme that could speed RBS back to popularity', *The Evening Standard* (16 June 2015), http://www.standard.co.uk/business/markets/ nick-goodway-a-radical-selloff-scheme-that-could-speed- rbs-back-to-popularity-10323690.html.

Gould, P., *The Unfinished Revolution: How the Modernisers Saved the Labour Party* (London: Random House, 2011).

Hannah, S. *A Party With Socialists In it: A History of the Labour Left* (London: Pluto Press, 2018).

Hardie, K., 'An Indictment of the Class War', *Labour Leader* (2 September 1904).

Harris, K., *Attlee* (London: Orion, 1995).

Harrison, B., 'Coalition Phobia', *London Review of Books*, 9/11 (4 June 1987), p. 10.

Haseler, S., *The Gaitskellites: Revisionism in the British Labour Party 1951–64* (London: Macmillan, 1969).

Hennessy, P., *A Duty of Care: Britain Before and After Covid* (London: Penguin, 2022).

Hennessy, P., *The Prime Minister: The Office and Its Holders Since 1945* (London: Allen Lane, 2000).

Hennessy, P., *Never Again: Britain 1945–51* (London: Penguin Books, 1992).

Howell, D., *British Social Democracy* (Oxford: OUP, 1976).

Howell, D., 'Ramsay MacDonald', in C. Clarke & T. James, eds., *British Labour Leaders* (London: Biteback, 2015).

Hutton, W., 'New Keynesianism and New Labour', *The Political Quarterly* (1999), 97–102.

Inman, P., 'Sowing seeds of next crash will not help young people', *The Guardian* (15 June 2015).

Jackson, B., *The Case for Scottish Independence: A History of Nationalist Political Thought in Modern Scotland* (Cambridge: Cambridge University Press, 2020).

Jackson, B., 'Getting Labour Together', *The Political Quarterly*, 91/1 (Jan.–March 2020).

Jenkins, R., *A Life at the Centre* (London: Methuen Publishing, 1987).

Jones, O., *This Land: The Struggle for the Left* (London: Penguin, 2021).

Kelly, M., 'Tories face losing most of their northern Red Wall MPs say polls', *Newcastle Chronicle* (19 January 2022), https://www.chroniclelive.co.uk/news/north-east-news/tories-red-wall-mps-polls-22800037.

King, M. & Kay, J., *Radical Uncertainty: Decision-Making for an Unknowable Future* (London: The Bridge Street Press, 2020).

Krebel, L., et al., 'Building a Green Stimulus for Covid-19' (London: NEF, 2020), https://neweconomics.org/2020/07/building-a-green-stimulus-for-covid19.

Kruger, D., 'Levelling Up Our Communities: Proposals for a New Social Covenant' (London: House of Commons, 2020).

Lansley, S., *Life in the Middle: The Untold Story of Britain's Average Earners* (London: Trade Union Congress, 2010), https://www.tuc.org.uk/sites/default/files/documents/lifeinthemiddle.pdf.

Leonard, D., *A Century of Premiers* (Basingstoke: Palgrave Macmillan, 2005).

Marquand, D., 'Political Biography' in M. Flinders, A. Gamble, C. Hay, M. Kenny, eds., *The Handbook of British Politics* (Oxford: Oxford University Press, 2009).

Marquand, D., *Britain Since 1918: The Strange Career of British Democracy* (London: Weidenfeld & Nicholson, 2008).

Marquand, D., 'Downhill', *London Review of Books*, 7/16 (19 Sept. 1985), 14.

Marquand, D., 'England, Our England: The Dilemmas of Revisionist Social Democracy', *Dissent Magazine* (Nov.– Dec., 1969).

Marquand, D., 'Inquest on a Movement: Labour's Defeat & its Consequences', *Encounter* (July 1979), p. 9.

Marquand, D., *Ramsay MacDonald: A Biography* (London: Heinemann, 1977).

Mattinson, D., *Beyond the Red Wall: Why Labour Lost, How the Conservatives Won and What Will Happen Next* (London: Biteback, 2020).

Mazzucato, M., 'Financing the Green New Deal', *Nature* (December 2021).

McKibbin, R., 'The Economic Policy of the Second Labour Government 1929–31', *Past & Present*, 68/1 (Aug. 1975) p. 114

McKibbin, R., *Parties and People: England 1914–51* (Oxford: OUP, 2008).

Moggridge, D. E., *Maynard Keynes: An Economist's Biography* (London: Routledge, 1995).

Morgan, K., *Labour in Power 1945–51* (Oxford: Clarendon Press, 1984).

Morrison, H., *Herbert Morrison: An Autobiography* (London: Odhams, 1960).

Peden, G., *Keynes, the Treasury and British Economic Policy* (Basingstoke: Palgrave Macmillan, 1988).

Pimlott, B., *Harold Wilson* (London: HarperCollins, 1992).

Pogrund, G. and Maguire, P., *Left Out: The Inside Story of Labour Under Corbyn* (London: Vintage, 2020).

Radice, G., *Odd Couples: The Great Political Pairings of Modern Britain* (London: IB Tauris, 2015).

Radice, G., *Trio: Inside the Blair, Brown, Mandelson Project* (London: IB Tauris, 2010).

Radice, G., *Friends and Rivals: Crosland, Jenkins and Healey* (London: IB Tauris, 2003).

Radice, G., *Offshore: Britain and the European Idea* (London: IB Tauris, 1992).

Radice, G., *Community Socialism* (London: The Fabian Society, 1979).

Rawnsley, A., *The End of the Party? The Inside Story of New Labour* (London: Penguin, 2010).

Rentoul, J., 'Tony Blair', in C. Clarke, T. James eds., *British Labour Leaders* (London: Biteback, 2015).

Rentoul, J., *Tony Blair* (London: Sphere, 2001).

Resolution Foundation, 'Painting the Towns Blue: Demography, Economy, and Living Standards in the Political Geographies Emerging from the 2019 Election' [report] (12 Feb. 2020).

Richards, S., 'Gordon Brown', in C. Clarke, T. James, *British Labour Leaders* (London: Biteback, 2015).

Richards, S., *Whatever it Takes: The Real Story of Gordon Brown and New Labour* (London: Fourth Estate, 2010).

Schlesinger, A., 'Appraisals of New Fabian Essays', *The Review of Economics and Statistics*, 35/3 (1953), pp. 200–10.

Shaw, E., 'The Labour Party and the Militant Tendency', *Parliamentary Affairs*, 42/2 (1989), pp. 180–96.

Shaw, E., *The Labour Party Since 1979: Crisis and Transformation* (London: Routledge, 1996).

Skidelsky, R., 'What would Keynes do?', *The New Statesman* (10 Sept. 2020).

Skidelsky, R., 'What Would Keynes Say Now?', *Project Syndicate* (December 2020), https://www.project-syndicate.org/commentary/keynes-how-to-pay-for-war-against-covid19-by-robert-skidelsky-2020–03.

Skidelsky, R., *Politicians and the Slump: The Labour Government of 1929–31* (London: Penguin, 1967).

Sobolewska, M. & Ford, R., *Brexitland: Identity, Diversity and the Reshaping of British Politics* (Cambridge: Cambridge University Press, 2020).

Starmer, K., *The Road Ahead* (London: The Fabian Society, 2021).

Tawney, R., 'The Choice Before the Labour Party', *The Political Quarterly*, 3/3 (1932) pp. 323–45.

Thorpe, A., *A History of the British Labour Party* (Basingstoke: Palgrave Macmillan, 2015).

Tomlinson, J., 'Why Wasn't There a "Keynesian Revolution" in Economic Policy Everywhere?', *Economy and Society*, 20/1 (1991).

Toye, R., 'The Labour Party and Keynes', in D. Tanner, E. H. H. Green, eds., *The Strange Survival of Liberal*

England: Political leaders, Moral Values and the Reception of Economic Debate (Cambridge: Cambridge University Press, 2007).

Watt, N., 'Hilary Benn makes emotional plea to bomb Isis "fascists" in Syria', *The Guardian* (3 Dec. 2015).

Webb, B., *The Diaries of Beatrice Webb*, N. & J. MacKenzie, eds. (London: Virago, 1985).

Whitehead, P., *Writing on the Wall: Britain in the Seventies* (London: Michael Joseph, 1988).

Williams, P., *Hugh Gaitskell: A Political Biography* (London: Jonathan Cape, 1979).

Index

General, Municipal and
  Boilermakers' Union (GMB)
  238
general elections
  1918 35
  1922 36
  1924 36
  1929 40
  1931 11, 50–51
  1945 12
  1951 14, 71, 82
  1955 71, 87–88
  1959 15, 71, 92–94, 96
  1964 16, 235
  1966 235
  1970 111–112, 113, 114, 115, 236
  1974, February 124–125
  1974, October 126
  1979 18, 136, 138, 164
  1983 19–20, 163, 164, 194,
    230–231
  1987 20, 165
  1992 165
  1997 169–170, 236, 243
  2001 172
  2005 180
  2010 22, 161, 183–184, 187, 246
  2015 23, 195–196, 246
  2017 185, 190–191, 201–205, 237,
    243, 246
  2019 185, 192, 210–213, 237, 239,
    246
general strike, 1926 2, 28, 34, 38,
  76
*The General Theory of Employment,
  Interest and Money* 54, 56
George V 36, 48, 49

German Social Democratic Party
  (SPD) 66, 94, 224
Gladstone, Margaret 30–31
gold standard 41, 46, 52
Goldthorpe, John 96
Good Friday Agreement (GFA)
  171
Gould, Philip 166, 170, 187
Graham, Andrew 171
Granita restaurant 167
Great Depression, 1929 10, 234
Green New Deal 255, 256
Green Party 191, 205, 220, 264
Greenwood, Arthur 47–48

H
Haines, Joe 17, 113
Hardie, Keir 3, 26, 29, 62, 239
Harris, Carolyn 216
Hartlepool by-election 213, 221
Hattersley, Roy 129, 146, 165
Hayek, Friedrich 62
Healey, Denis 19, 106, 113, 114,
    121–122, 125, 132–134
  on 1978 autumn election 137
  and 1979 defeat 138, 139
  on Benn 123
  on Callaghan 131
  chancellor 125, 126
  and Crosland 154
  defence secretary 115
  and deputy leadership 109,
    150–153
  and electoral college proposal
    144
  on European Community
    119–120

M

MacDonald, James Ramsay 3,
26–27, 28, 29–32, 34–37, 38, 39,
41–45, 46–47
and ethical socialism 62
and Howell 51–52
and Keynes 53
and Morrison 48–50
and National Government
11–12
and Snowden 234
and Wertheimer 9–10
won 1929 election 40
MacDonald, John 29
Macmillan, Harold 71, 75, 93, 100
Macmillan Committee 53
Macmurray, John 162
Maguire, P. 215
Major, John 168
The Manchester Guardian 49
Mandelson, Peter 166, 177, 190,
195, 209, 238
manifestos
1945 68
2017 202–203, 230
Starmer's leadership 217
Margate conference 88
Marquand, David 3–4, 29, 39,
106, 107, 231
Marshall Plan 71
Mason, Paul 216–217
Mattinson, Deborah 251, 259
Maxton, Jimmy 105
May, George 43
May, Theresa 185, 190, 191, 192,
201, 202, 204
and Brexit 205–207

resigned the premiership 209
May Committee 43
McDonnell, John 193, 194, 196,
201, 203, 215, 216
McFadden, Pat 199, 208–209
McKibbin, Ross 199
Mear One, anti-semitic mural
supported by Corbyn 207
Middle Temple 214
Milburn, Alan 238
Miliband, David 184, 195
Miliband, Ed 23, 184–185, 189,
195, 197, 233, 237
Militant Tendency 144
Milne, Seumas 199
Momentum 198, 202, 226
Monetary Policy Committee
(MPC) 171
Morecombe conference, 1952 83
Morgan, Lord Kenneth 66, 70–
71, 72, 79, 80, 118
Morrison, Herbert 14–15, 49–50,
51, 55, 58, 74
on 'consolidation' 72, 85–86
defeated in leadership election
89
on NHS 74
Mosley, Oswald 45, 55
Mullin, Chris 194
Must Labour Lose? 92–93

N

Nandy, Lisa 216
Nasser, Gamal Abdel 89
National Cyclists' Union 30
National Enterprise Board (NEB)
123